DARK MATTERS

DARK MATTERS

An Unofficial and Unauthorised Guide
to Philip Pullman's Internationally Bestselling
His Dark Materials Trilogy

Lance Parkin and Mark Jones

For Lorraine and Olivia Jones and
Gabrielle Lewis

This updated paperback edition first published in Great Britain in
2007 by
Virgin Books Ltd
Thames Wharf Studios
Rainville Road
London
W6 9HA

First published in 2005 by Virgin Books Ltd

ISBN 978 0 7535 1331 6

The paper used in this book is a natural, recyclable product made
from wood grown in sustainable forests. The manufacturing
process conforms to the regulations of the country of origin.

Typeset by TW Typesetting, Plymouth, Devon

Printed and bound in Great Britain by
CPI Bookmarque, Croydon, CR0 4TD

1 3 5 7 9 10 8 6 4 2

CONTENTS

Introduction 1

Part One: Philip Pullman 5

Part Two: The Stories 13
1. The Novels 15
   Northern Lights 15
   The Subtle Knife 22
   The Amber Spyglass 27
   Lyra's Oxford 41
   The Book of Dust 42
2. The Audio Versions 43
   The Talking Books 43
   The Radio Dramatisations 44
3. The Stage Play 48
4. The Movie 61

Part Three: The A–Z of *His Dark Materials* 71
1. Characters and Creatures 73
2. The Worlds 162
3. Beyond the Books 229

**Part Four: The History of Lyra's World,
as Far as it is Known** 251

INTRODUCTION

What makes a classic?

The reviewers of Philip Pullman's three books *Northern Lights*, *The Subtle Knife* and *The Amber Spyglass*, which make up the *His Dark Materials* trilogy, were quick to compare his work to modern children's classics like the books of J. K. Rowling, Ursula Le Guin, Susan Cooper and Alan Garner. By the time *The Amber Spyglass* was released, the stakes had been raised, Pullman was said to rank along with J. R. R. Tolkien and C. S. Lewis, and talk was of future generations enjoying it.

It's impossible to say which books will still be popular in a hundred years. Will people still listen to the Beatles or thrill to *Star Wars* in 2107? Ask the people of 1907 to name a vampire story, and every one of them would have said *Varney the Vampire*, not *Dracula*. No one in 1957 would have predicted that *The Lord of the Rings* would now be topping poll after poll of 'Best Loved novel of the twentieth century'. For that matter, if anyone had told Pullman, a stalwart children's writer in 1997 that his fifteenth or so book would become a huge international bestseller, making him the darling of the literary scene and the subject of multi-million-dollar film deals, then he might not have believed it either.

His Dark Materials looks to have the makings of enduring success. Simultaneously, it deals with the big, ageless issues of growing up, forming an identity, challenging beliefs and authority while also being very much of its time, featuring a thoroughly post-feminist heroine who travels in a world with a collapsing environment where the forces of religious totalitarianism jostle with underfunded quantum physicists over a fragmented 'truth'. It's a big, bold, daring saga, one that dares to take on questions about God and the individual when most thinkers have left all that to the religious, and sections of the religious have rediscovered the value of the mob and the death threat. It's a profoundly utopian book at a time when, across politics, art and intellectual life, utopianism is out of favour. It doesn't just tell us the world's a mess; it invites us to do something about it.

And it's a children's book. In an age where politicians seem to think that the most a child should aspire to is a C at GCSE, and most children's entertainment involves members of boy bands being covered in gunge, Pullman is not afraid to write a book for an intelligent eleven year old that deals with identity, authority, abuse, rebellion, sexuality and politics. It's no wonder when most adults' entertainment involves chick lit and lads' mags that grown-ups have flocked to the books and found something profound there, too. It's impossible to say what people will think of these books in a hundred years, but they are certainly important *now*.

Our book is intended as a companion for the original novels, not any form of substitute. This is a guide to the *His Dark Materials* saga, in all the various forms it appeared in. We use the British title for the first novel, *Northern Lights*, throughout. In America and some other parts of the world, it is called *The Golden Compass* (we explain why the title changed on page 42).

The first section is a brief biography of Philip Pullman.

The second includes detailed but brief synopses and analyses of the three novels, as well as the audio adaptations, the stage play and the forthcoming movie.

The third section is a comprehensive A–Z of all the places and characters encountered in the books that goes into more detail than the synopses, and hopefully will demonstrate the range and breadth of Pullman's sources and imagination.

The fourth section is a detailed timeline of events in the world of the novels.

Part One

PHILIP PULLMAN

Philip Nicholas Pullman was born on 19 October 1946 in Norfolk.

His parents were called Alfred and Audrey, and his father was a Flight Lieutenant in the Royal Air Force. Profiles and biographies make much of his family history, choosing to see parallels between his life and Lyra's relationship with her parents in the *His Dark Materials* books. Superficially, this is appealing. The young Philip Pullman rarely saw his father, who was always travelling to exotic parts of the world. Alfred was killed in a plane crash in Kenya when Philip was seven or eight. His mother moved to London, sending Philip and his brother Francis to live with her parents. When put like that, it's hard not to see the origins of Lord Asriel and Mrs Coulter, absent parents who are terribly important and always off somewhere interesting. However, as Pullman has pointed out himself, many children's books have absent parents – it's almost a necessary part of the story, as it allows the young heroes and heroines to have adventures. There is perhaps a risk of reading too much into this early life story. The news that his grandfather was an Anglican chaplain fascinates critics looking into the anti-clericalism of *His Dark Materials* . . . but almost every educated person of Pullman's generation questioned the religious certainties of their parents and grandparents.

There's a real danger that certain facts from Pullman's life
are given as 'explanations' for the contents of his books, but
we can take this too far into the territory of mythologising or
pop psychology. The profiles rarely mention the differences
between the experiences of Lyra and her creator. Usually, the
Pullman family would travel as a unit (when Philip was two,
the family was posted to Rhodesia). Audrey Pullman remarried
within a year – to another RAF man – and soon the family
were travelling the world together again, including a posting to
Australia. But they settled in North Wales in 1957, and
remained there at least until Philip went to university. That
said, travel was clearly an important influence on his writing,
not only because of the experiences he had and landscapes he
saw, but because it exposed him to a variety of stories he
wouldn't otherwise have seen. He has spoken passionately
about an Australian radio series about a resourceful kangaroo,
and while in Australia he first read American comic books, far
more lurid and colourful than most British ones of the time.
One thing that has characterised all of his work – and, of
course, that of many of his contemporaries – is that he wears
his influences on his sleeve, borrowing from dozens of diverse
sources.

Pullman went to Exeter College, Oxford, in 1965, but didn't
thrive there, and ended up with a third-class degree. After
finishing his course, he married and began his first novel, which
was published in 1972 as *The Haunted Storm*. This, like most
first novels, didn't sell well, and Philip has condemned it as
'terrible'. The book is now a collector's item, and one online
bookseller is asking over £5,000 for an unsigned copy. After
doing a number of the kind of jobs recent graduates find
themselves in, Pullman became an English teacher. Pullman
seems to think more of his second novel, *Galatea*. He seems to
like it more than his first, but is also quoted as saying it was
'rubbish', and that it didn't sell. Copies of *Galatea* are
relatively easy to come by, and it's a pretty good example of
the sort of British magic realist novel that was emerging at the
time from Pullman's contemporaries like Angela Carter and
Salman Rushdie (who is the same age and was at Cambridge

while Pullman was at Oxford). Had he been able to pursue that career, he would no doubt have carved out a small niche in that literary scene. Instead, he concentrated on his teaching, writing occasional articles and books such as a guide to the *Junior Oxford Dictionary*.

He found an outlet for his creativity by writing school plays. In 1982, an adaptation of one of those, *Count Karlstein*, was published. Another play he adapted into a children's novel, *The Ruby in the Smoke*, was published in 1985. This was the first book to feature Sally Lockhart, and this time Pullman scored enough of a success to give up full-time teaching. He took a part-time job at Westminster College, and began producing roughly a book a year. It was, ironically, his least typical or timeless novel, *How to be Cool*, that was adapted for television (in 1988) and brought him to the attention of the larger audiences that that medium attracts. His books were aimed at children, but they fell into distinct strands – there was the Victoriana and near-fantasy of the *Sally Lockhart* and *New Cut Gang* series, the fairytale storybooks like *Count Karlstein* and *Clockwork, or All Wound Up* and 'realistic' teen novels *The Broken Bridge* and *The White Mercedes*. His books occasionally appeared under the name Philip N. Pullman. This body of work established him as a children's author, but he was barely known outside those circles and like many jobbing writers was at the mercy of his publishers' whims. A proposed series of six New Cut Gang books was ended after two volumes when his editor at Puffin left.

The publication of *Northern Lights* in 1995 radically improved his fortunes. At first, while it got good reviews, there was no sign that the book would sell any better or gain more attention than the Sally Lockhart novels. Gradually, though, word-of-mouth began spreading. The book won the *Guardian* Fiction prize and the Carnegie Medal. By the time the paperback of *The Subtle Knife* was released in 1998, though, the series was an unprecedented hit for Pullman, who was now being feted by the media. *The Amber Spyglass* was eagerly anticipated, and the hardback sold in huge numbers. By now, the series was clearly as much for adults as children.

What happened to create this success? One unavoidable answer is: Harry Potter. *Harry Potter and the Philosopher's Stone* was published in June 1997 in Britain, and became the centre of a bidding war for the American publishing rights. Scholastic eventually paid $100,000, a vast amount that required them to really push the book in America to recoup their investment. This set off an extraordinary self-sustaining hype for the books. In Britain, the interest in the American success of the books became a story in its own right, and – absolutely crucially – adults on both sides of the Atlantic started buying the novel to see what all the fuss was about. By the time the sequel was released, a bona fide phenomenon had exploded in Britain. *Northern Lights* was the natural candidate for a book to give to children who had enjoyed Harry Potter and were now looking for something else to read. By now, children's book sales were booming, especially those tinged with fantasy. In America, the *Series of Unfortunate Events* books, by 'Lemony Snicket' became a hit in their own right. In Britain, Pullman benefited enormously from the added attention from bookshops and journalists – and got a large advance for the American rights. There's a distinct sense in the reviews and articles about Pullman that his work is more deserving of its success than J. K. Rowling's. While some have seen adults reading Harry Potter as a rather worrying sign, there's been no such reservation about Pullman's work, which genuinely deals with big issues. Or, as Claudia Fitzherbert put it in the *Daily Telegraph* (23 January 2002) 'Adults read J. K. Rowling because she is not complicated; children read Philip Pullman because he is.' Like the Harry Potter books, *His Dark Materials* is available with 'grown-up' covers for those adults who don't want to be seen reading children's books in public.

The attempts by right-wing and Christian critics to paint Pullman as some form of frothing subversive who's leading the children of Britain to Hell itself inevitably backfired. Pullman, while clearly enjoying his fame and fortune, comes across as self-deprecating and articulate. He is passionate about children's education, an advocate for people reading broadly and thinking intelligently, a man of firm beliefs at a time of moral relativism. He continues, as he has done for years, to write a thousand words a day (about three pages) in a heated 'shed' in his house in Oxford, which has among its features a six-foot stuffed rat from the first production of his Sherlock Holmes play, *The Limehouse Horror*. He is married and has two grown sons. One of his current projects is *The Book of Dust*, a further exploration of Lyra's world (but not a sequel). He is now regularly heard on the radio; he often gives lectures and talks. He has been the subject of a *South Bank Show* profile, and the accolade of being the author of the first children's novel to win the Whitbread Prize. He has been condemned as 'the most dangerous author in Britain' by the *Mail on Sunday*, surely a prize above rubies. The stage version of *His Dark Materials* has been an enormous critical and commercial success for the National Theatre. The movie version of *Northern Lights* is being touted as potentially as lucrative as *The Lord of the Rings* films. The irony, for an author who clearly started out trying to be a serious, literary novelist, is that he is now – 20 years on – among the most talked-about and important of contemporary British writers.

Published books by Philip Pullman

The Haunted Storm (1972)
Galatea (1978)
Using the Oxford Junior Dictionary (1979)
Ancient Civilisations (1981)
Count Karlstein (1982, revised editions 1991, 2002)
The Ruby in the Smoke (1985, revised edition 1987)
The Shadow in the Plate (1986, revised as *The Shadow in the North* 1988)
How to be Cool (1987)
The White Mercedes (1988, revised as *The Butterfly Tattoo* 1992)
Springheeled Jack: A Story of Bravery and Evil (1989)
Frankenstein (play, 1990)
The Broken Bridge (1990)
The Tiger in the Well (1991)

Sherlock Holmes and the Limehouse Horror (1992, revised edition 2001)
Thunderbolt's Waxwork (1994)
The Tin Princess (1994)
The Firework Maker's Daughter (1995)
The Gas-Fitter's Ball (1995)
Northern Lights (1995, published in America as *The Golden Compass*)
The Wonderful World of Aladdin and the Enchanted Lamp (1995)
Clockwork, or All Wound Up (1996)
The Subtle Knife (1997)
Mossycoat (1998)
I Was A Rat! or The Scarlet Slippers (1999)
The Amber Spyglass (2000)
Puss in Boots (2000)
Lyra's Oxford (2003)
The Scarecrow and His Servant (2004)
The Book of Dust (forthcoming)

Part Two

THE STORIES

1. THE NOVELS

NORTHERN LIGHTS

The first novel in the *His Dark Materials* trilogy, first published in 1995. It has the alternative title *The Golden Compass* in North America.

Synopsis

Part One: Oxford – Lyra Belacqua is hiding in the Retiring Room at Jordan College when she sees the Master of the College poisoning a drink intended for her uncle, Lord Asriel. She warns Asriel, then hides to see the presentation he has come to Oxford to make.

Asriel has been searching the frozen North for the Grumman expedition. There he has discovered evidence of Dust, and of an otherworldly city visible in the northern lights. He asks, and receives, money from the College to investigate. When Asriel and Lyra have left, the Master confides to the Librarian that he wants to protect Lyra from Asriel and the Oblation Board.

Lyra and her friend Roger explore the catacombs under the Oratory. Meanwhile, rumours reach Oxford that the Gobblers are coming. For several months they have been blamed for children going missing all over the country. Sure enough, one of the gyptian children, Billy Costa, goes missing. Lyra searches for him, but two more children – one of them Roger – also vanish. Her desperate search is cut short when she is ushered to the Master's Lodgings for dinner. There she is introduced to Mrs Coulter.

Lyra is enthralled by Mrs Coulter. She is upset but excited to discover that the Master has arranged for her to go and stay with Mrs Coulter. The Master is clearly reluctant to let her go; he gives her an alethiometer but is unable to tell her how to use it – Lyra must learn that in time. She and Mrs Coulter take the zeppelin to London, where Lyra marvels at the surroundings. That night, alone in her room, Lyra examines the alethiometer in more detail but is unable to make it work.

After six weeks in London, living in luxury, Lyra is punished by Mrs Coulter, whose golden monkey dæmon savagely attacks Pantalaimon. Shortly afterwards, Mrs Coulter holds a cocktail party, attended by the great and the good. Lyra overhears Professor Docker talking about Dust. Docker also suggests that Gobblers is a corruption from GOB, the General Oblation Board, Mrs Coulter's pet project. Lyra is ushered to see Lord Boreal. When asked what she has been studying, Lyra boldly says the Oblation Board and Dust. Boreal unwittingly confirms that Mrs Coulter has been taking children to assist in the Oblation Board's investigation into Dust. Later, Lyra also hears that Lord Asriel has been taken captive and is being held by the armoured bears of Svalbard, who also supposedly killed Grumman. Mrs Coulter's true nature revealed, Lyra makes her escape.

Lyra makes her way across London, uncertain where to go. She is pounced on by two Turk traders at a wharf. It is only the quick action of Tony Costa, killing the two attackers, that saves her. Back at Tony's mother's narrowboat, Lyra rests. The next day, the gyptians tell Lyra that they are en route to the Fens for a gathering. They have lost many children to the Gobblers and have decided to take action. Tony Costa hopes they will send a rescue party north.

The gyptians know that Lyra is wanted by the police, and she fails to blend in. John Faa tells the assembled gyptians that they will keep her safe. At the end of the meeting, Ma Costa introduces Lyra to John Faa and Farder Coram. Faa tells Lyra the truth about her origins – she is the daughter of Lord Asriel and Mrs Coulter. Asriel deposited Lyra in the care of Jordan College and the gyptians have watched over her ever since. Farder Coram gives her some rudimentary understanding of how the alethiometer works.

As the gyptians prepare for their expedition, Lyra asks Ma Costa more about her past and experiments with the alethiometer. The gyptians want to rescue the children, but aren't planning to help Lord Asriel.

Lyra fails to inveigle her way into the gyptians' expedition. She studies the alethiometer with Farder Coram, slowly finding ways to interpret its movements. She successfully predicts the failure of a spying mission and her eerie accuracy earns her a place on the expedition. Using the alethiometer, Lyra learns Mrs Coulter is looking for her. Lyra is attacked by clockwork beetles on the deck of the ship. The gyptians capture one, deducing it is one of Coulter's spy-flies. The expedition joins a ship, heading across the German Sea to Lapland.

Part Two: Bolvangar – The gyptian expedition heads for Trollesund. Farder Coram intends to befriend the witches, or at least ensure their neutrality. Lyra befriends an able seaman called Jerry whose dæmon fixed as a seagull. On arrival at Trollesund, Farder Coram and Lyra make for the Witch Consulate. They meet Dr Martin Lanselius who agrees to contact a witch Coram once saved, Serafina Pekkala, on their behalf. Serafina is now a Clan-Queen. Lanselius tells Coram and Lyra that the Oblation Board is working locally through a company called the Northern Progress Exploration Company. After seeing her operate the alethiometer, Lanselius sends Lyra from the room, and tells Coram Lyra is the girl of whom the witches have prophesied. She must fulfil her destiny, in full ignorance, for the sake of all. When Lyra returns, Lanselius suggests that the gyptians obtain the services of an armoured bear, and recommends Iorek Byrnison. Byrnison is first unwelcoming and refuses to work unless his armour is returned to him.

Lyra sees the Aurora for the first time. Serafina's great grey goose-dæmon, Kaisa arrives, and Farder Coram tells him that they intend to rescue the children from the Oblation Board and asks for information. The witches know the Oblation Board as Dusthunters and that they have taken the children to a purpose-built base, The Station, known locally as Bolvangar. Kaisa also reveals that the witches know of Other Worlds that exist parallel to ours. The gyptians meet Lee Scoresby, who agrees to help them go North in his balloon. Lyra discovers where Iorek's armour is, and the bear crashes in, taking it back. With Iorek and Scoresby, the gyptians and Lyra head for Bolvangar.

En route, Lyra uses the alethiometer to find out more about Bolvangar's defences but there is a confusing reading: nearby there is a village by a lake, which is troubled by a child. She convinces Faa to let her travel on Iorek's back to the village to investigate. As they head there, they see hundreds of witches flying North, to war. The villagers are frightened of a spirit in the fish house and Lyra promises to take the spirit with her. Slowly she musters up the courage to enter the fish house and is horrified to see a boy, Tony Makarios, without a dæmon. This is a severed child – the result of intercision.

Lyra forces herself, despite feelings of anguish and sickness, to take Tony Makarios back to the gyptians. The gyptians' reaction is much the same as hers. Lyra wakes the next morning to hear that Tony Makarios died shortly after they returned.

The gyptians prepare for an assault on Bolvangar, but are ambushed by Samoyed Hunters. Three gyptians are killed and John Faa is injured. Lyra is captured and taken to Bolvangar. Lyra convinces Sister Clara that she is Lizzie Brooks, the daughter of a trader, and a slow-witted child. The personnel at Bolvangar, or the Experimental Station as Sister Clara calls it, are pleased that her dæmon has not fixed its form. There are around forty children held at Bolvangar. Lyra learns that they are uncertain why they are being held, but notes that the staff check for Dust and measure their dæmons. Mrs Coulter is expected tomorrow – and her arrival always means some of the children will disappear.

Lyra sees Roger, and their dæmons meet up to make sure Roger doesn't blow her cover. A girl called Bridget tells Lyra about Tony Makarios's last moments in the Station. She overheard a nurse explaining that Tony and his dæmon would be operated on to fix his dæmon's state and make him a grown up. Lyra meets Billy Costa, and tells him the gyptians are on the way. Lyra's examination by a doctor is interrupted by a fire drill. From there, she meets up with Roger, Billy and Kaisa to explore the Station. They find a small building where the severed dæmons of children are kept in glass cages. Kaisa leads the dæmons to safety. As Lyra and her friends go back to the main group of children, Mrs Coulter's zeppelin arrives.

Lyra prepares to instigate a mass escape from the Station. She sneaks in to spy on Mrs Coulter. Her mother has learned that the dæmons have escaped, and asks about a 'new separator'. A senior figure at the Station explains that they have developed a guillotine to separate body and dæmon. Coulter reveals that Asriel is being held at Svalbard: he continued his philosophical researches against instructions and now the Consistorial Court of Discipline is discussing his execution. Once Mrs Coulter has retired for the night, Lyra is discovered, and one of the scientists grabs Lyra's dæmon – breaking a taboo. They set her up on the guillotine, but Mrs Coulter hears them and intervenes. Lyra is sent to bed.

Lyra awakens to find Mrs Coulter preparing a drink. Mrs Coulter insists that Dust is an evil thing that affects grown-ups. When body and dæmon are separated, Dust cannot affect the child. Lyra is silently horrified. Mrs Coulter demands the alethiometer, but Lyra hands over an identical tin containing the spy-fly. The children make their escape, pursued by the Tartar guards, but they are rescued by the witches. Serafina Pekkala takes Lyra and Roger to Lee Scoresby, and they and Iorek escape in the balloon. The gyptians raze Bolvangar to the ground.

Part Three: Svalbard – As the balloon heads towards the pole, Lyra, Roger and Iorek sleep. Scoresby, who had wondered if Asriel's account of Grumman's death was genuine, asks Pekkala about what lies ahead. Pekkala explains that they are all at war, whether they know it or not; their destiny is set. Lyra learns Iorek was exiled for killing a young bear, and Iofur became the new king. Pekkala notes that Iofur has the cunning of a human, and talks of establishing embassies with human nations and working with human engineers. He even lives in a purpose-made palace, forsaking the ice forts of bears.

The balloon judders, and Scoresby has to descend. They are attacked by cliff-ghasts, and Lyra and Pantalaimon tumble from the balloon. An unfamiliar bear emerges through the snow and fog. They are taken to Iofur's palace at Svalbard. It resembles a human palace, but is filthy and filled with a pungent smell. Lyra is thrown in a cell with Santelia, who confirms that Iofur is forcing the bears to adapt to human ways. Iofur has isolated Asriel but has let him continue his experiments. Lyra develops a plan – if Iofur wants to be human, he'll want a dæmon. She has an audience with Iofur and convinces him that she is Iorek's dæmon, but wants to become Iofur's. She uses the alethiometer to answer trick questions Iofur asks to try to disprove her. Lyra tells Iofur to defeat Iorek in single combat so Iofur orders the way cleared for Iorek to enter.

Lyra worries for Iorek when she sees Iofur in his full armour, but, although the fighting is vicious, Iorek wins, eating Iofur's heart to prove his victory. The bears welcome their new king. Lyra is reunited with Roger, and Scoresby is also safe. The alethiometer says Mrs Coulter with an army of Tartars is a few hours away in pursuit, intent on seizing power from Iofur; Mrs Coulter seeks to kill Lord Asriel, to prevent him undertaking an experiment that she too wishes to undertake – to reach the city in the Aurora. Both Asriel and Coulter want Lyra for something she has, but Lyra is not sure it is the alethiometer. Nevertheless, she determines to take the device to Asriel before Mrs Coulter can get her hands on it.

Lyra, Roger and Iorek travel into the interior of Svalbard. Amid the jagged precipices and ice floes, they find a house, with large glass panes and a small courtyard. Lyra is greeted by Thorold, who is surprised to see her. She is ushered through to her father, but he cries out in anguish, insisting that he had not sent for her. Lyra is stunned, but when Roger comes to her side, Asriel calms down. He explains that Dust *is* the substance that moves the alethiometer, but it is more than that. Mrs Coulter, hungry for power, established herself as an expert in Dust. The Magisterium, terrified of Dust, funded her investigations. Asriel intends to make a bridge to the other world, to cross it and to destroy Dust – the source of misery, destructiveness and death. He refuses the alethiometer and leaves. Lyra sits by the fire, bewildered.

Lyra is awoken by Thorold, who explains that Asriel has left with Roger. Suddenly Lyra realises what Asriel is intending – he will sever Roger's dæmon to release the power to create the bridge to the other world. Quickly, she dresses and is carried by Iorek, and accompanied by other armoured bears, in pursuit of Asriel's sled. En route, the Aurora springs into life, but, as they finally catch sight of Asriel's sled disappearing over the horizon, the party is attacked by a witch clan. Mrs Coulter's zeppelin approaches and, while the bears battle the witches and hold down the advancing army, Iorek and Lyra continue their pursuit. Iorek halts suddenly before a bridge of compacted snow – Asriel's sled crossed the weak bridge, but an armoured bear would be too heavy. Lyra crosses the perilous bridge, which collapses behind her. Iorek returns to fight alongside his fellow bears and Lyra is alone.

Pantalaimon soars high and sees Asriel and Roger over the next hill. Suddenly, the Aurora seems to flicker, and then disappears. Lyra rushes forward to see Asriel, aided by a witch, wiring the Aurora to the equipment on his sled. Asriel completes the circuit and the Aurora returns – he is controlling it, or drawing power from it for his equipment. Lyra takes Roger's hand and they run. Suddenly, as Roger and his dæmon are parted, a surge of power leaps up and into the Aurora and sunlight leaps through from the other world. Lyra, now caught on a ledge of ice holding Roger's lifeless body, can only stare in astonishment at Mrs Coulter and Asriel locked in a passionate embrace. Asriel asks Mrs Coulter to join him, assured that together they can find and destroy the source of Dust. But, fearful of the Church, despite his appeals, she refuses to go. She sobs as Asriel crosses to the other world, a world of sunlight, palm trees and sun-soaked buildings, then leaves. Lyra is broken from her anguish by Pantalaimon, who makes a startling suggestion: if their enemies all fear Dust, perhaps it is something to be sought and cherished? Lyra breathlessly agrees – perhaps they could prevent its destruction. Lyra carefully lays Roger's body down before she and Pan walk into the sky.

THE SUBTLE KNIFE

The second novel of the *His Dark Materials* trilogy was first published in 1997.

Synopsis

Will goes to his former piano teacher and asks her to look after his mentally ill mother. They have both been menaced by men looking for Will's father and, when Will returns home to look for his father's papers, he is interrupted by men breaking in. He finds his father's writing case, and pushes a man down the stairs, killing him, as he escapes. Guilt-ridden and afraid the police will come after him, he makes his way to Oxford. On the outskirts, he makes a strange discovery – a window in the air. He finds himself in a deserted coastal town, which seems Mediterranean. The streets and cafés are empty, food left to go stale on plates, but in a café he is confronted by a ferocious young girl in tattered clothes, accompanied by a large wild cat. The girl introduces herself as Lyra Silvertongue, an inhabitant of another world joined on to this one. As they talk, Lyra comes to realise that Will's dæmon is inside him and that he has not been severed from it. They eat and Will quickly falls asleep. Lyra, however, asks the alethiometer about Will – the device answers that Will is a murderer. Lyra takes heart at the news: at least he's no coward.

Blown out to sea by the blast of Asriel's experiment, the witches have regrouped with Scoresby. One witch is missing. The warm air pouring through the window from the other world has formed a thick fog. Serafina spies on Mrs Coulter, who is in conference with Cardinal Sturrock and other members of the Church, including Fra Pavel. Serafina watches, horrified, as Mrs Coulter tortures the captured witch who reveals only that Lyra has a name in the prophecy that she will not reveal. Serafina kills the witch and the Cardinal, and barely escapes with her own life. Serafina consults Dr Lanselius, who knows only that the Magisterium is gathering a massive army and suggests that Serafina consult Thorold. After she helps Thorold despatch a flock of cliff-ghasts, he tells her his suspicions that Asriel's target is not the Church, but the Authority Himself.

Serafina convenes a witch council, with two guest speakers. The first, Ruta Skadi, urges the witches to join forces and travel north in search of Lyra. The second, Lee Scoresby, believes that there is some connection to Grumman and determines to head to Nova Zembla, Grumman's last known whereabouts.

Will and Lyra hear some children talking and gingerly make contact. Angelica and Paolo are suspicious. They reveal that the town, Cittàgazze, is overrun by Spectres. These Spectres can only be seen by adults and can only harm adults: they eat them out from inside. Will and Lyra go to Will's Oxford looking for a scientist to tell them about Dust. Lyra, rushing ahead, walks in front of a car and is knocked down. Though she is only bruised, Lyra is perplexed: this is a very different Oxford and she feels lost, a little girl in a strange world.

While Lyra looks for a scientist, Will calls the family lawyer, then consults the local history library and finds out that his father had been hired as part of a dig in the north of Alaska sponsored by the Institute of Archaeology. He visits the Institute and discovers that the man who broke into his house has also been asking questions there. As Will heads for the lawyer's office, he sees the man who broke into his house. Meanwhile, Lyra visits the Pitt-Rivers Museum, where she finds some trepanned skulls. The alethiometer reveals that there is a high volume of Dust around the skulls. She is interrupted by a man called Charles, who offers to tell 'Lizzie' about them, but she is suspicious of him. Later, the alethiometer tells her where she can find a scientist – Dr Mary Malone – who knows about Dust. Malone realises Dust is what she calls Shadow Particles or Shadows. Lyra discovers that she can control Malone's computer – the Cave – just as she can the alethiometer.

Lyra and Will head back to Cittàgazze. While Lyra sleeps, Will reads the letters he rescued from his house. They are the final messages from John Parry to Will's mother. In the letters, Will's father describes a mysterious anomaly on a ridge that the Eskimos believe is a doorway to the spirit world. Parry seems to be the only member of the expedition aware of the anomaly, but later letters reveal that Nelson, a physicist on the team, is searching for the anomaly on the orders of the Ministry of Defence. As the letters end, John Parry prepares to pass through the window. Will is excited – his father discovered a window, just as he had done, and they might meet again.

Lee Scoresby consults Sam Cansino at Nova Zembla and discovers a great deal about Grumman, who is known there as Jopari. Scoresby comes to realise Grumman was investigating Dust. On his way back, Scoresby is attacked by a Skraeling but manages to shoot the man. Meanwhile, the witch clan fly into the world of Cittàgazze. They witness a Spectre attack and learn from a local man, Lorenz, that angels have recently reappeared, en route to the Pole. Ruta intercepts five angels, who explain that they are responding to a call. She follows them. After two nights they pass through an invisible gateway to a new world, where flights of angels are converging on an enormous fortress, responding to a call from Lord Asriel.

Lyra makes her way to Mary's office again. Mary warns Lyra that two strangers want to ask her questions. They make a grab for her, but Mary helps Lyra leave. Unable to escape her pursuers, Lyra is relieved when a dark-blue Rolls-Royce pulls up and Charles offers her a lift. Charles drops her off and, after a while, Lyra makes for the window and returns to the world of Cittàgazze and Will, but realises that Charles has stolen the alethiometer. Lyra has Sir Charles Latrom's business card so she and Will go to Latrom's house and ask him for the alethiometer, though Lyra accidentally reveals her real identity. Latrom says the device will fit well with his collection of scientific instruments. As they argue, Will is disturbed to see a black snake nestling in the sleeve of Sir Charles's jacket. Sir Charles proposes a bargain: Will and Lyra can have the alethiometer back if they bring him an object from a place he cannot go – a knife from the Torre degli Angeli in Cittàgazze.

The children pass back into the world of Cittàgazze and make for the tower. At the top of the stairs they see an old man bound and moaning but are interrupted by a mad young man, Tullio, who climbs the stairs armed with the knife. There is a brief fight, during which Will overpowers Tullio, who runs away, only to be taken by the Spectres. In the aftermath, they discover that Will is injured: the little finger and the finger next to it on his left hand are missing, severed by the knife. The old man, Giacomo Paradisi, explains that the knife can cut through anything, even a hole from this world into another. Lyra is disturbed at the thought of leaving Paradisi prey to the Spectres now he no longer has the knife, but, with the knife, Will intends to return to Latrom's house and retrieve the alethiometer.

After a little trial and error, Will and Lyra cut through and find themselves in Latrom's study. They wait quietly, either side of the window, and eavesdrop. Lyra recognises Latrom – he is Lord Boreal – and he is talking to Mrs Coulter. She reveals that Asriel is preparing to finish a war that began in heaven aeons ago. Boreal also talks about Cittàgazze – the crossroads where all windows converge – and the Spectres. He is intrigued by the possibility that Coulter's bodyguards – men who have had their dæmons removed – may not be susceptible to the Spectres and could protect them in that world. Lyra distracts them, Will recovers the alethiometer and they return to Cittàgazze. Lyra fears that the world of Cittàgazze presents just as much danger as Will's world and, sure enough, they are interrupted by the sound of children approaching, brandishing weapons. A volley of arrows from the witch clan ward off the children, while Will and Lyra retreat to a cave, where Will has to tend the wounds he suffered in his fight with Tullio.

Lee Scoresby arrives at the Yenesei village, on the trail of Grumman. The tribesmen introduce him to Grumman – their shaman, Jopari. Grumman reveals that he is actually John Parry, and from another world. Parry has discovered much that makes sense of physics, but he is fearful of the Magisterium. He is also aware of Asriel's plan, describing it as the greatest activity undertaken in human history. He knows about the subtle knife, and gets Scoresby to agree to help him take the bearer of the knife to Lord Asriel. They get past the Imperial Guard of Muscovy to retrieve Scoresby's balloon and make their escape.

Mary Malone eagerly tells her colleague Dr Payne about Lyra. Payne struggles to take in the apparent confirmation of their research and ultimately is unconvinced. Sir Charles Latrom arrives and offers to help them secure their continued research funding. Later, however, Mary makes adjustments to the Cave and is surprised when she starts receiving messages; the Shadows confirm that they are Dust or Dark Matter. More astonishingly, they reveal that they are also angels, uncountable billion beings of spirit that intervened in human evolution for vengeance. The angels tell Mary that her work here is done and that she has an important part to play – she must play the Serpent. They tell her to prepare for a long journey, and to destroy the Cave. She heads to a new world.

The witches give Will a potion to help his hand heal. The next day they report that they have sighted Lee Scoresby's balloon but they are soon interrupted by the sounds of a battle in the air. The witches fly up, leaving two to guard Will and Lyra. After a short battle with cliff-ghasts, the witches regroup and Ruta rejoins them. She tells them how she marvelled at Asriel's preparations and how she feels these must have been taking place over aeons. She made her way to Asriel's innermost chambers where he asked her to rally the witch clans to join his battle against the Authority. Serafina tells Ruta that her clan cannot join Asriel now – they are committed to helping Lyra reunite Will and his father.

Scoresby and Grumman continue to fly over Cittàgazze. Grumman explains how the Spectres feed on a conscious and informed interest in the world. Soon they are being followed by four zeppelins, and are approaching a storm. One of their enemies is destroyed by lightning, but they are forced to ditch. Grumman manages to wipe out all but one of the zeppelins and they make their way up a mountain. After a ferocious battle, in which Scoresby buys time for Grumman to escape, Scoresby and his dæmon Hester kill all their pursuers, but suffer mortal wounds.

Witch Lena Fledt finds an encampment of soldiers with their dæmons cut away. Making herself invisible, she investigates further and finds Mrs Coulter seducing Lord Boreal. Once she knows about the subtle knife, Coulter poisons Boreal. Coulter interrogates the witch and discovers that Lyra, Will and the knife are nearby. Lena, crippled in agony, reveals that Lyra is known to the witches as Eve. Though taken aback, Coulter realises her purpose: she must find Lyra and kill her – Eve cannot fall again. She calls to the Spectres to rise into the air and seek out the children.

Will meets Grumman, who soothes Will's fingers with bloodmoss. Knowing that he has found the bearer, Grumman tells Will the purpose of the knife – it alone can kill the Authority, and must, therefore, be taken to Asriel. Just as Will and Grumman realise they are father and son, a witch's arrow kills Grumman outright. Will makes his way back to the camp and sees two men in the shadows. They explain that they are angels, come to take Will to Lord Asriel. He continues back to find Lyra, but soon sees witches standing around. Airborne Spectres have killed the guard, and only a few have survived. Will finds the alethiometer . . . but Lyra is missing.

THE AMBER SPYGLASS

The third novel in the trilogy was first published in 2000.

Synopsis

Mrs Coulter is in hiding in a cave, high in the Himalayan mountains in Lyra's world. She is visited by Ama, a young girl from a nearby village who brings food. Mrs Coulter is keeping Lyra sedated but it is clear that Mrs Coulter's golden monkey dæmon is discontent with Mrs Coulter's decision to hide Lyra and herself from the Church. In a dream state, Lyra is contacted by the ghost of Roger. He tells her that he is in the land of the dead. He hates it and is scared.

Ama goes to a healer, a monk, and asks for medicine for Lyra. She returns to the cave and is shocked to see that it is Mrs Coulter who is keeping Lyra sedated. She decides to wait until Mrs Coulter goes, and then free Lyra. Lyra struggles, but Roger urges her to stay asleep – he's worried she'll think he's only a dream if she wakes.

The two angels, Balthamos and Baruch, urge Will to come with them to Asriel, but Will says he must find Lyra. Balthamos leads him to an abandoned camp where Will practises with the subtle knife and discovers he can cut through to many different worlds. Baruch continues the search for Lyra and returns to say he has located her in the Himalayas of her world. They are attacked by an angel loyal to someone known as 'the Regent'; Will kills it with the knife and they escape to another world. Balthamos recounts the origins of the Authority and explains that he has devolved his power to Metatron; it is Metatron who has tracked them down. They must find Asriel and tell him that Metatron's Clouded Mountain is moving. Will also learns that those that die go to a prison camp, the land of the dead. Balthamos stays with Will to rescue Lyra; Baruch sets off for Asriel.

Baruch is attacked and caught by hunters. He finds himself at Asriel's fortress, a huge basalt creation, seemingly thrown up over millions of years. The fortress sits at the border of a great plain and huge valleys, and is gearing up for war. A sentry realises the ragged figure is an angel.

Asriel takes a briefing from Lord Roke, a Gallivespian. Roke explains that Lyra is the cause of much consternation within the factions that make up the Magisterium. A crisis will come and all will depend on how she behaves at that point. Roke also has a spy in the Consistorial Court of Discipline – Chevalier Tialys. The Court is conducting an investigation into events at Bolvangar. Roke believes that the Society will locate Lyra first but will do nothing; the Court will take longer to find her but will act decisively. Asriel is puzzled by Lyra's importance, believing that she was destined only to bring Roger to him at Svalbard. His musings are cut short as Baruch is brought to him.

The angel is mortally wounded but explains how he and Balthamos discovered the Authority within his crystal chamber deep in the Citadel. Metatron plans to relocate the Authority to a permanent Citadel and then to turn the Clouded Mountain into an engine of war, with which to subdue the independence of human beings, starting with Asriel's republic. Next he explains about the subtle knife and its wielder, Will, the son of Stanislaus Grumman. Asriel is taken aback. Finally Baruch tells Asriel about Lyra, her location in the Himalayas and her friendship with Will. The angel cannot hold his frame together any longer and dissipates. Asriel orders a squadron of gyropters to the Himalayas. He calls for Teukros Basilides and orders him to pinpoint the exact location in the Himalayas where Lyra can be found.

In Geneva, the Consistorial Court of Discipline hears the evidence of Fra Pavel. Father MacPhail insists they must bear their true purpose in mind – the destruction of Dust – and to that end he proposes radical action. He orders Father Gomez, youngest of the Court, to seek out and kill Lyra before she can be tempted and fall. The Court's assent is overheard by a Gallivespian spy. Father MacPhail talks to Dr Cooper, a survivor from Bolvangar, and learns what he can of the work there.

Mary Malone is in Cittàgazze. Remembering Lyra's use of the Cave and the alethiometer, she decides to use the principles of the I-Ching to take guidance. The brief moment of contemplation puts Mary in mind of a window to another world, and she soon finds one. Mary finds herself in the strange world of the Mulefa, and discovers a mysterious seed pod. The Mulefa are friendly, and take her to their village.

Balthamos feels the pain of Baruch's death but Will is able to convince him that finding Lyra would be a tribute to Baruch.

They find the village of Kholodnoye in disarray. When Asriel opened the bridge to the other world, an earthquake hit the village, leaving its tall buildings and spires at peculiar angles. The local priest, Semyon Borisovitch, believes that the earthquake foretells the coming of the Apocalypse of St John. He warns that the town is troubled by Armoured Bears, heading south from the Arctic in a steamship. Two hours later, a bitter battle between the townsfolk and the bears flares up. Will demonstrates his strength by cutting a piece of a bear's armour – this is Iorek, who had been told about what had happened by Serafina Pekkala; Will had also heard all about Iorek from Lyra. The bears are looking for a new home and Iorek agrees to grant Will passage on their steamer.

Iorek agrees to look for Lyra, and they soon arrive at the foothills of the Himalayas. King Ogunwe leads the squadron of gyropters and the fuel zeppelin over Svalbard. The news from Asriel is disconcerting: The Lady Salmakia witnessed the Church factions put aside their differences and join forces in pursuit of Lyra, and the Court has sent Swiss Guards after her; the Church also know of Asriel's plan to rescue his daughter. Now it is a race. But Asriel's forces have to rescue Lyra; the Church has only to kill her. The Gallivespians race to Lyra's aid, but no member of Asriel's forces is aware of Father Gomez and his deadly mission . . .

Father Gomez arrives in Cittàgazze in search of Mary Malone. Angelica and Paolo, the children who had pursued Lyra and Will, remark on seeing Mary days before. Mary, meanwhile, has learned the Mulefa have a society and fire – they are better understood as people than creatures. She slowly learns to communicate, much to their mutual delight. That night she discovers why the Mulefa take such great care of the seed pods: the wheel-pod trees are dying, and the Mulefa depend on them to live.

Ama is startled to come across Iorek and Will, but it is Will who makes her feel most uncomfortable. However, she leads him to Lyra's cave. Once satisfied that Lyra is safe, Will and Mrs Coulter talk, although he is determined not to be taken in. She explains how she has turned her back on the Church to save Lyra and asks Will to use the knife to save them by taking them into another world. Will makes his excuses but, on his return to Balthamos, it is clear that Mrs Coulter has bewitched his senses. Will, however, still has enough sense to hatch a plan, and intends to cut through to another world and there to sneak to a place to cut through and rescue Lyra, while Iorek presents a distraction.

Will and Ama sneak through the forest and find a place for Will to make the first window. The other world has a dry rocky surface and is bathed in moonlight, which Will realises will shine through like a torch when he cuts the window at the back of the cave. He cuts a peep hole: Mrs Coulter is asleep but he can't see Lyra; he and Ama pass through. They hear the sound of zeppelins approaching. Will finds Lyra, but he is reminded of his own mother when he sees Mrs Coulter. With Will distracted, the subtle knife breaks, trapping them all in the cave.

The African forces of King Ogunwe engage the Swiss Guard of the Consistorial Court outside the cave. Will gathers the pieces of the knife and accuses Coulter of breaking it, but she wanted it to aid their escape. As the battle rages, Chevalier Tialys reveals himself, threatening Mrs Coulter and creating a stand-off.

Will attacks the gold monkey and he and the Gallivespians make their escape. They do not get far: three Swiss Guards stand in their way, with their wolf-dog dæmons beside them. Will calls for Iorek but it is Balthamos who intervenes, temporarily scaring the guards before becoming too terrified and flying away. As Ama flees to the village, Will, Lyra and the spies cross into the other world.

Lyra uses the alethiometer; though she finds it more difficult to interpret, she is delighted to discover that Iorek is nearby – he can mend the knife. Lyra explains about her dream, the conversation with Roger and the land of the dead. The alethiometer reveals that they can travel there but that only their consciousness can enter that world. The Gallivespians try to take them to Asriel, but Will fends them off; they must travel to the land of the dead for Roger.

Back in Lyra's world, they make their way through the wreckage of the battle; after a long walk, they find Iorek. The bear king, however, is minded not to mend the knife; he believes it is the most dangerous weapon ever invented and has intentions that Will does not know. Lyra consults the alethiometer to discover what to do, which proves more difficult than before. The knife determines the outcome of a fine balance – it can do good or not, and Will is key to the outcome. Lyra secretly tells Will that the alethiometer has said that the knife will be the death of Dust but will also keep it alive. They are unsure what to make of the message.

Iorek repairs the knife, as only he could, and talks to Lyra about their plan to visit the land of the dead. Lyra is insistent that she must keep her promise. Iorek realises now that bears cannot live in the mountains and plans to return home with his compatriots where he may be needed by Serafina Pekkala, John Faa and the gyptians. Before leaving, Iorek warns Lyra that, if she cannot escape the land of the dead, they may never see each other again. However, Iorek believes in Will and would trust her with no other.

Taking the knife, Will tells the Gallivespians that they are going to cut through to another world. The Gallivespians are incensed but Will tells them that they can choose to come with them or go back to Lord Asriel.

Mrs Coulter is Asriel's prisoner. He studiously ignores her appeals to be released. Lord Roke, King Ogunwe and Xaphania, leader of the angelic forces, arrive for the briefing. Asriel is unhappy that he now has no spies in the Church. After reviewing Ogunwe's garrison, Asriel and his commanders decide to view the intention craft, a new weapon developed by the armoury. En route to the armoury, Mrs Coulter discovers that Asriel is not seeking to destroy the Authority, but to create a world where the Authority does not exist. The world of the adamant fortress is free of consciousness and they can build again. The armaments are to prevent the Authority from defeating them, if he ever intended to try. She also discovers that Xaphania was one of the first rebelling angels and that the Authority is not the Creator, as the church had thought. The workmen reveal the intention craft, which Mrs Coulter steals . . . just as Asriel had planned. Unbeknown to her, Lord Roke is a stowaway on the craft. Asriel heads back into the armoury where the latest, more advanced, model of the intention craft awaits his inspection.

Mary Malone is constructing a mirror to see Shadows. The notion came to her when she realised that the Mulefa can see Shadow Particles. Mary starts to find connections with her previous research as she listens to the Mulefa legends. The Mulefa help Mary to create a spyglass but it is only when Mary accidentally covers one sheet in the amber seed-pod oil, that she sees Shadow Particles, few on young Mulefa but more rich and dense around adults. The Mulefa ask her to help them find a cure for the sickness of the trees, or they shall all die. Meanwhile, Father Gomez makes his way into the mountains close to Cittàgazze.

Lyra gets guidance from the alethiometer how to proceed. She and Will are wary around the Gallivespians but, recognising they need the little spies, they make a trade: they will tell the spies what they intend to do, but must keep control of the lodestone resonator in return. Tialys and Salmakia are shocked to hear of their plans but concede the resonator. Will cuts a window to a world of hundreds of ghosts, all of whom are trudging towards a refugee camp by a river. They have found the land of the dead. At the outskirts, the children are stopped by a living man at a run-down customs building; they must go to a holding area, a long walk away, to await entry. Lyra learns that people's Deaths follow them around, and makes a deal with hers to enter the land of the dead.

Mary's studies with the amber spyglass reveal an underlying current to the movement of *sraf* – it is slowly moving out to sea, against the wind. The movement cannot be seen on the ground but is more pronounced from among the tree branches. The change in direction means fewer seed pods are germinated. Mary tells the Mulefa that she must make many more observations, and asks that they help her to make a platform in the trees on which she can sleep. Father Gomez finds the window from Cittàgazze to the world of the Mulefa through which Mary passed.

Will, Lyra, Pantalaimon and the spies make their way to the jetty in the oily sickly river, led by Lyra's Death. The boatman tells them that Lyra must leave Pantalaimon behind. Fighting her every instinct, Lyra puts Pan on the shore, promising to return one day to find him. As she is separated from her dæmon, Lyra screams and it is echoed from the bank by Pan. But she is not alone: Will also feels a tearing at his chest, as though his heart is being pulled away.

Suddenly, a creature – a harpy – flies down through the mist. The harpy seeks some kind of payment and Lyra offers a story. When the harpy agrees, Lyra eagerly gets to work, her mind racing, but the harpy suddenly lunges, taking a clump of hair from Lyra's head. The harpy screams 'Liar' at her over and over again, the scream added to by the harpy's unseen sisters. The travellers find themselves on a great plain, covered in mist and a strange, dingy half-light. All around them are ghost people, barely moving, only whispering. Ushered by the ghosts, Lyra confides to Will that perhaps they should free all the ghosts. Will gives a smile that makes Lyra feel pleasantly different. She wishes Pan was here to tell her what it meant.

After a long walk, Lyra finds herself face to face with Roger. In secrecy, Lyra tells Roger her plan to free all the dead; this, she believes, is the witches' prophecy – her destiny. The ghosts will simply dissipate if they leave, becoming part of the world. The Gallivespians realise at once that with this act, they will issue a blow from which the Authority will not recover. Lyra makes a deal with the harpies that they will escort the ghosts from the land of the dead if the ghosts tell them their stories. The harpies show Will where to cut an escape route.

Mrs Coulter lands the intention craft in Geneva. The President hides his surprise when Mrs Coulter is ushered before him and calmly remarks that she is under arrest. The President listens impassively as she describes how she kept Lyra hidden in the cave away from the serpent and how she feels the President's action allowed Lyra to escape with Will. She also describes Asriel's war efforts and her escape. The President believes Asriel intends to kill the Authority.

He has Mrs Coulter locked in the guest room. Lord Roke introduces himself to a stunned Mrs Coulter and calmly passes on a message from Lord Asriel that he awaits her report. Some time later, Brother Louis retrieves a locket from around Mrs Coulter's neck, and Lord Roke follows him. Dr Cooper intends to use the lock of Lyra's hair from the locket to create a bomb, based on Lyra's genetic pattern. It can be detonated anywhere and will instantly cause Lyra's death. Roke quickly retrieves the hair and returns to Mrs Coulter but he only has half the hair: there must be more somewhere.

The President's zeppelin arrives at Saint-Jean-Les-Eaux, buffeted by fierce sleet and hail. Hidden inside Mrs Coulter's coat, Lord Roke watches the guards unload the crate containing the bomb. Mrs Coulter feigns clumsiness in an effort to persuade her guard to release her handcuffs. She fails, but the guard mentions the location of the sergeant who has the key. Lord Roke runs out across the landing point to the sergeant and stabs him with his sting. He does the same to a concerned guard, but makes it back to Mrs Coulter who, quietly, escapes. She learns that the President intends to separate her from her dæmon in order to release enough energy to detonate the bomb. Roke has to despatch another guard, but this alerts the President, who calls to, and is immediately joined by, a witch. The witch reports that something else is approaching from the north. Father MacPhail orders the witch to find and kill Mrs Coulter. In the absence of Mrs Coulter, the President will sacrifice himself to detonate the bomb. There's a struggle, in which Roke is killed, but the President manages to complete the circuit. There is an explosion, and Asriel arrives to rescue Mrs Coulter and destroy the zeppelin.

Will and Lyra are into dark caves, where they meet the ghosts of Lee Scoresby and John Parry. Will's father orders him to cut Lyra's hair and put it in another world, severing the link between the lock of hair the Church has. They escape the blast, but it has created a vast, black and endless abyss. Parry believes that some of the ghosts should not pass through into the other world to dissipate, but should hold back to help Asriel in the final battle. If Asriel is to battle the Spectres, then ghosts, who have no dæmons to attract them, will be the ideal opponents. Scoresby and the Gallivespians agree to help. John Parry wants Will to help the ghosts to escape then to return to the land of the dead to cut a window to Asriel's world where the remaining ghosts can help in the battle and where the children can find their dæmons. Parry explains that while people can travel between worlds their dæmons can only live their full lives in their own. For that reason, Lord Asriel's great plan will fail: you cannot build the republic of heaven in another world, only in your own, for there is no elsewhere.

The first of the ghosts to leave the world of the dead is Roger, who grins delightedly at Lyra as he evaporates into the world of the living – a green savannah world with huge tall trees. The ghosts begin leaving their prison.

Mary looks through the amber spyglass and sees that the movement of *sraf*, Shadow Particles or Dust is no longer a slow, but a deliberate, movement, as though the floodgates have opened. Mary feels light-headed, released from her body, and senses herself being pulled with the Dust. By concentrating on what it feels like to be in her body, she steadies the flow and realises that the Dust is helping her. It is *alive*. Back on the platform, she realises that the particles know what is happening and are sorrowful. Meanwhile, Father Gomez finds himself at the headland that Mary first saw many days previously. He kills a Tualapi bird with his rifle.

Asriel and Mrs Coulter return to the fortress. The cloud on the horizon shows that Metatron is about to attack Asriel with the Clouded Mountain. Should he succeed, he will unleash an inquisition more terrible than before. Asriel admits that his forces did not know what they were entering into but notes that the Authority did not know what he was facing with Lyra. Asriel intends to destroy Metatron and believes that the republic may have been called into being for one purpose alone: to enable his child, and Will and their dæmons to escape safely into another world. Asriel orders King Ogunwe to lead the defence of the fortress and sends his Gallivespians to look for Will and Lyra and their dæmons. The dæmons are spotted by the east gate.

Will has finally reached the point where he can cut through to the world of Asriel's republic. The children and the ghosts are immediately disorientated by the noise of battle. Legions of troops from both sides are facing each other on the plain. Asriel is losing . . . and then there is an uneasy calm and the Kingdom's forces hold back. Suddenly, the Kingdom unleashes an army of Spectres. Will leads the ghosts into battle. Scoresby and Parry grapple and tear at the Spectres in hand-to-hand combat. The republic's witch clans fly at the cloud carrying flaming torches of pitch pine and are met by the Kingdom's angels. Soon the sky is filled with angels falling to the ground, their wings ablaze.

Mrs Coulter pilots the Intention Craft to a terrace on the Clouded Mountain. She hides to one side as a group of angels pass carrying a large crystal litter. The figure inside is indescribably aged and decrepit – the Authority. Mrs Coulter finds herself before an armed angel. With great self-confidence, she demands that the angel take her to Metatron. When Metatron asks for Lyra, Mrs Coulter says that she does not have Lyra but knows that Asriel has her dæmon and she can take Metatron to it. Metatron, looking into Mrs Coulter and seeing the depth of her selfishness and depravity, believes that she is capable of betraying her own daughter.

Meanwhile, Xaphania and her angels have discovered a crack at the side of the basalt fortress that leads to the abyss. Asriel walks down to investigate. Mrs Coulter and Metatron reach the abyss. Mrs Coulter hurries to Asriel and tells him it is time to destroy Metatron and preserve Lyra's future. Mrs Coulter calls for Metatron and at once Asriel is upon him, pinning the angel's arms and wings to his waist, trying to throw him down the abyss. Despite his efforts, the angel is able to lift up. With her last effort, Mrs Coulter leaps at Metatron and holds his head back for Stelmaria to savage the angel's throat. Their combined weight pulls the Regent into the abyss and all three plunge to oblivion.

Lyra and Will stumble through mud and rocks in search of their dæmons. They hide and watch as the cavalry surround the crystal litter. Will and Lyra turn, only to find themselves in the midst of the troop. Will and Lyra frighten off the retinue guarding the crystal litter and Lyra tries to soothe the panicky occupant. The Authority is released but this aged figure is scared of the children and dissipates into the wind. Lyra is left with the impression of release. The Gallivespians lead Will and Lyra towards their dæmons, meeting Iorek on the way. They sense their dæmons are in danger in the great battle between Spectres and Ghosts. Will and Lyra grab the dæmons, only to realise that they are holding each other's. They quickly break their gaze and jump through to the safety of another world. Lyra and Will say their short final goodbyes to Lee Scoresby and John Parry.

Lyra and Will are in a world of tall trees. Mulefa arrive and take them to Mary Malone. Will and Mary meet for the first time and shake hands. Mary feeds them, though they find the food rich, and patiently answers their questions about the Mulefa without quizzing them about their adventure. The Mulefa warn Mary that the Tualapi have become more violent in the last day or so.

Lyra wakes naked, and goes swimming. She feels self-conscious. Before, she'd swum with other children, but it wouldn't be the same if she did that with Will. Will wonders whether Mary stopped believing in good and evil when she stopped believing in God, but Mary knows now that good and evil is in what people do; it doesn't exist independently of people. Mary leaves the village, experiencing the evening. There is a sense of purpose in the air. She takes out the amber spyglass and looks at the sky. She sees two movements: the clouds and wind, rushing in one direction, and Dust moving inexorably the other way and out of the world. And then, possessed of the facts from Will and Lyra's stories, the pieces fall together. Mary sees that the clouds, the trees, the grass – all are working in vain to prevent the loss of Dust. Matter loves Dust, she realises, and this is the great purpose that she sensed in the air.

Mary begins to head back to the village. On the horizon she sees the white sails of the Tualapi and, getting from the back of one, a man. She uses the spyglass and sees that he is carrying a rifle and heading towards Mary's hut. Mary wants to shout but she might give away Will and Lyra. The figure enters Mary's house and, shortly after, leaves, remounts one of the Tualapi and sails away.

Lyra tells Mary that she and Will are going for a walk to look for their dæmons. Mary warns them to be wary of the man, but Lyra dismisses him as an innocent traveller who chanced upon an open window. The children set out in search of their dæmons, and recall, with embarrassment and excitement, when they picked up each other's by mistake. The children make their way down a valley and into a small wood of silver-barked trees. From the valley's ridge, Father Gomez watches their progress. He has tracked them all day and is convinced that they are walking into sin. Gomez is concerned not to hurt the boy – he has not been absolved of his murder – but knows he must kill the girl. Reaching for his rifle, he feels his dæmon grasped; gasping, he turns to find his assailant but there is nothing. From the air, Balthamos's voice tells him to keep still.

Will and Lyra rest beside a trickling stream. They are hungry and reach for the food Mary packed for them. Lyra, her heart beating fast, holds the little red fruit to Will's lips. They know what is happening and both are brimming with happiness. They kiss, and say they love each other. The whole world seems to hold its breath.

Balthamos, having dragged Gomez's dæmon away from the children, with what strength he has left, holds the priest's head down in the water until his beetle-dæmon vanishes. Balthamos calls to Baruch – he can do no more – and dissipates to join his lost loved one.

Using the spyglass, Mary sees that the great outflow of *sraf* has now stopped to a faint trickle. Dust is falling like snowflakes on to the upturned flowers on the Mulefa's seed-pod trees. And there, in the distance, Will and Lyra are walking back, hand in hand. Mary knows that if she used the spyglass the children would be a radiant gold colour. They have come into their inheritance and Dust has found a living home again.

The dæmons approach the village and find Will and Lyra asleep in each other's arms. They are taken aside by Serafina Pekkala who tells them that their forms will soon fix. Mary tells Serafina that Will and Lyra have prevented the outpouring of Dust, and shows the witch Dust for the first time through the amber spyglass. Serafina has met Xaphania in her travels and relays that the angels are closing the abyss in the underworld. On the ridge overlooking the wood of silver-barked trees, the body of Father Gomez is devoured by lizards.

The young lovers are reunited with their dæmons, but Pan is in distress because, every time a window was created, Dust leaked out of the world into the same emptiness as the abyss. They must close every last window. But, if Will and Lyra can create enough in their own world, by teaching people to open their minds and be curious, they may be able to keep one window open. Their hearts leap until they realise that the one window they must leave open is that from the world of the dead. Will and Lyra are in torment but know they must return to their own worlds and never see each other again. They wish this night would last forever but know the gyptians' arrival tomorrow is not far away. As they comfort each other, Pan and Kirjava return, Pan as a graceful pine-marten and Kirjava as a cat with lustrous fur. Will reaches out and touches Pan, conscious of his actions, and Lyra, heart racing and joyful, responds. They know now that their dæmons will not change, and wonder if any lovers before them had made the same blissful discovery.

The gyptians arrive with Serafina Pekkala to take Will and Lyra back to Oxford. Mary says goodbye to Atal and the Mulefa, and receives seeds from the wheel trees to take home. The two-week journey passes all too quickly for Will and Lyra. Once all the windows are closed the two Oxfords will align once more, but never touch again. Mary tells Serafina she will help Will to deal with all the inevitable questions and has promised Lyra to be his friend. Lyra travels into Will's Oxford with Mary and Serafina and they head to the Botanic Garden. Lyra is delighted to find it is just the same as in her world – even down to the wooden seat at the far end of the garden. Lyra suggests that once a year, at midday on Midsummer's Day, they return to this place to be together and not together again. Will readily agrees. Will cuts a window through to Cittàgazze to let Lyra and Serafina back into their world. Will and Lyra share a last kiss then, holding back their emotions, watch each other as Will seals the window. Will tries to break the knife but thinking about his mother does not help. Kirjava suggests that he think of Lyra and it works. Mary and Will head back to her flat for a cup of tea.

A little later, Lyra and Pan slip out of Jordan College and down to the Botanic Garden. She wonders what Pan and Kirjava did on their travels, but the dæmons have promised only to tell Will and Lyra in time. Lyra is pleased that she and Will share something again. She knows now that they could not be together – no one could build what they must if they put themselves first. Pan asks what they must build. 'The republic of heaven,' answers Lyra.

LYRA'S OXFORD

A small hardback book published in 2003 by David Fickling books, with engravings by John Lawrence. It's packed with a pretty fold-out map of Oxford (and a rather more functional one of Oxfordshire on the reverse); adverts from Lyra's world; details of the SS *Zenobia* cruise to the Levant; a postcard from Mary Malone to Angela Gorman; and two pages from a guide book to Oxford. Most importantly, it contains the short story 'Lyra and the Birds', set after the *His Dark Materials* trilogy.

In that, Lyra is on the roof of Jordan College when she sees a flock of starlings attacking a witch's bird dæmon. She rescues the dæmon from the real birds, and it tells her to find a man called Makepeace. This turns out to be the reclusive alchemist Sebastian Makepeace. But the witch is trying to kill Lyra and frame Makepeace for the murder. Defeating the witch, Makepeace asserts 'everything has a meaning, if only we could read it.' Lyra is unsure what it means that the real birds were protecting her, though . . .

THE BOOK OF DUST

Philip Pullman is working on a new book set in the worlds of *His Dark Materials*. He has said that it isn't a sequel; it is a short story collection that acts as a companion piece. Some of the stories will fill in some of the gaps in the history of *His Dark Materials*, and it is believed that the centrepiece will be a longer story set after *The Amber Spyglass*, featuring Lyra. 'Lyra and the Birds' in *Lyra's Oxford* would seem to act as a bridge to this story.

Comment

In America, the first novel was renamed *The Golden Compass*. According to Philip Pullman, this was because the American editors at the publisher Alfred A Knopf got confused – 'The Golden Compasses' was Pullman's original title for the whole trilogy. It has led to the further confusion that the compass being referred to is the alethiometer when, in the original quote from Milton, it's the instrument God used to create the universe. Between books two and three, Pullman publicly adopted the title *His Dark Materials*, another quotation from *Paradise Lost*. The foreign editions of the book were split between the two titles (so that the German version is *Der Goldene Kompab*), with a slight majority preferring the title that means 'Northern Lights'. The French version of *The Subtle Knife* is called *La Tour des Anges* – 'the Tower of Angels'.

2. THE AUDIO VERSIONS

There are two versions of the books available on CD. The first is a reading of the books, narrated by Philip Pullman with a full cast. The second is a dramatisation, first broadcast on BBC Radio 4 in 2003.

THE TALKING BOOKS

The talking book version of the trilogy is unabridged, and as such is very long. The adaptation of *Northern Lights* is ten hours and 49 minutes, *The Subtle Knife* is eight hours and 55 minutes and *The Amber Spyglass* is fourteen hours and 55 minutes – a total of more than thirty-four hours and 30 minutes.

Narrated by Philip Pullman, the dialogue is acted by a large cast, many of whom play more than one part. Lyra is portrayed by Joanna Wyatt; Stephen Thorne played the Master, Coram, Charles, Thorold, the Inquirer and Sattamax; Sean Barret played Asriel and Iorek; Susan Sheridan played Serafina and Roger. There were occasional cast changes between books, so that Stephen Webb played Will in *The Subtle Knife*, Peter England played him in *The Amber Spyglass*. Pantalaimon was played by three actors over the course of the three books: Rupert Degas, Paul Panting and Richard Pearce. Stephen Greif (Lanselius and Metatron) went on to play the President and John in the stage play. Other notable parts were taken by Alison Dowling (Mrs Coulter), Kate Lock (Mary) and Julian Glover played Grumman.

The director was Garrick Hagon and the music was by Peter Pontzen.

Comment

This is, in many ways, the definitive version of the story, a complete reading, with Philip Pullman providing (presumably) the correct pronunciations for tricky names like 'Cittàgazze' and 'Iorek'. This version is available on both CD and cassette, and – in both formats – as individual books and a boxset collection of all three.

THE RADIO DRAMATISATIONS

Radio Four broadcast three plays, each 160 minutes long, on consecutive weeks at the beginning of 2003. The radio plays were dramatised by Lavinia Murray, produced by Janet Whitaker and had music by Billy Cowie. They are available from BBC Audiobooks, both individually and in a boxset with an exclusive interview disc.

Northern Lights – first broadcast on 4 January 2003.
The Subtle Knife – first broadcast on 11 January 2003
The Amber Spyglass – first broadcast 18 January 2003

These are faithful, if pared-down versions of the stories. As with the stage play, most of the cuts to *Northern Lights* are to Lyra's carefree life in Oxford, which is a shame because the books depend on showing this childhood to contrast it with what Lyra has lost, or grown out of. As might be expected, the longest book, *The Amber Spyglass*, sees the most cuts. Most of the politicking of the Church and Asriel's commanders is lost, and there's little detail of Mary Malone's life among the Mulefa.

This is the only version of the story where Mrs Coulter's golden monkey dæmon is given a name: Ozymandias. There is the only description of the Magisterium's uniforms – the senior members have 'gold robes', the more junior ones 'plain vestments'. The film Lyra and Will see when they first go together to his world is specified as *ET: The Extra-Terrestrial* (Steven Spielberg, 1982).

The episodes are narrated by Balthamos, a recording angel.

Comment

These are perfectly acceptable adaptations of the stories, but they aren't quite as epic or impressive as the novels, or the clearing of the Radio 4 schedules they entailed, demanded. Barring the odd example of new dialogue that doesn't quite work or is downright jarring, such as Lee Scoresby declaring 'If we carry on going up, I won't be an aeronaut, I'll be an astronaut', the scripts are solid. The music works, but the rest of the sound design isn't as imaginative as it needs to be, and it feels very studio-based and more than a little stagey. A slightly shorter running time and a slightly faster pace would have helped tremendously; they don't hold up well to, say, the BBC's 1970s radio adaptation of *The Lord of the Rings*.

Lulu Popplewell sounds very young as Lyra, and indeed was only eleven years old when she played the part. Central to the story, it's a fine performance. The actress has since gone on to parts in *Love in a Cold Climate* and *Love, Actually*. Terence Stamp (Asriel), has had a long film career, from the title role of *Billy Budd* in 1962, via General Zod in *Superman II* to *The Adventures of Priscilla, Queen of the Desert* (1994) and *Elektra* in 2005. On paper, it's excellent casting for Asriel but, for some reason, the layers of the character don't come across.

The other main parts were played by Ray Fearon (Balthamos), Emma Fielding (Mrs Coulter), Daniel Anthony (Will) and Philip Madoc (Metatron).

The only Mulefa to speak has a Welsh accent.

These are worth a listen, but aren't a very good introduction to the stories. A lot of the alterations are made in order to speed up the pace of the story. In *Northern Lights*, Tony Makarios is kidnapped from Oxford, not London, allowing all the abductions seen in the book to take place in a short space of time. Mrs Lonsdale is both the housekeeper and the cook, allowing one character to fulfil two roles. Similarly, one of the burglars at the beginning of *The Subtle Knife* is explicitly Walters. The children of Cittàgazze know the story of the Guild, which greatly speeds up the explanation of the subtle knife and how it works, and the witches know of angels. Some sequences are entirely removed, for example, the Imperial Muscovite Academy in *The Subtle Knife*, while Lyra and Will's passage through the Land of the Dead and Mary's time with the Mulefa are heavily curtailed.

Other changes have been made to improve on the internal logic of the novels. Asriel immediately rationalises the Master's motives for the attempt on his life, rather than allowing Lyra to stew on the matter. Serafina Pekkala visited Lanselius and left a spray of cloud-pine because she knew that Farder Coram was en route to Trollesund. The Windsuckers – ghostly creatures in the north of Lyra's world known to the gyptians – are revealed as Spectres. Ama's dæmon, Kulang, is also female, making her the only character in the radio dramatisations with a dæmon of the same sex (Bernie Johannsen, the pastry cook, does not appear).

The dramatisations also have some new thoughts on dæmons. Human and dæmon share a sense of taste; when Wren's dog laps at the Tokay, his human tastes the poison. Hopefully, dæmons don't eat according to their form or the poor butler may become partial to Pedigree Chum. The closeness of the link is further implied when Pan describes Asriel and Coulter to Lyra as 'our parents'. The severed dæmons in the dæmon cages are described as translucent, as though made from stained glass. They are also described as a mixture of animals: half-bird, half-rodent, etc. A number of dæmons are also given names: Roger's dæmon is called Salcilia, the Master's raven dæmon is Leonore (a reference to Edgar Allan Poe), and, most significantly, the golden monkey is here called Ozymandias. Despite the fascination with the dæmons, one element that does not translate so strongly to the radio serials is the touch taboo; there is a rather glaring moment early in *The Subtle Knife* where Pan touches Will, and in *The Amber Spyglass* touching is simply frowned upon. Yet, at the end, the taboo still retains its sexual significance.

Then there are the downright peculiar differences. Dr Lanselius has daughters; their mother is Ruta Skadi. The alethiometer is explicitly gold, not brass. And in *Northern Lights*, Lyra was not deposited with the Sisters of Obedience at Watlington but with a St Michael's and All Saints in Babacombe!

3. THE STAGE PLAY

HIS DARK MATERIALS

A two-part stage play, an epic adaptation of the whole *His Dark Materials* trilogy by Nicholas Wright, directed by Nicholas Hynter, first performed by the National Theatre in 2003. The story is an exceptionally faithful, but pared-down version of the novels.

Story

Part One, Act One – Twenty-year-old Will and Lyra talk to each other from their different worlds on Midsummer's Day. Both are now undergraduates, and Lyra is studying at Jordan College.

Lyra remembers growing up there . . . and we see something of her at twelve, playing and studying with other children. She meets Roger Parslow, and they sneak into the Retiring Room, where they see the Master of the College drop poison into the wine of her uncle, Lord Asriel. Lyra warns Asriel, but he refuses to take her with him on his next expedition. Asriel goes on to give the assembled scholars a lecture illustrated with slides showing that a colleague, Jopari, has shown him how to make photograms of Dust. More than that, he has taken pictures of a city in the Arctic, proof of a gateway to another world. Asriel convinces a majority of the scholars that Jordan should fund his next expedition there.

Six weeks later, children have begun to mysteriously disappear, including Roger. Lyra is called to the Master's office, where he introduces her to Mrs Coulter, Chief Executive of the General Oblation Board, who offers Lyra the chance to go to the Arctic with her. The Master takes Lyra aside, and gives her an alethiometer. We see Mrs Coulter packing the missing children onto a boat. In Mrs Coulter's house, Lyra uses the alethiometer to try to find Roger, but Mrs Coulter interrupts. Mrs Coulter takes a lock of Lyra's hair and the bag with the alethiometer. They attend a dinner party, where Lyra meets Boreal, who boasts that Asriel is in prison and admits the General Oblation Board are taking the children. Meanwhile, the Master is visited by Fral, who reveals that an alethiometer has warned the Church of a witch's prophecy that Lyra is a child of destiny, who will either redeem the Church or destroy it. Lyra has a secret name that will reveal which one it shall be. As Lyra takes a walk, she's attacked by two Tartars and their dæmons, but she's saved by two gyptians, Tony and Ben. They've heard that the missing children are being 'cut up' in the Arctic. Lyra is taken to John, leader of the gyptians, whose seer, Coram, teaches her to use the alethiometer.

They head to Trollesund, the nearest port to the Oblation Board's laboratory, but they don't yet know where the laboratory is. They are being spied on with spy-flies. As they arrive, Lyra sees Iorek breaking up an iron buoy and offers him work. Iorek refuses, as his armour has been stolen by the locals. Lyra finds it with the alethiometer. The gyptians find their children's belongings, and it is all Coram can do to prevent them from taking their revenge on the town. They are joined by Kaisa, the dæmon of the Queen of the Lapland witches, Serafina, who has been sent to guide them to Bolvangar the 'fields of evil', where the children are. Kaisa reveals that the witches know of millions of other worlds. Iorek joins them, as does Lee, a Texan balloonist who fought with Iorek in the Tunguska campaign. Iorek tells Lyra that Mrs Coulter supported a rival to his throne of Svalbard, Iofur Raknison, making him bold with poison and promising to give him a dæmon. The armoured bears are now employed to guard Asriel in his prison.

The gyptians find Billy, one of the missing children, but he is missing Ratter, his dæmon. That is what Mrs Coulter is doing – cutting the link between the children and their dæmons. Lyra is captured by Tartars, and wakes in the dismal camp where the missing children have been taken. Kaisa finds Lyra and tells her the gyptians and witches are both coming to rescue her. The doctors decide to cut off Lyra's dæmon, but they are interrupted by Mrs Coulter. She stops them performing the operation on Lyra, but insists that the experiments are for the betterment of humankind – they make children safe from Dust, which she says is an evil force that affects people at puberty. Mrs Coulter goes on to reveal that Asriel is Lyra's father ... and that Mrs Coulter is her mother. She was married to another man when Lyra was conceived, and Asriel killed her husband in a duel. The resulting trial cost Asriel his lands and fortunes, and that was when he placed Lyra under the protection of Jordan College. As Mrs Coulter tries to take the alethiometer, Lyra manages to escape and free the children. Amid the confusion and gunfire, witches swoop down and Serafina rescues Lyra and Roger, taking them to Svalbard.

Part One, Act Two – An older Will tells Lyra that he killed a man, and while he was running away he found the window to Cittàgazze. Lyra resumes her story. Serafina tows Lee's balloon, with Lee, Lyra, Iorek and Roger on board. Serafina shows Lee her amber spyglass, given to her by a traveller from another world, and capable of seeing Dust. The witches believe that Lyra could annihilate death and lead to the 'triumph of Dust'. They are attacked by cliff-ghasts as they approach Svalbard. Brought before Iofur, Lyra claims to be Iorek's dæmon, answering questions only a dæmon would know using the alethiometer. Iorek gives Lyra a new name: Silvertongue. Iorek and Iofur fight a duel. Iorek wins, eating Iofur's heart.

He is restored as king of the bears. They free Asriel, who has managed to maintain a library and laboratory during his imprisonment. He is unimpressed by Lyra's efforts until she shows him that she had brought the alethiometer. He tells her that Dust makes the device work, and that it is the physical proof that something changes when innocence becomes experience. He is not interested in Mrs Coulter's experiments, except that he's learned that when the link between child and dæmon is cut, it creates a burst of energy that, as Lyra guesses, will allow people to travel between worlds. On one of the worlds is the origin of original sin. Asriel wants death to die. Stelmaria warns him not to say more, and he sends Lyra away. Back in Bolvangar, Mrs Coulter is faced by a surprise inspection from Fra. He tells Mrs Coulter that they have been watching Lyra her whole life. They interrogate a captured witch, trying to find Lyra's mystery name, but she is killed by Serafina, who has been invisibly watching the exchange. Asriel cuts Roger's link with his dæmon, killing Roger. Mrs Coulter catches up with them in time to see the window to another world opening in the Northern Lights. Asriel confesses to Mrs Coulter that he's going to search from world to world until he finds the Authority, then he's going to kill him with the knife *aesahaettr*. Mrs Coulter thinks he's insane. Fra arrives in an armed Church zeppelin. Lyra steps through the window. Meanwhile, the witches have captured Lee. They learn of Asriel's plan to kill the Authority, and despite an impassioned speech from Ruta Skadi pleading for them to join his cause, they are deeply divided. Serafina reveals that, using the amber spyglass, she's seen Dust flowing out of the world, through the windows. The world is being drained of Dust. The witches agree to find Lyra and lead her to her destiny. They seek out Jopari.

In Cittàgazze, Lyra meets and tussles with Will, who doesn't have a dæmon. He's come from another world. There are only children here – the adults have been killed or driven away by Spectres. Lyra uses the alethiometer to discover that Will is a murderer, on the run from the police, but that she should help him. Mrs Coulter is brought before the President of the Consistorial Court of Discipline. Mrs Coulter asks the Church to stop pursuing Lyra, in return for her telling them Asriel's plan. The Court consults Lord Boreal, who says that not only does he know about the other worlds, he regularly visits another Oxford, where he is known as Sir Charles Latrom. No one at the Court can tell if Asriel's plan will work. Fra thinks not, but Boreal believes that the knife sounds like one he knows of in Cittàgazze. Fra is forced to hand his alethiometer to Brother Jasper, who is able to make faster interpretations.

Lyra and Will cross over to Will's Oxford. Boreal is there, and tells Will that his father, Major John Parry, disappeared on an expedition to the Arctic where he was on the trail of a door to the spirit world. Charles steals the alethiometer. In Cittàgazze, the witches find Jopari, who tells them about a knife which can cut windows to other worlds. It is kept in the Tower of Angels on this world, in the keeping of Giacomo. Will tells Lyra about Latrom, and they go to his house – where Lyra recognises him as Lord Boreal. He tells her she can have the alethiometer back if she goes to Cittàgazze and gets the knife for him – she'll be safe from the Spectres. Will fights Tullio, who is trying to steal the knife, and loses two fingers, but as he wins the knife, he is now the bearer, the one person who can use the knife. Paradisi shows him how to open and close windows with the knife. Outside the Tower, the witches see angels massing, ready to join battle. As everyone prepares for the fight, Brother Jasper announces that he now knows Lyra's secret name .

Part Two, Act One – The President assembles the Council. Asriel has built a huge fortress and rebel angels are flocking to his cause. They are planning to attack the Authority in his citadel, the Clouded Mountain. He reveals that no one in the Church has had contact with the Authority since the time of Pope John Calvin. Boreal is brought before the Council, and tells them he is still trying to acquire the subtle knife, the only weapon that the Authority cannot defend against. There is great agitation when it's realised that Lyra is involved in his scheme. Her secret name is Eve and, like her namesake, she will control the fate of Dust. They give him absolution for the future murders of Will and Lyra.

Will – whose hand is still bleeding – and Lyra use the subtle knife to create a window from Cittàgazze to Will's world, stealing the alethiometer from under Boreal and Mrs Coulter's noses. They eavesdrop, and learn that Will's father is still alive. Serafina tracks down Will and Lyra, and asks Lyra what she thinks of him. She pledges to protect the children.

Asriel tells his troops that his fortress is built on the 'edge of reality', the last world before the domain of the Authority. It is a deliberate provocation, a symbol of human free will and defiance – and as such, something the Authority will not tolerate. He tells them about the subtle knife, neglecting to mention that he doesn't yet possess it. His army is joined by the Gallivespians.

In Cittàgazze, Mrs Coulter throws Giacomo to the Spectres, with whom she has reached an arrangement, and questions the children about the whereabouts of the knife. Nearby, the witches are protecting Will and Lyra and they shelter from a storm. Will has come to realise that there are dæmons and Spectres in his world, they just aren't visible. Ruta finds them and excites them by saying that Asriel has issued a call to arms. They are interrupted by Jopari, whose balloon is in difficulty in the storm. Sheltering from the storm, Mrs Coulter threatens to throw Boreal to the Spectres unless he gives her Lyra's true name. He tells her, but she lets the Spectres have him anyway, and takes his gun.

Will's wound still hasn't healed. Jopari uses an ointment on it, and reveals that he is Will's father. Ruta kills him – John rejected her for Will's mother. Meanwhile, Mrs Coulter has found Lyra and massacred the witches protecting her. She takes her daughter to a remote cave. Serafina and Will see the devastation, and retrieve the alethiometer. They are joined by two angels, Baruch and Balthamos, who have come here for the knife, which they say they want to give to Asriel. Lyra sees Roger's ghost. The angels tell Will that when people die, everyone, whether good or evil, is sent by the Authority to the world of the dead, 'a prison camp'. Baruch heads off to Asriel, while Balthamos remains with Will.

The Court hears from Dr Sargent, who explains the theory of quantum entanglement. The President is not interested, and vows to send zeppelins to kill Lyra, who Jasper has found with the alethiometer. They have also developed a bomb. The Gallivespians are watching, and send a report to Asriel, who is baffled by the Church's interest in Lyra. Baruch has been mortally wounded reaching Asriel's fortress, but he can point to a map to show where Lyra is. Asriel orders gyropters to search for his daughter.

Will is ambushed by bears, including Iorek. He threatens them with the subtle knife, and Iorek concedes the fight when Will shows he can slice through his armour. Iorek learns that Will is Lyra's friend. He tells Will that the Arctic doorway to sunny Cittàgazze that Asriel opened has melted the ice, and the bears have left their kingdom, hoping to live in the mountains. Balthamos is grief-stricken as he senses that Baruch has died, and joins them in their search for Lyra.

Jasper briefs the Council. The Church is aware of the various forces converging on Lyra, which includes Will and the subtle knife. The President wants the knife, and Lyra's head.

Will's party finds Lyra and Mrs Coulter just as the gyropters approach. Mrs Coulter tells him to cut an escape route to another world. She threatens Will with a gun, but is stung by the Gallivespians. As Will tries to cut a window to make his escape, Mrs Coulter impersonates his mother, distracting him, and the knife breaks. Asriel's forces and those of the Church arrive. In the confusion, the bears spirit Will and Lyra away.

Part Two, Act Two – Asriel remembers the defeat of a rebel angel, years ago. The recording angels always blame the losing side. In his war-room, he receives a report from the Gallivespians. Mrs Coulter has been captured, but the children got away with the subtle knife. Asriel's vast army of men, angels and monsters is assembled.

Lyra and Will inspect the broken knife. Lyra thinks Iorek will be able to fix it. When the Gallivespians approach to take her and the knife to Asriel, she agrees, but only if they find Iorek first. While they go to fetch him, Lyra and Will agree to go to the land of the dead to rescue John and Roger. Iorek arrives, and doesn't want to fix the knife – he believes it would have been better had it never been made in the first place. Lyra consults the alethiometer, which tells her that the slightest thought might tip the balance between the knife being used for good or ill. Lyra asks Iorek to mend the knife, and he agrees.

Asriel is informed of this. He is worried about the Church's bomb. Mrs Coulter is dragged before him in chains. Once released, she tells him what she knows about the bomb, which is in Geneva. Asriel has no spies there, and Mrs Coulter convinces him that she now hates the Church and will go there on his behalf.

Iorek, Will and Lyra remake the subtle knife, although it now looks 'wounded'. The children cut their way to the land of the dead.

The President confronts Mrs Coulter, suspicious of how easily she escaped Asriel's fortress. She tells him that before that, she was protecting Lyra from the Church, who has a feverish interest in sex. She tells him that she believes the Authority to be feeble, and his murder to be a mercy killing. The Church gets its bomb ready.

Lyra and Will discover living people being held on the outskirts of the land of the dead. They are accompanied by their Deaths, which haunt them. Lyra meets her own Death. To cross the river into the land of the dead, Lyra has to agree to leave her dæmon behind.

The Church has stolen Mrs Coulter's locket, and the lock of Lyra's hair within it. They can use the genetic information to aim the bomb at Lyra.

In the land of the dead, Lyra can no longer tell a lie, but she finds Roger and Will's father. Unable to cut their way out, Lyra makes a deal with the harpy guards – they must free all the prisoners from now on, once they have told the harpies their stories. Lyra leads the ghosts of the dead out into the open, where they dissolve, becoming part of the world.

Mrs Coulter is about to be severed from her dæmon by the Church. The energy released will power the bomb. When Coulter escapes, the President sacrifices his own life to power the bomb. Asriel's men arrive just as the power builds up.

Will's father gets Will to use the knife to take the piece of scalp that the lock of hair came from, and throw it into another world. The bomb detonates there. The explosion has formed a vast abyss, through which Dust is falling.

Serafina brings Pantalaimon to Asriel's fortress to prove that Lyra is still alive. The only way for the abyss to be sealed is for Eve to Fall again. As he absorbs this news, the Clouded Mountain, surrounded by flocks of angels, moves to attack the fortress. Asriel addresses his army, and Mrs Coulter – soon there will be no kingdoms or kings, bishops or priests; everyone will be free citizens of the Republic of Heaven. Asriel gives the signal to engage the Authority.

As Will's father dissolves, he tells Lyra that people have to stay in the world in which they were born, or their life drains away. Asriel will fail, as we must each build the Republic of Heaven where we are, not elsewhere.

Lyra and Will emerge onto the battlefield, and quickly meet Iorek. Asriel's fortress has been destroyed, the Clouded Mountain has retreated, and it is impossible to say who has won. Iorek wants to return to his ruined kingdom, to make a life there. They discover a crystal casket containing an incredibly old man. Voiceless, he wants someone to kill him, but soon expires anyway. Asriel and Mrs Coulter appear, and announce that the old man was the Authority. Lyra tells him she has annihilated death by freeing the prisoners of the land of the dead. The Kingdom of Heaven is over, the Church has no power. Asriel's dæmon warns Will not to give Asriel the knife. He tells Will and Lyra to leave. Asriel agrees with Mrs Coulter that Will will put it to better use – that if he becomes the bearer of the knife, he will simply replace the Authority, not destroy it. Their work is done; the world is now their children's. Together, they jump into the abyss, and oblivion.

Lyra and Will eat fruit and make love. Serafina watches Dust fall in new patterns on the Earth, 'like rain on the poor, parched throat of the earth'.

The next morning, Lyra is reunited with Pantalaimon, and Will also finds that he has a dæmon, Kirjava; both are fixed in the form of cats. Serafina tells them that the triumph of Dust is not complete; it is still flowing away, through all the windows. Every time a window is made, a Spectre is created.

Will and Lyra must return to their worlds, having closed all the windows, forever. Lyra turns to the alethiometer for guidance, but now she has lost her innocence, she can no longer use it – not without years of study.

Lyra and Will vow to talk to each other once a year, between worlds. Balthamos leads Will home and they seal the window. Will thinks of Lyra, and the subtle knife shatters.

We're back with the older Lyra and Will as they end their annual talk between worlds. There is no elsewhere, so here they will build and share the Republic of Heaven. They pass each other as they leave the stage.

Major Cast and Crew

Anna Maxwell Martin was 25 when she played 12-year-old Lyra in the first run of the play. She had previously appeared in *The Little Foxes* at the Donmar Warehouse, and since *His Dark Materials* has appeared in *North and South*, *Midsomer Murders* and *Doctor Who* on television, as well as having a small part in the film *Enduring Love*.

Timothy Dalton (Lord Asriel) is most famous for playing James Bond in *The Living Daylights* and *Licence to Kill* in the late eighties. This represents a couple of years of a long career, encompassing movies from the sublime *Lion in Winter* and *Cromwell* to the ridiculous *Flash Gordon* and *The Beautician and the Beast*, television roles such as Rhett Butler in *Scarlett* and a long history of acclaimed Shakespearean theatre.

Patricia Hodge (Mrs Coulter) is a familiar face on television, appearing in many series, including *Rumpole of the Bailey*, *Holding the Fort* and *The Lives and Loves of a She Devil*. Her career in theatre is at least as extensive.

Other main parts were taken by Samuel Barnett (Pantalaimon), Dominic Cooper (Will), Danny Sapani (Iorek), Stephen Greif (The President and John Faa), Niamh Cusack (Serafina Pekkala) and Chris Larkin (Jopari). Behind the scenes, the main designers were Giles Cadle (Sets), Jon Morrell (Costumes), Jonathan Dove (Music) and Michael Curry (Puppets).

The second run of the play started in time for the Christmas season 2004, and had a completely new cast, except for John Carlisle (Lord Boreal and the Boatman). The main cast were: Elaine Symons (Lyra), David Harewood (Lord Asriel), Adjoa Andoh (Serafina Pekkala), Jamie Harding (Pantalaimon), Michael Legg (Will) and Lesley Manville (Mrs Coulter).

Comment

Nicholas Wright states that his adaptation is 'written for a theatre with vast resources' and even this is something of an understatement. The plays require a cast of about 30, extensive use of puppetry and special effects, as well as a drum-revolve stage. A drum-revolve stage can have two sets up at one time: it rotates to allow one set of scenery to be removed from view and replaced without slowing down the action. It's thought that the National Theatre is the only theatre in the world equipped with one.

The two plays take six hours to perform in total (including a twenty-minute break between acts) but, even given that, the story has to be cut down a great deal (compare the unabridged reading, which lasts thirty-five hours).

The first play ends in roughly the same place as Chapter Eight of *The Subtle Knife*, but the first appearance of the angels is held back until this point to strengthen the cliffhanger.

Beyond making the material more concise, as the synopsis demonstrates, there are some fairly radical alterations – Lee Scoresby becomes a minor character in a few scenes in the middle of Part One, and Mary Malone and the world of the Mulefa do not appear at all. The only angels to speak are Baruch and Balthamos, meaning that there is no place for Xaphania or Metatron. Those are omissions; the main *change* is that the absence of Metatron affects Asriel and Mrs Coulter's motive for jumping into the abyss. They now go because their time has passed, which – while moving – doesn't seem quite as satisfying as the visceral, immediate reason in the book. It also makes the Church Council the main 'bad guys', and so there is a larger role to the President and Fra Pavel. Another significant change is that Asriel knows about the subtle knife and what it can do before the story starts, whereas he learns about it during the course of the books.

There are also a few small differences: Dr Cooper becomes Dr Sargent, presumably because 'Cooper' and 'Coulter' sound similar. Pantalaimon settles in the form of a cat, not a pine marten as in the books.

The play quickly pins down some of the more opaque aspects of the novels – within the first minute, the audience is told that Lyra's dæmon is her 'soul', and Serafina describes Lyra and Will's action at the end as 'two children are making love in an unknown world'.

The adaptation is an extraordinarily intelligent and dramatic version of the story, which streamlines the events of the novels without losing any of the spirit or complexity of the plot, any of the ambitious scale and without toning down any of the more controversial aspects of the story. The first run was rightly acclaimed, with Anna Maxwell Martin holding the whole thing together as Lyra, and Timothy Dalton and Patricia Hodge as Asriel and Coulter providing much entertainment for the adults in particular. The production was intelligent, and manages to avoid the excesses of NSC staginess or West End showiness. The music, design, costumes and – particularly – the puppetry all add up to a very clever use of theatre. It's no surprise it was a massive hit, and even children who can't be used to sitting still for so many hours were enthralled during performances. Deliberately pitched at many levels, from the purely spectacular to the deeply personal, unafraid to take risks or to talk about God and teenage feelings – or to change the source material in the name of better drama or to speed things up – this is easily the best adaptation of the stories into another medium.

Further Reading

The rehearsal script, with cast details and a brief afterword, is published by Nick Hern Books.

The Art of Darkness, by Robert Butler and published by the National Theatre and Oberon Books charts the staging of the play and interviews the key players.

The show's *Programme*, in addition to the usual cast list and biographies, includes a short piece on the props by Jonathan Croal, extracts from interviews from *The Art of Darkness* and a short glossary, as well as interesting historical and literary quotes and pictures. There are also some interesting new pieces from Philip Pullman himself: drawings, and three short text pieces on the Gallivespians, the history of the Magisterium and – perhaps best of all – a fold-out guide to the alethiometer and how it works.

```
*** TRANSIT SLIP ***
*** DISCHARGE ON
ARRIVAL ***

Author: Parkin, Lance.
Title: Dark matters : an
unofficial and unauthorised
gui
Item ID: 204762229Y
Transit to: DOHQ
```

4. THE MOVIE

The production of a movie version of *Northern Lights*, with the American title *The Golden Compass*, was first announced on 11 February 2002, by New Line Cinema, who were keen to demonstrate that they had other big projects underway as their highly successful *The Lord of the Rings* trilogy drew to a close. Originally, talk was that the film would be in cinemas for Christmas 2004, but this release date would soon start slipping, and there was a long period when it seemed the movie would never see the light of day. While most films have a long production process, it does seem fair to say that this movie has had a particularly difficult gestation.

Tom Stoppard, who, as well as receiving a knighthood for his stage plays, has also written or co-written some of the cleverest movies of recent years, like *Brazil* and *Shakespeare in Love*, wrote an early draft of the screenplay. This version was lauded by the film studio and Philip Pullman, but was turned down by Chris Weitz when he was appointed director, in favour of a script he wrote himself.

Chris Weitz, director of *About a Boy* and *Down to Earth*, was hired in May 2004. He resigned from the film in December of that year, saying that he was not the man to meet the 'technical challenges' of the film: 'I didn't feel like I was willing to undertake the sheer scale of this. It's a remarkably daunting challenge for me'. His departure came a week after he had stated that his movie would tone down the anti-religious aspects of the story, sparking a great deal of negative comment, including an article in *The Times*. Weitz's stepping down came hot on the heels of that news story, but it is difficult to interpret if and how the story might have played a role in his departure. It may be that the studio was looking for someone more willing to tackle the religious side of the story, or it might be the complete opposite – they may have felt Weitz had already proved too controversial. Or we could take Weitz's comments at face value – his previous work had been small-scale and involved minimal special effects.

There was little news after Weitz's departure in December 2004 until the announcement on 8 August 2005 that Anand Tucker was in negotiations to direct. Like Weitz, Tucker was mainly known for smaller films – he'd started out making arts shows for television, then directed the Oscar-nominated *Hilary and Jackie* (1998), and *Shopgirl* (2005, based on the novel by and starring Steve Martin). Philip Pullman welcomed the appointment on his website. Tucked away in the press release was a quote from New Line's president of production, Toby Emmerich, that the company 'will be bringing all three of Philip Pullman's bestselling *His Dark Materials* stories to the big screen'. While New Line had optioned all three books, previous statements had tended to suggest they would see how successful the first film was before committing to the sequels. From this point, some of the studio publicity started to refer to the project as *His Dark Materials: The Golden Compass*.

Tucker worked closely with Weitz (despite the latter's departure as director) and together they developed Weitz's screenplay. It appears that Tucker was also planning to build on the pre-production work Weitz had done (including the concept art and visual effects), rather than start from scratch.

Early April 2006 saw four open auditions for the key role of Lyra in Cambridge, Kendal, Oxford and Exeter in the UK. Ten thousand girls and young women showed up, and the process garnered a lot of media coverage. It was several months before an announcement was made about the casting directors' decision.

The next big news about the movie, though, came on 7 May, when it was announced that Chris Weitz was once again on-board to direct the film. Reports emerged that Anand Tucker left because of unspecified 'budgetary constraints' and 'creative differences', and fans and journalists who had been following the movie's development assumed that production had stalled once again. However, the project now had momentum and it was announced filming would start in September of that year, with the film scheduled for release in Autumn 2007.

The filmmakers now also had their Lyra: it was announced on 29 June 2006 that Dakota Blue Richards, a twelve-year-old from Brighton who'd attended the Cambridge open audition, had got the part. This audition, at the Cambridge Corn Exchange on 4 April, had been the first to be held and Richards had been one of two actors that the makers and Pullman had independently singled out from that day. Reports said that Richards had never acted before, wouldn't have gone to the audition if it had been raining – it rained on all of the other three days auditions were held – and that her mother accidentally hung up on the director (presumably Weitz) when he rang to tell them she had got the part. Dakota Blue Richards was born 11 April 1994, which was after Pullman began writing *Northern Lights*.

With the Lyra problem solved, the adult members of the cast began to fall into place. Philip Pullman had long stated that Mrs Coulter was based, at least in part, on Nicole Kidman. He'd singled out her performance in *To Die For* on more than one occasion as a big influence. Long-rumoured for the role, Kidman's casting was announced on 17 July 2006. The British press reported that there had been 'complex' negotiations, but, boiling it down, it seems that if there were sticking points they were the traditional ones involving money and the actress having to commit to the sequels and agree a fee before knowing how successful the movies would be.

The role of Lord Asriel proved less straightforward. Pullman had previously mentioned Jason Isaacs, and Eric Bana was apparently approached. The press were convinced that Paul Bettany had secured the role and that Kidman had only signed up because her friend Bettany was on board. The fee was again an issue – it must have been complicated by the fact Asriel only has a small part in the first book, isn't in the second, but is a major protagonist of the third (although even that might change in the movie – Asriel has a much smaller role in the BBC Radio version, for example, and the makers might choose to focus on Lyra's story). In the event, the producers announced on 18 August 2006 that they had picked Daniel Craig, who had just finished filming his first movie as James Bond, *Casino Royale*. His casting as Bond was proving controversial among online 007 fans, but he would be spectacularly vindicated by the box office performance and critical reception of the Bond movie when it came out in November 2006. Daniel Craig was a genuine fan of Pullman's novels, and was keen to win the role. On 2 August it had been announced that Craig's co-star in *Casino Royale*, Eva Green, had been cast as Serafina Pekkala. This was touted in the press as the only time a Bond had ever reunited with one of his Bond girls on a different film – in reality this wasn't quite true, as Sean Connery had gone on to work with Honor Blackman on *Shalako* after working with her on *Goldfinger*. Interestingly, Asriel was played by another James Bond actor, Timothy Dalton, in the original run of the stage play.

It was reported that Ian McShane, famous in Britain as Lovejoy and in the US for Deadwood, was voicing 'a talking bear' for the movie – the initial assumption was that he was playing Iorek, but it transpired that he was playing Iofur, the rival bear-king, and that, to avoid confusion over two similar-sounding names, his character had been renamed Ragnar Sturlusson. Stage actor Nonso Anozie was soon confirmed as playing Iorek. Sam Elliott was cast as Lee Scoresby, after some speculation that Samuel L Jackson was in the running for the role.

A fine cast of character actors had been assembled:
Nicole Kidman (Mrs Coulter)
Daniel Craig (Lord Asriel)

Dakota Blue Richards (Lyra)
Eva Green (Serafina Pekkala)
Sam Elliott (Lee Scoresby)
Ian McShane (Ragnar Sturlusson)
Adam Godley (Pantalaimon)
Simon McBurney (Fra Pavel)
Magda Szubanski (Mrs Lonsdale)
Jim Carter (John Faa)
Tom Courtenay (Farder Cordam)
Clare Higgins (Ma Costa)
Nonso Anozie (Iorek)
Jack Shepherd (Master)

Filming finally began on 4 September 2006 and would continue until the end of February the following year with, as usual for a major movie, various re-shoots and pick up shots done over the summer. Where possible, the film was shot at the actual locations in the book, mainly Oxford, including the real Pitt-Rivers Museum, with extensive shooting in the Bodleian Library and Christ Church College (although not the dining hall, which had doubled for Hogwarts in the Harry Potter films, and was felt to be too recognisable); the Fens and even Svalbard. The Old Royal Naval College in Greenwich doubled as Jordan College, and other 'Arctic' scenes were filmed in Norway and Switzerland.

The first official photographs promoting the film were released at the end of October 2006, and included the first image of Dakota Blue Richards as Lyra. These were received enthusiastically online, not least because they were the first concrete proof that the movie was actually being made. At the beginning of January 2007, a second batch of pictures was released. These were more formal publicity portraits, including the first pictures of Daniel Craig's Asriel, and gave a much better idea of the 'look' of the film. It was also confirmed around this time that the movie would be called *The Golden Compass* throughout the world, even in countries – like Britain – where the book was named *Northern Lights*.

In March, a 'proto trailer' appeared on the official website. It showed scenes from the film without completed special effects and allowed viewers their first chance to see the main characters in action ... and particularly to judge Dakota Blue Richards' performance, as she was central to a number of the scenes. In April, it was revealed that the screenplay for the adaptation of *The Subtle Knife* was being written, as was a treatment for the third in the series, *The Amber Spyglass*.

May 2007 saw a new burst of activity. The first teaser poster – a shot of Lyra in the Arctic with Iorek looming over her – was released on 5 May. This was the opening shot in a publicity campaign centred around the Cannes Film Festival, where ten minutes of footage was unveiled. This included a two minute teaser trailer and eight minutes of clips from the film itself. The taglines for the movies were also revealed as 'There are worlds beyond our own – the compass will show the way' and 'It is the Alethiometer. It tells the truth. As for how to read it, you'll have to learn by yourself'.

As with most blockbuster movies, the studio has signed dozens of merchandising deals, and forthcoming products include a videogame, action figures, high-end prop replicas, trading cards, playsets and board games. Not to be left out, Scholastic, the American publisher of the trilogy (and co-producer of the movie) announced it would be releasing a raft of tie-in books, aimed at all ages.

New Line had always made it clear they wanted *His Dark Materials* to appeal to the people who'd flocked to their *The Lord of the Rings* trilogy. The teaser trailer couldn't make the comparison any more explicit – it starts with an image of a golden ring that spins until it becomes an aleithometer, with a caption reading 'In 2001, New Line Cinema opened the door to Middle-earth. This December, they take you on another epic journey'. The trailer was released in time for it to be shown in front of one of the big summer movies, *Pirates of the Caribbean III*, and stressed the parallel worlds aspect of the story.

So ... will it be any good? While Philip Pullman is very confident about New Line and their ability to translate his work onto the big screen, even an 'epic' adaptation of the books will require a lot of material to be trimmed and simplified. Philip Pullman has talked about reading being a 'democratic' process, where each reader comes to their own understanding of the material. In those terms, though, the film will necessarily be one reading of the book. The material requires a sensitive and imaginative reader – and, therefore, a sophisticated and imaginative director to bring it to the screen.

With a projected budget of US$150 million, New Line are looking for a huge hit. It's unclear, however, what sort of story the company thinks it has bought. There are two ways to adapt the book – as a dark, complex treatise on growing up and religious faith (the Stoppard script was rumoured to be that), or as a straightforward action story about a young girl going on an adventure with a talking polar bear. Both could make for a good film or a bad film, depending on the script and the performances, but fans of the books are worried that a lot of what makes the books so good will be missing from the movie.

The makers of the movie have a big problem, though – currently, the religious Right in America are extremely vocal and influential. President Bush's electoral victory in 2004 was felt to be on the back of 'moral issues' and Mel Gibson's *The Passion of the Christ* demonstrated that there was an army of Christian filmgoers. A film – a children's film – in which the Christian church and God are the enemy, and are destroyed at the end, would be mired in controversy. Historically, having groups of people screaming that a film should be banned has actually been pretty good for business. But as many of these groups feel *Harry Potter* borders on the satanic and dangerously subversive, it's clear that the *His Dark Materials* films could act as a lightning rod for the debate.

This has led to anxiety from fans of Philip Pullman that aspects of the books – the depiction of religion, the violence and the sexuality – will all be toned down for the movies. This isn't simply the usual lament of fans reluctant to see any changes at all to the thing they love. Part of the power of the novels is that they are uncompromising and challenging, but Hollywood adaptations often involve a smoothing over of the difficult bits, and the removal of anything too dark or downbeat. Many Hollywood films value a simple message about the power of faith, spirituality and belief – precisely the sort of empty thinking Pullman's work despises. This is simple business sense: if a studio spends US$150 million on a movie, it has to try to make its money back, and that involves getting as many people as possible into cinemas. That's done by giving people something they will like, not something they will be offended by.

So, as *The Times* put it, 'Chris Weitz, the director, has horrified fans by announcing that references to the church are likely to be banished in his film. Meanwhile The Authority, the weak God figure will become "any arbitrary establishment that curtails the freedom of the individual."' Weitz invited great mockery by going on to say that the Authority could equally well be a communist as a Christian. Pullman's agent added 'You have to recognise that it is a challenge in the climate of Bush's America.' Online fans were quick to register their own horror at this development. On his website, Philip Pullman criticised *The Times* article for taking his words out of context – both what he had said in interviews, and in his books. He loathes those who 'insist on a literal interpretation of every single word, a point-by-point identification of this with that, a "correct" reading that's authorised and approved and certified by the authorities they submit to. People like that don't understand irony or implication or subtlety of any kind.'

The problem is, though, that film is a concrete medium. Some of the things that the books leave vague or open to interpretation will have to be depicted in a literal way in the movie, and this will seriously affect the way the movie is 'read'. To take one example, what will the churchmen wear? Will their costumes have crucifixes? Will the buildings they meet in have Christian symbols and images displayed? Will the designers draw on one particular type of Christian tradition for the look of the Church in the film, so that the members can be identified as Catholic priests or Puritan ministers? Will they mix-and-match different Christian looks? Or will they simply downplay the link to Christianity, dressing them in something austere but religiously 'neutral'? The books leave a lot of this sort of picturing to the reader, but that will be impossible in the film, and every design choice will mean the makers of the movie are imposing their own reading of the stories. While it's possible for some ambiguity and hidden meaning, the sort of blockbuster cinema New Line has in mind is not terribly good at the form of nuances Pullman talks about.

Evidence that the makers might be on the right track can be detected in the casting of Lyra. By picking Dakota Blue Richards, they have rejected the easier option of casting an older actress to play a teenager. Lyra is thirteen in the books, and looks young for her age, but by the end of the trilogy she is aware of her sexuality. She is possibly even sexually active – although it's safe to assume that the film of *The Amber Spyglass* will steer well clear of that reading of the ending of the book. The usual practice is to cast someone in their late teens to play young teenagers. There are good practical reasons for that – child actors are limited in the number of hours they can work, and still have to be tutored. Plus, of course, older actors are more experienced and have learned more about acting. The first actress who played Lyra in the stage play, Anna Maxwell Martin, was in her mid-twenties. But film is a very literal, visual medium. To have had a Lyra who looks sixteen or seventeen would have been quite a significant change.

None of this is actually that much of a problem in the first book. *Northern Lights* is a fairly straightforward adventure story. The Oblation Board are evil, but at a distance from the church. Lyra has no strong romantic feelings (Will first appears in *The Subtle Knife*). Even Asriel's revelation that he plans to destroy the Church is fairly mild compared with what is to come. It would make for an exciting children's film without ruffling too many feathers. The main problems will come with *The Amber Spyglass*, with the good guys fighting the forces of heaven, priests torturing prisoners to death, the death of God, not to mention thirteen year old children skinny dipping and disappearing off into the woods together. It's difficult to find parts of *The Amber Spyglass* that could be adapted without causing at least some parents to get worried. Perhaps New Line hope that, by then, the success of the previous movies will ensure the audience will come back to see the conclusion to the saga.

Whatever happens, the books will still be there, in the form Philip Pullman wrote them. The movie will lead many more children to the original stories, especially in America, where sales have been healthy but Pullman is still very much a relative unknown. Done right, though, the movie adaptations have the potential to be truly important and influential pieces of cinema.

Part Three

THE A–Z OF *HIS DARK MATERIALS*

In these A–Z sections we reference specific moments in the books, indicated by the initials of the book (NL for *Northern Lights*, for example) followed by the chapter number. The text in **bold** indicates that the subject has its own entry in the A–Z.

1. CHARACTERS AND CREATURES

The *His Dark Materials* novels have a large cast of characters and races. In this chapter you will find biographical entries on all the people and peoples who appear, or are mentioned, in the *His Dark Materials* trilogy and Lyra's Oxford.

A

AGNES, SISTER – One of the stenographers at the **Consistorial Court of Discipline**. She was from the order of **Saint Philomel** and had sworn an oath of silence [AS, 6].

ALEXANDROVNA, LYDIA – An elderly servant of **Father Semyon Borisovitch,** the Siberian priest who helps **Will** find a passage to the **Himalayas**. She has a sister who knew of the boat of **armoured bears** and their journey south [AS, 8].

ALLAN – **Lord Boreal'**s chauffeur in **Will'**s world [SK, 7].

AMA – A young girl, aged nine or ten, who helps **Will** to rescue **Lyra** from **Mrs Coulter**. Ama brings food to Mrs Coulter in her Himalayan cave hideout, believing her to be a holy woman engaged in meditation [AS, 1]. There she is told that Lyra is under an enchantment that cannot be broken. Ama takes it upon herself to visit the **Pagdzin** *tulku*, a Tibetan Monk famed for his abilities as a healer, from whom she obtains an antidote [AS, 4]. On her return, Ama discovers that Mrs Coulter is responsible for keeping Lyra unconscious. She subsequently helps Will and **Iorek Byrnison** to rescue Lyra using the **subtle knife**. Once Will and Lyra are safe, Ama returns to her village where she believes that the children are devils [AS, 14. Her **dæmon** is called **Kulang** [AS, 4]. Ama's father is a herdsman and has a crow dæmon [AS, 1].

ANDERSSON, ERIC – One of the guests **Mrs Coulter** considers inviting to her cocktail party. Andersson is the latest fashionable dancer [NL, 5].

ANFANG – The pinscher **dæmon** of **Lord Asriel**'s manservant, **Thorold** [NL, 21].

ANGELICA – A young girl of **Cittàgazze**. She has a younger brother, **Paolo**, and an older brother, **Tullio**. It is Tullio who breaks into the **Torre degli Angeli** and steals the **subtle knife** from **Giacomo Paradisi**. After **Will** becomes the bearer of the knife, Tullio flees from the Tower and is killed by **Spectres**. Maddened, Angelica leads a hunt for Will and **Lyra** from which they barely escape [SK, 11]. Angelica willingly gives information about Will and Lyra to **Father Luis Gomez** on his passage through Cittàgazze, hoping that he will kill them [AS, 10].

ANGELS – aka *bene elim*, **Watchers** [SK, 6]. Beings of pure spirit. Their preferred name for themselves is *bene elim* (SK, 6), Hebrew for 'sons of God'. The vast majority of angels are created from **Dust**, when matter becomes conscious of itself: the **Authority** was the first and **Xaphania** one of the earliest thereafter. A small minority of angels were once men, that is the descendants of Adam: **Metatron** was originally a man called Enoch, six generations from Adam [AS, 28], and **Baruch** was his brother. How some men came to be angels is unclear, but it would seem to have something to do with the freedom of one's **ghost** after death: thanks to **Balthamos'** intervention, Baruch's ghost did not travel to the **world of the dead** and he became 'angelic' [AS, 2]. Ghosts and spirit would seem to be connected.

As with all the angels in *His Dark Materials*, there is some ambiguity over their physical appearance. They are invariably described as being like humans but taller, naked and muscular with wings from their shoulder blades. Beyond that, the details are hazy: Xaphania is said to have a face that is old and young together [AS, 16, 36] while Balthamos is apparently ageless, having lived thousands of years and being capable of living for thousands more [AS, 8]. They are all said to glow but to different extremes as their luminescence implies rank: while Xaphania glows with a shimmering light [AS, 16], Balthamos and Baruch are barely visible except for during the half-light of dusk or dawn. The two angels admit that they are 'not of a high order among angels' [AS, 2]. We later discover that there are many kinds of angels, with different allegiances, factions and feuds [AS, 16].

In fact, the exact nature of angels cannot easily be described by reference to the physical. Angels are beings of 'intelligence and feeling' [SK, 6]. Their touch is light and cool [AS, 1]. They are capable of changing their form: Balthamos becomes a bird to pretend to be **Will's dæmon**, though he finds it 'unspeakably humiliating' [AS, 2]. It is stated that they only appear as humans to human eyes [SK, 6].

Nevertheless, angels have some physicality, even though their 'flesh' is not the same as that of humans. They need to eat, although they need little nourishment [AS, 2]. They can be fought and killed: Will is able to bear one angel assailant to the ground and kill him with the **subtle knife** [AS, 2] while Metatron's angels are set alight by the burning torches of the witches at the **Battle on the Plain** [AS, 29]. Whatever form angels take, human beings are ultimately stronger: it is for this reason that Will is able to command Balthamos and Baruch.

Although they may be physically 'weaker', angels possess a number of talents lacking in humans. They can travel at great speeds. They have an awareness that extends to the far-reaches of the universe [SK, 6]: Balthamos immediately senses the death of Baruch, although he does not know when or where [AS, 8]. The only place they cannot see is the world of the dead [AS, 11]. Angels are also capable of seeing **windows** between worlds [SK, 6] although they are not wholly reliant on them: Xaphania indicates that humans can learn to transport themselves between worlds as angels do. **Major John Parry** is adept at this [AS, 37]. It is for this reason that the angels can undertake to close all the windows, save that from the world of the dead.

While it is implied that angels have been seen in all the worlds, legends of their presence do not appear everywhere. The **witch** clans of the north, including those of **Serafina Pekkala** and **Ruta Skadi**, know nothing of them [SK, 2], although their prophecies are based on the 'immortal whispers' of the beings who pass between worlds [NL, 10]. Even **Mrs Coulter** believes angels to be an invention of the 'Middle Age' [AS, 16]. Nevertheless, angels are known to many cultures and appear in many religions.

The depiction of angels in *His Dark Materials* owes a lot to **John Milton**'s epic poem on the **Fall** of Man, *Paradise Lost*. Milton went far beyond the Bible in describing the nature and history of angels as well as the exploits and personalities of the principal figures. Milton's angels are beings of intelligence, made not of physical matter but of 'ether' or 'spirit'. They are capable of travelling at great speeds, can change form and can undertake either good or evil purposes. Although spirits, they maintain the powers and qualities of human beings, and need to eat and can love as men do. Milton's angels also have rank although nothing as strict as the hierarchy of the Seraphim put forward by his contemporaries.

Pullman, like Milton, implies that man is in some ways superior to angels, having been created by God to replace and improve on the fallen. In *His Dark Materials*, angels are usually subservient to man. **Lord Asriel** believes that Metatron's hatred of man is based on envy of their bodies that are so well suited to the earth. The critical factor is flesh: Lord Asriel insists that this is what makes man superior and will enable him to defeat the Authority [AS, 28]. This is because angels are one part of the elements of human beings: spirit, body and soul – or ghost, body and dæmon in **Lyra**'s world view.

ANNIE – A tall red-haired girl from London who is captured by the **General Oblation Board** and taken to **Bolvangar**. The experimental theologians at Bolvangar experiment to see how far her **dæmon** can get away from her. Her dæmon's name is **Kyrillion** [NL, 14, 16].

ARCHBISHOP – One of the guests **Mrs Coulter** invites to her cocktail party. It seems the invitation is given for political reasons and not for pleasure: Mrs Coulter actually thinks that he is a 'hateful old snob' [NL, 5].

ARMOURED BEARS – *See* **Bears**.

ARROW, DR BROKEN – *See* **Broken Arrow, Dr Leonard**.

ASRIEL, LORD – **Lyra**'s father. Lord Asriel is one of the chief protagonists in *His Dark Materials*, and one of Philip Pullman's greatest creations. From the moment he appears in the Retiring Room at **Jordan College**, tall and powerful, with a dark face and black eyes that flashed with 'savage laughter . . . a face to be dominated by, or to fight: never a face to patronise or pity', Asriel holds the reader in awe [NL, 1]. Lyra is meant to look like him, and has dark gold hair, so perhaps Asriel does. His **dæmon**, a powerful snow leopard with green eyes called **Stelmaria**, is the perfect shorthand for his character. As **Thorold**, Asriel's manservant of 40 years, said: 'he's Lord Asriel, he's not like other men' [SK, 2].

Asriel was born into the nobility; his brother was Count Belacqua [NL, 5]. He was 'a high-spirited man, quick to anger, a passionate man'. When he was young, Asriel explored the north and returned with a great fortune, which may have bought or supplemented his Oxfordshire estate [NL, 7]. He became a member of the **Royal Arctic Institute** and a member of Jordan College (his visits to the College were rare but always valued) [NL, 2]. He also sat in Parliament where he defeated the Watercourse Bill to the **gyptians**' lasting benefit. Indeed, the gyptians regarded Asriel as a stout friend for having given them a free passage across his estate, interceded with a Turk for the life of Sam Broekman and fought in the **floods of '53** to save the lives of two young gyptians [NL, 8]. By the time of Lyra's adventures, Asriel was a member of the **Cabinet Council**, the Prime Minister's special advisory body which also included the **Master of Jordan College** [NL, 1].

Most of all, Asriel was an opponent of the **Church**. Thorold said that Asriel had nursed a rebellion for as long as he had known him. At one point, Asriel had even considered making it an issue of force but believed the Church itself to be too weak. Instead, Asriel set his sights on the root cause, on the **Authority** Himself [SK, 2]. But how? Asriel became fascinated by the **Barnard–Stokes** heresy, the notion of other **worlds** existing parallel to his own, perhaps believing that in one he might find and kill the Authority. Asriel also investigated **Dust**, developing an entirely different idea of its nature that the Church would condemn as profoundly heretical [NL, 16]. It would take many years before he could put these pieces together.

But Asriel had more earthly concerns too. Around fourteen years before his war against the Authority, he met a fellow scholar, **Marisa Coulter**. It may have been at Oxford or at the Royal Arctic Institute where they were both members. Wherever it was, they fell in love at once. However, Marisa was already married to **Edward Coulter**, a powerful member of the **King**'s party who was destined for high office. Marisa became pregnant but did not tell her husband that Asriel was the father. When Lyra was born, it was obvious that Edward was not the father. Marisa claimed that her daughter had died in childbirth and sent her to Asriel's Oxfordshire estate where she was cared for by **Ma Costa**. Edward Coulter found out and came to the estate in 'a murderous passion'. Edward shot at Asriel and missed; Asriel seized the gun and shot Edward between the eyes, dashing his brains out [NL, 7, 8].

The subsequent court case lasted for weeks. In the end, the judges ordered the confiscation of Asriel's land and property. Lyra, abandoned by her mother, was sent to the **Sisters of Obedience** at **Watlington** (an attempt by Ma Costa to take custody of Lyra was rejected by the court). However, Asriel, consumed by a burning hatred of monks, priors and nuns, rode to Watlington and took his daughter, depositing her with the Master of Jordan College. Asriel's sole condition was that Marisa should never be allowed to see her daughter [NL, 7].

It was presumably at this time that Asriel chose to disguise his identity as Lyra's father, claiming instead that she was the daughter of the Count and Countess Belacqua, Asriel's brother and sister-in-law, who had died in an 'aëronautical' accident in the north. [NL, 5]. From then on he would visit Jordan College and Lyra on 'irregular occasions' [NL, 3]. Although Lyra came to imagine her 'uncle' as a heroic adventurer, the reality frightened her [NL, 1]. Asriel certainly never showed more than a passing interest in Lyra, and was always ready to scold her. When news of Lyra's importance reached him, it came as a complete surprise [AS, 3].

Asriel returned to his researches, seeking the destruction of the Authority and the Church. He continued to explore the north and at some time became the lover of the Latvian Witch-Queen **Ruta Skadi** [SK, 2]. Then, twelve months before the start of Lyra's adventure, he made some significant discoveries. Asriel went north, supposedly on a diplomatic mission to the King of **Lapland**, but in fact on a mission to investigate the mysterious disappearance some six months earlier of **Stanislaus Grumman**, a fellow explorer and academic. In one of his last reports, Grumman had told of a city behind the **Aurora**, proof that the 'heretical' Barnard–Stokes hypothesis was true. Asriel developed a new emulsion that enabled him to take **photograms** of Dust and more importantly the city itself. On his return, he presented these photograms – and the decapitated head of Grumman – to the scholars at

Jordan College. They readily funded a second expedition so Asriel could find out more [NL, 2]. Asriel, however, had more than research on his mind – he intended to build a bridge between his world and the world beyond the Aurora, to find the Authority and kill Him [NL, 11].

But Asriel was not the only person investigating Dust. By this time, Mrs Coulter had created her own power base within the Church, the **General Oblation Board**, which was set up to explore the connection between Dust and the fixing of dæmons during puberty. Using the precedent of circumcision, Mrs Coulter had argued that separating child and dæmon before the dæmon had fixed would keep the child in a state of innocence, free of **original sin**. Fearing the consequences of Asriel's plan, Mrs Coulter made a pact with **Iofur Raknison**, an ambitious armoured bear, to capture and imprison Asriel on **Svalbard**. Iofur's price was Mrs Coulter's assistance in the expulsion of another bear, **Iorek Byrnison**. Coulter readily agreed; Iorek was overthrown and Asriel was captured [NL, 11].

Imprisoned on Svalbard, Asriel was placed under a suspended sentence of death by the **Consistorial Court of Discipline** and ordered to discontinue his philosophical researches. In fact, he did nothing of the sort. 'Haughty and imperious', he forcibly argued with Iofur for a concession, persuading the new bear king to build his accommodation on a headland facing north, with large windows of real glass overlooking the Arctic ocean. Asriel was even able to have visitors. **Santelia** claimed that Iofur was actually playing Asriel and Mrs Coulter off against each other for his own benefit [NL, 19]. Whatever the case, within six months Asriel had assembled from various sources a laboratory with all the equipment he needed to complete his research. All he needed was one last thing – a child who, severed, would release enough energy to create the **bridge** [NL, 21]. Somehow, the Oblation Board discovered Asriel was close to achieving his task. The Consistorial Court began to debate his death sentence with all probability that it would be carried out [NL, 16].

In the event, the Court's decision, if it was ever made, came too late. Lyra travelled to Svalbard, succeeded in restoring

Iorek to power and unwittingly brought to Asriel the child he needed to complete his experiment. For one brief moment, Asriel betrayed his feelings for Lyra, horrified that his own daughter was the child he was to sever. His relief when he saw **Roger Parslow** was palpable [NL, 21]. On the frozen wastes, Asriel succeeded in creating a bridge to another world. He tried to persuade Mrs Coulter to join him, claiming that together they could 'find the source of Dust and stifle it forever' but was unsuccessful [NL, 23]. Lord Asriel crossed the bridge and entered another world.

What happened to Asriel thereafter is unclear. Evidently he passed into the world of **Cittàgazze** and from then into a world without consciousness. There, at the western end of a mountain range, Asriel built an enormous basalt fortress and began amassing his forces. In the **Adamant Tower**, built on the highest rampart, Asriel and his **high commanders** planned their war [AS, 5]. Ruta Skadi was astonished by how advanced Asriel's preparations were: 'he must have been preparing this for a long time, for aeons . . . I think he commands time, he makes it run slow or fast according to his will' [SK, 13]. However it was achieved, Asriel's forces were formidable and focused on one task: resisting the Authority and creating a world free from His influence [AS, 16]. Mrs Coulter correctly deduced that Asriel's plan was none other than to complete a war fought in Heaven aeons ago [SK, 9].

Although he didn't know it, Asriel's great endeavour was doomed to failure. As **Major John Parry** explained, individuals cannot live in another's world for any length of time: 'we have to build the **Republic of Heaven** where we are, because for us there is no elsewhere' [AS, 26]. Nevertheless his actions helped secure the second **Fall** of Man, occupying the forces of **Metatron** for such time as to let **Will** and Lyra escape. Most significantly, Lord Asriel achieved what he sought out to do – an end to the Authority Himself, or at least his **Regent**. With Mrs Coulter's help, he dragged Metatron into the abyss, dooming himself to an eternity of falling without release [AS, 31].

Asriel is an extremely well-crafted anti-hero. He has the characteristic determination, moral certainty and single-mindedness of classical heroes, with more than a hint of dismissiveness, obsessive fanaticism and arrogance. Utterly fixed on his task, Asriel has little time for anyone that might stand in his way, including his own daughter. His view of Lyra – 'impulsive, dishonest, greedy' and not very clever – is not retracted [AS, 16]. Indeed, his interest in her is only awakened when he discovers her importance. And yet there is a hint that he is secretly ashamed of his actions: when Lord Roke claims to know more of Asriel's daughter than Asriel himself, the Gallivespian soon realises he has overstepped the mark [AS, 5]. Nevertheless, this is an utterly dysfunctional relationship – indeed it's barely a relationship at all: he and Lyra only meet at the beginning and end of *Northern Lights*. He is not seen at all in *The Subtle Knife*, and although he sends spies and agents after his daughter, he doesn't come face-to-face or talk to her in *The Amber Spyglass*. It is peculiar to think that Lyra's last sight of her father is his attempt to reunite with Mrs Coulter shortly after Roger is killed.

Equally perplexing is Asriel's relationship with Dust and how this is presented in the books. In *Northern Lights*, Asriel boldly states that Dust comes through the Aurora. He is intent on finding 'the origin of all the Dust, all the death, the sin, the misery, the destructiveness in the world'. After he has opened the bridge, Asriel appeals to Mrs Coulter to come with him: 'We could find the source of Dust and stifle it forever.' But is this really what he intends? Let's go back to the first quote. After railing against the horrors apparently associated with Dust he says: 'Human beings can't see anything without wanting to destroy it, Lyra. *That's* original sin. And I'm going to destroy it. Death is going to die' [NL, 21]. It seems that he is seeking to destroy the desire to kill Dust, the Church's obsession with eliminating what it sees as original sin. When in the Adamant Tower, Mrs Coulter questions Asriel on his intention to stifle Dust at its source, he simply says it was a lie to tempt her to come with him [AS, 28].

Are we to believe Asriel or is this just Philip Pullman correcting a mistake? It seems unlikely that Asriel's words were not deliberately chosen for two principal reasons. First, a scientist at **Bolvangar** suspects that Asriel has an entirely different view of the nature of Dust that is profoundly heretical [NL, 16]. Whatever his precise understanding of Dust, Asriel's ideas would not find favour with the Church. Second, Asriel seems to have some sense of what is to come, even if it is not complete: Lyra suggests that 'Death is going to die' is a reference to freeing the ghosts in the land of the dead [AS, 23]. Third, before Asriel creates the bridge, **Pantalaimon** suggests to Lyra that Mrs Coulter's attempts to destroy Dust must mean it is good, something to be 'sought and welcomed and cherished' [NL, 23]. Pullman is clear at the end of *Northern Lights* that Dust is a positive force. And yet Asriel's motivation still seems unsatisfactory.

Lord Asriel is named after Azrael, the angel of death in the Book of Tobit which is regarded as apocryphal by Protestants. In the Book of Tobit, Azrael is an angel under the command of God. In the Qur'an, he is an archangel. Peculiarly, the modern first name Azriel means 'God helps' in Hebrew. This Azriel is named after one of the tribe of Manasseh in the Bible (I Chronicles, 5:24).

One of the peculiar unknowns about Asriel is his age. In the stage play, Lyra reckons he's 'old, dead old, forty at least', but it is said in the novels that he's helped rescue two young gyptians in the floods of '53, some 43 years before Northern Lights takes place, and that Thorold has served him for 40 years. Assuming he could have been no older than Lyra at the time of the floods, this would make him 56 years old. When performed, he has been played by actors of a similar age: Timothy Dalton was 57 when he played Asriel in the stage play, Terence Stamp was 63 in the radio version. Daniel Craig was 39 when he made *The Golden Compass*, roughly the same age as Nicole Kidman's Mrs Coulter.

ATAL – A female **zalif** (one of the **Mulefa**) who befriends **Dr Mary Malone** [AS, 10].

AUTHORITY – aka God, the **Creator**, the Lord, Yahweh, El, Adonai, the King, the Father, the Almighty. The Authority is the first **angel** to be formed from **Dust**. He tells the angels that come after him that he has created them but this is a lie. One angel, **Xaphania**, knows the truth and is banished from Heaven [AS, 2]. The resulting rebellion, witnessed by the oldest **cliff-ghast**, is unsuccessful and the fallen angels are forced to flee [SK, 13]. So the Authority's dominance and the **Kingdom of Heaven** is cemented [AS, 16]. Ruling from the **Clouded Mountain**, the Authority creates the **world of the dead** during the early ages of his rule as a prison camp for the spirits of the departed [AS, 2]. Four thousand years before the events of *The Amber Spyglass*, the Authority takes **Metatron** into his kingdom to rule by his side as Regent [AS, 5]. Then the Authority withdraws, leaving his priests to maintain his order [AS, 28].

By the time of *His Dark Materials*, the balance of power in the Kingdom of Heaven has shifted. 'Together', the Authority and Metatron intend to subdue Man's independence and restore their power by intervening directly in human affairs and establishing a permanent Inquisition [AS, 5]. However, it is clear that the Authority is in no fit state to command – indeed **Lord Asriel** refers to the first angel as the 'old Authority' clearly implying that Metatron has taken his place [AS, 28]. Encased in a crystal litter, the Authority is demented and powerless, an indescribably aged creature of 'terrifying decrepitude' that can only mumble in pain and misery [AS, 30, 31]. Once the crystal case is opened, the Authority dissipates into nothingness in the wind [AS, 31].

So, is the Authority God? As ever, there are no simple answers. He is certainly the biblical figure who banishes the fallen angels from Heaven, who turns Enoch into Metatron and makes him his Regent and the focus of worship for the Churches of the world. Yet he is explicitly not the Creator [AS, 16]. What is more interesting is the question of whether or not there *ever* was a Creator. **King Ogunwe**'s comment that the Authority 'came into being' shocks **Mrs Coulter** who always saw God as the creator of worlds [AS, 16]. By suggesting that matter can become conscious of itself and therein form itself into beings, Philip Pullman puts forward an alternative, secular view of creation.

Strangely, given the amount of time spent discussing religion in the books, there's no sense given of how and where ordinary people worship the Authority. In the stage play, there are a couple of references to 'prayers' to the Authority and someone says grace – 'for what we are about to eat, we thank the Authority'.

B

BALTHAMOS – An **angel** who is a somewhat haughty and disdainful character. Balthamos is an angel conceived of **Dust**. By the time of the second **Fall**, he had been alive for many thousands of years [AS, 7]. Four thousand years before *The Amber Spyglass*, Balthamos prevented **Baruch**'s ghost from entering the **world of the dead**, transforming Baruch into an angel [AS, 2]. From then on, they 'loved each other with a passion', feeling as one, and become lifelong companions [AS, 2]. Balthamos and Baruch serve the rebel angel **Xaphania** and it is in this capacity that they track **Major John Parry** to **Will** in order to bring the **subtle knife** to **Lord Asriel** [AS, 2]. Balthamos is heartbroken by the death of Baruch at the hands of the **Authority**'s angels [AS, 8] but continues to help Will, as Baruch would have wanted. Balthamos is able to assist by transforming into an animal to pretend to be Will's **dæmon** and translating languages [AS, 2, 8]. It is Balthamos who ultimately secures the second Fall of Man by killing the assassin **Father Luis Gomez** [AS, 35]. His task complete, Balthamos vanishes, to join his beloved Baruch once more.

Balthamos and Baruch clearly love each other but whether this is homosexual or brotherly love is questionable. The use of the word 'passion' might indicate the former, but it may be different for angels.

Balthamos is the narrator of the radio version, where he was played by Ray Fearon.

BARUCH – An **angel** and beloved of **Balthamos**. Baruch is younger and more powerfully built than Balthamos, and has a simpler nature [AS, 2]. Four thousand years ago, he lived as a man, the brother of **Enoch** who became **Metatron**. On his death, his **ghost** was saved from entering the **world of the dead** by Balthamos and Baruch became an angel. Like Balthamos, Baruch serves the rebel angel **Xaphania** in the battle against the **Authority**. Baruch is attacked by four of the Authority's angels on his way to **Lord Asriel**'s **fortress** to relay the location of **Mrs Coulter**'s Himalayan cave [AS, 5]. He had barely completed his mission before dying.

Baruch appears in the Bible as the friend and scribe of Jeremiah (Jeremiah, 32:12, 36:4). He is purported to be the author of the Book of Baruch which is included in the canon of the Roman Catholic and Eastern Orthodox Churches but considered by the Protestant Church to be apocryphal. The Book of Baruch is essentially a message of hope to the Jewish community set against the backdrop of the Babylonian exile. There are other mentions of Baruch in the Hebrew Bible and it is not clear which, or whether any of them, was the brother of Enoch. Baruch is Hebrew for 'blessed'. The name is pronounced bah-rouk.

BASILIDES, TEUKROS – **Lord Asriel**'s **alethiometrist**. Basilides is a thin, pale man, who has dark eyes and a nightingale **dæmon** [AS, 5, 28].

BASILISK – A mythical creature in our world, but the **dæmon** of one of the former **Masters of Jordan College** [NL, 3]. The basilisk was supposedly king of the serpents and is usually depicted as a giant snake with the head of either a human or a cockerel. In art, it usually symbolised the devil but to Protestants was also the symbol of the Papacy.

BEARS – aka **Armoured bears, Panserbørne**. The armoured bears of the north are one of the most impressive and terrifying sights for the brave traveller. Around ten feet tall on their hind legs, these giant polar bears are immensely strong and resilient, capable of travelling great distances through the arctic wastes without rest. Their home, **Svalbard**, is regarded by **Lee Scoresby** as the most inhospitable place he visited on his travels. The armoured bears are capable fighters, regarded by the **gyptians** as being vicious and pitiless in their raids against the **Skraelings** whom the bears had fought for centuries [NL, 6]. Bears are also talented metalworkers: according to the gyptians they had hands like men and learned the trick of working iron 'way back' [NL, 6]. **Lyra** marvels at **Iorek Byrnison**'s ability to use his opposable claws to bend and shape thin metal into a tin for the spy-fly [NL, 13]. Most notably, Iorek is able to repair the **subtle knife** with immense precision.

The bears are most famous for their armour which they fashion from 'sky-metal' or 'sky-iron' (meteorite rock). Iorek's armour is a mass of sheets and plates of rust-red iron, laid over each other and crudely riveted together. The bears use seal blubber to lubricate the armour. The helmet is pointed like a muzzle with slits for eyes and an exposed jaw for tearing at opponents. There is a weak point between the shoulder and helmet [NL, 11]. But for bears, armour is more than defence. 'A bear's armour is his soul, just as your **dæmon** is your soul', he tells Lyra. Indeed, there may be something quite literal to this: the priest holding Iorek's armour believes that there is a spirit in it and is trying to conjure it out [NL, 11, 20].

Bear society is highly structured and governed by ancient rites and rituals. Both Iorek Byrnison and **Iofur Raknison** are princes among the Svalbard bears and deserving of respect and obedience. When disagreements arise between bears, the weaker must back down. Bears have ways of turning away their anger with each other [NL, 13]. Killing another bear is a major offence punishable by the removal of the bear's armour and exile. She-bears are taken as wives and mothers: bears are brought up by their mothers, and seldom see their fathers [NL, 19].

Bears are also famously difficult to trick, as Iorek demonstrates by parrying aside Lyra's attempts to fence with him. 'We see tricks and deceit as plain as arms and legs,' Iorek tells her. 'We can see in a way humans have forgotten.' [NL, 13]. Lyra is able to trick Iofur because he behaves like a person [NL, 18]. The exchange is an interesting one in two important respects. First, it intimates that this way of seeing is the same employed by Lyra to read the **alethiometer** – a kind of **negative capability**. This ability to command a state of grace or 'innocence' is a recurring theme. Second, the encounter is informed by **Heinrich von Kleist**'s *On A Marionette Theatre*, one of only three authors whom Philip Pullman credits as influences at the end of *The Amber Spyglass*. In Kleist's story, a bear can fight instinctively, without the limitations of self-consciousness.

BELISARIA – The seagull **dæmon** of **Jerry**, the able-seaman **Lyra** befriends on her journey to the north [NL, 10].

BELLA – A 'friendly, plump' girl with dark hair, who is captured by the **General Oblation Board** and taken to **Bolvangar** [NL, 14].

BENE ELIM – See **Angels**.

BETTY, SISTER – A nurse at **Bolvangar** who measures **Lyra** for **Dust**. She has a pretty bird **dæmon** [NL, 15].

BLACK SHUCK – A great ghost dog in the tales of the **Fen**-dwellers [NL, 7]. The story of Black Shuck is a Norfolk folk tale and is believed to be one of the inspirations for Sir Arthur Conan Doyle's *The Hound of the Baskervilles*.

BOATMAN – An ancient figure, 'aged beyond age', who transports **ghosts** across a lake to the **land of the dead** [AS, 21]. Crippled and bent, and clothed in sacking, the boatman has bony hands and 'moist pale eyes sunk deep among folds and wrinkles of grey skin'. The boatman has transported millions of ghosts and though threatened on many occasions cannot be hurt.

In Greek mythology, Charon, the ferryman of Hades, takes the newly dead ('shades') over the river Acheron on their journey to the land of the dead. He is often depicted as a cranky, skinny old man but sometimes as a winged demon.

Charon is often mistakenly believed to transport people across the River Styx but this is one of the later rivers of Hades that borders the earth. In Dante's *Inferno*, the Acheron borders Hell.

BOREAL, LORD CARLO – aka **Sir Charles Latrom**. A powerful member of the **Council of State** in **Lyra**'s world, and **Mrs Coulter**'s lover [NL, 23; SK, 9]. In his late sixties, with grey hair and dark eyes, Boreal exudes prosperity, confidence and power [SK, 4, 12]. Lyra first encounters Boreal at Mrs Coulter's party in London where he claims that he and the **Master of Jordan College** are old friends [NL, 5]. In fact, Boreal lives a secret second life. Many years prior to meeting Lyra, Boreal finds his way to **Will**'s **Oxford**, most likely via **Cittàgazze** [SK, 9]. There he becomes Sir Charles Latrom CBE, taking residence at **Limefield House** in Old Headington, where he is chauffeured about in a dark-blue Rolls-Royce [SK, 7]. It is unclear whether his knighthood and CBE were invented or earned as Boreal insinuated himself with the intelligence services, working for many years as a spy for the British government against the Soviet Union (**Muscovy** in Lyra's world). After the decline of the Soviet empire, Boreal continued to keep in contact with those who ran the listening posts from whom he learned the consequences of **Lord Asriel**'s **bridge** [SK, 9]. As Latrom, Boreal steals Lyra's **alethiometer** and seeks to trade it for the **subtle knife**. Will, however, is able to use the knife to retrieve the alethiometer and escape to safety. Once Mrs Coulter extracts the truth about the knife from Boreal, she poisons him seeking to take it for herself [SK, 15]. His **dæmon** is a serpent with a mailed head and gold-rimmed black/green eyes [NL, 5; SK, 7].

Boreal's name seems to be laden with hidden meaning. Boreal is perhaps a corruption of the Latin 'boreas' meaning the north. Latrom is 'mortal' backwards, a hint at his imminent demise.

BORISOVITCH, FATHER SEMYON – An immense grey-bearded Siberian priest who tells **Will** how to find a passage south to the **Himalayas**. His servant is **Lydia Alexandrovna**. He has a crow **dæmon** [AS, 8].

BRAKS, ADRIAAN – A **gyptian** who questions whether the gyptian families are duty-bound to rescue **Lord Asriel** from his imprisonment in **Svalbard** [NL, 8].

BREATHLESS ONES – According to **Tony Costa**, the Breathless Ones are warriors, half-killed, whose lungs are extracted by Northern **Tartars**. Whole platoons of Breathless Ones can occasionally be encountered in the forests of the north [NL, 6].

BROKEN ARROW, DR LEONARD – A **Skraeling** and member of the **Royal Arctic Institute**. He was famed for mapping the ocean currents in the Great Northern Ocean [NL, 4]. He is the author of 'The Proto-Fisher People of L'Anse aux Meadows' [LO].

BROOKS, LIZZIE – Pseudonym used by **Lyra** when she is captured by the **Samoyed Tartars** [NL, 14]. Lyra pretends that her father has brought her to the north while trading New Danish **smokeleaf** and buying furs [NL, 14]. Lyra continues to use the name Lizzie in **Will's Oxford**.

BYRNISON, IOREK – King of the **armoured bears** of **Svalbard**. Ten feet tall on his hind legs and possessing tremendous strength, Iorek is a dominant member of the **Panserbørne**. His size is matched equally by his deep, booming voice, so flat that it is difficult to sense any inflection or expression in his words [NL, 10]. As befits the armoured bears, Iorek is a gifted metalworker, capable of constructing everything from his own impressive armour to small tin boxes to house the **alethiometer** and the **spy-fly**. But he also stands apart from them: **Lyra** notes that other bears are not so 'pure and certain and absolute' [NL, 20]. His long-time friend and ally, **Lee Scoresby**, who Iorek fought beside in the **Tunguska Campaign**, vouches for the bear king's honesty and integrity without hesitation [NL, 12, 13].

Above all, Iorek is a committed and ferocious fighter and friend: 'War is the sea I swim in and the air I breathe' [NL, 10]. It is a skill that would come in useful on many occasions.

Iorek history is known to the **witches** of the north though he was not quick to disclose it himself. Iorek is high-born, a prince destined for the highest office. His throne is stolen from him by another prince, **Iofur Raknison**. Iofur is a bear of cunning and deceit, of 'humanness', who wishes above all to have a **dæmon** of his own. When establishing **Bolvangar, Mrs Coulter** cultivates a relationship with Iofur, promising him that one day he will be baptised as a Christian by the **Magisterium**. Her price is the bears' protection for her experiments. To that end, she helps Iofur to overthrow Iorek. When Iorek and **Hjalmur Hjalmurson** clash over a she-bear, Iofur secretly feeds Hjalmur a drug that Mrs Coulter provides. Hjalmur is enraged and in this induced state refuses to recognise Iorek's superior strength and forces a fight. Iorek, for his part, loses control of his anger and kills Hjalmur. Iorek is stripped of his wealth, rank and armour and sent out to live at the edge of the human world. It is a punishment that he later accepts is just, although he knows nothing of Mrs Coulter's hand in the affair [NL, 13, 18].

Now no longer a Svalbard bear, Iorek travels south. On the way he makes new armour from **sky-metal**. At **Trollesund**, the local men allow him to drink himself into a stupor then take his armour away, intending to keep him in the town for his metalworking skills. When he discovers the theft, Iorek goes on the rampage, breaking open the police house, the bank and other places in search of his armour. At least two people die [NL, 10, 11]. Eventually, unable to find his armour, Iorek becomes resigned to his fate. He finds employment with the sled depot in **Langlokur Street** where he provides his metalworking services in exchange for his keep and liquor from **Einarsson's Bar** [NL, 10].

It is here, in this sorry state, that Lyra meets Iorek Byrnison, the rightful king of the Svalbard bears, for the first time. Lyra recovers Iorek's armour, for which he is indebted to her. Together they travel to Bolvangar where Iorek plays a part in the destruction of the base. Later, Lyra helps Iorek regain his throne when she tricks Iofur into a battle with Iorek. Although the battle is closely fought, Iorek emerges as the victor, ripping Iofur's jaw from his head and tearing at his opponent's throat. Iorek releases Iofur's human prisoners and orders Iofur's marble palace to be abandoned in favour of the traditional ice structures of the Svalbard bears. In honour of her help, Iorek gives Lyra the surname 'Silvertongue'. She becomes one of only three non-bears for whom Iorek ever expressed any regard, alongside Lee Scoresby and **Serafina Pekkala** [AS, 9].

After **Asriel** opens his **bridge**, Lyra and Iorek part company and Iorek returns to rule the bears. However, the changes wrought to the parallel worlds by the creation of the bridge have disastrous consequences on the bears' home as the ice-caps begin to melt. Iorek leads some of his comrades south to the high mountains of the **Himalayas** in search of a new home [AS, 9]. Breaking their journey in the Siberian wastes, Iorek meets **Will** who immediately impresses the bear king with his strength of purpose. Iorek is able to help Will in his daring rescue of Lyra from Mrs Coulter and the **Church**'s forces. Iorek also repairs the **subtle knife**, although he senses in the blade a purpose of which none are aware. He is proved right. Iorek and the bears try to find a new life in the Himalayas but are unsuccessful. Iorek, Will and Lyra come to realise that they must make their own lives where they are. Iorek returns to Svalbard.

The character of Iorek is undoubtedly one of Philip Pullman's greatest triumphs. In the bear king's assuredness of purpose and integrity, one gets a character of moral purity to match Will and Lyra. To complement them, Iorek is also astoundingly wise: his reflection on the subtle knife and its secret intention (the creation of **Spectres** and the loss of **Dust**) echoes of foreboding. Pullman's great skill is in giving Iorek all these attributes while keeping him distinctly unhuman. We are never left unaware that Iorek is the product of centuries of bear culture and custom, living a life by rules completely separate from those of humankind. He remains to the end a step removed from the human characters, inherently alien to our ways of doing and thinking. The filmmakers would do well to preserve Iorek's impassive face and unfeeling directness.

In both the talking book and radio versions, the name is usually pronounced Yorrick, but sometimes Your-rick.

C

CALVIN, POPE JOHN – The last pope in **Lyra**'s world. Calvin moved the seat of the Papacy to **Geneva** and set up the **Consistorial Court of Discipline**, after which 'the **Church**'s power over every aspect of life had been absolute'. After Calvin's death, the Papacy itself was abolished and replaced by the collection of courts, colleges and councils known as the **Magisterium** [NL, 2]. During his lifetime, Calvin was reputed to have ordered the deaths of children [AS, 16].

Philip Pullman's Calvin is based on the great French Protestant theologian and reformer of the same name. He (1509–64) was one of the principal figures in the Protestant Reformation, the movement to reform the Roman Catholic Church that took place in the sixteenth century and resulted in the emergence of several other Christian Churches including those of the Lutherans, Anabaptists and Calvinists. In 1536, he was persuaded by Guillaume Farel (1489–1565) to assist in the reformation in Switzerland where the people of Geneva had won their independence from the Duke of Savoy. Calvin's order of moral severity provoked a backlash and he and Guillaume were expelled in 1538. Nevertheless, in 1541, he created a powerful theocracy – a political system based on the Church – that operated through the office of ministers, the College of Pastors and Doctors and the **Consistorial Court of Discipline**. His absolute supremacy was confirmed in 1555, after almost a decade and a half of struggles with the Libertines. Material provided by Pullman in the programme for the stage play states that his Calvin ascended to the Papacy in 1555. Calvin brought to Protestantism a clarification of its doctrine and ecclesiastical discipline and is one of the most significant figures in Protestant and sixteenth-century history.

Pullman's reference to Calvin poses some interesting questions. It could be interpreted that the Church we see in *His Dark Materials* is the Roman Catholic Church as reformed by Calvin on a much greater scale – the institution of the Calvinist Genevan theocracy across all Europe. If so, the Church of Lyra's world, which to the casual reader can appear to be Roman Catholic, is rather a peculiar hybrid.

CANSINO, SAM – A black-bearded, Texan fur-trader and old acquaintance of **Lee Scoresby**. Cansino met **Stanislaus Grumman** five years before the events of *The Subtle Knife*, at the northern end of the Urals where Stanislaus had fallen foul of a trap laid by **Yakovlev**. Sam, like most Arctic drifters, is an occasional resident at the **Samirsky Hotel** in **Nova Zembla** [SK, 6].

CANZONA, MICHAEL – A senior **gyptian** and second in command to **John Faa** during the rescue of **Lord Asriel** from **Svalbard**. It is Canzona's job to liaise between the gyptian heads of family and to take command if John Faa dies [NL, 8].

CARBORN, COLONEL J. C. B. – A member of the **Royal Arctic Institute**. Carborn was the first man to make a balloon flight over the North Pole [NL, 4]. He is the author of *By Zeppelin to the Pole*, where his full name and title is given as Lt-Col J. C. B. Carborn, GM, OS, FRAS [LO].

CASSINGTON SCHOLAR – One of the positions at **Jordan College**. According to **Lord Asriel**, the post is traditionally given to a free-thinker whose job it is to challenge the faith of the other scholars. The current Cassington scholar tells **Lyra** that the story of Adam and Eve is not literally true [NL, 21].

CASTOR – The name of the **dæmon** that once belonged to one of the **ghosts** in the **land of the dead** [AS, 22].

CAWSON – The **Steward** at **Jordan College**. As a superior servant, he has a superior dog as a **dæmon**, a red-setter. The

Steward had a long-standing rivalry with the Butler [NL, 1]. He is probably the 'Mr Cawston' (*sic*) referenced later [NL, 3].

CENTAURS – The **Authority**'s army apparently consists of these creatures, half-human half-horse [AS, 30].

CEREBATON – The **dæmon** of Simon Le Clerc, a former **Master of Jordan College** 1765–89 [NL, 3]. The name is probably a play on the Latin word 'cerebrum', meaning 'brain'.

CHAPLAIN – A scholar at **Jordan College** and a leading light among experimental theologians. His chapel is surrounded by philosophical equipment. Jordan College's reputation lay in no small part to his researches [NL, 3].

CHARLIE – A **gyptian** boy who sees the **Gobblers** abduct a little boy in Banbury [NL, 3].

CLARA, SISTER – A nurse who works at **Bolvangar**. She has a little white dog **dæmon** [NL, 14].

CLAY-BURNERS – A name given by **Lyra** and the children of **Oxford** to the people who process clay on the claybeds near Oxford. Lyra, **Roger** and the Oxford 'townies' temporarily join forces to wage a successful war against the clay-burners' children [AS, 23].

CLIFF-GHASTS – Stinking predators found in the frozen north, particularly around the palace of the **bear** kings at **Svalbard**. Cliff-ghasts are typically half the size of a man, with leathery wings and hooked claws. Their heads are flat with bulging eyes and froglike mouths. They are equally renowned for the 'wafts of abominable stink' that accompany them, presumably from their diet of carrion, and for their shrieking 'yowk-yowk' cries. **Lyra, Iorek Byrnison** and **Lee Scoresby** are attacked by the cliff-ghasts en route to Svalbard [NL, 18]. The cliff-ghasts also attack **Lord Asriel**'s servant, **Thorold**, and a party of **witches** [SK, 2, 13]. According to **Ruta Skadi**, the cliff-ghasts may not be of Lyra's world or that of **Cittàgazze** [SK, 13]. Indeed, they may originally be from the world in which Lord Asriel builds his army. It is in this world that Ruta Skadi encounters the oldest of the cliff-ghasts, older than humankind, where she overhears the story of **Æsahættr**, also known as the **subtle knife**. This creature is known to the other cliff-ghasts as 'grandfather' [SK, 13].

CLIFFORD, SERGEANT – A female police sergeant who, with **Inspector Walters**, questions **Dr Mary Malone** [SK, 7]. As she is sent by **Sir Charles Latrom,** it is unclear whether they are genuine police officers.

COKE, MICHAEL – A famous flautist in **Lyra**'s world who performs a recital at the Musical Society of **Saint Sophia's** College [LO].

COLE, IGNATIUS – **Master of Jordan College**, 1745–48. His **dæmon** is called Musca [NL, 3].

COLLEGERS – The name **Lyra** uses to describe the children from **Oxford** who traditionally battle with the **gyptian** children over the summer months [NL, 3].

COMMEDIA PLAYERS – Occasional visitors who came from **Bergamo** to **Cittàgazze** before the arrival of the **Spectres** [SK, 6]. Commedia was a style of Italian comic theatre popular between the sixteenth and eighteenth centuries.

COOPER, DR – A senior **experimental theologian** at **Bolvangar** who conducts experiments on children [NL, 16]. After the destruction of Bolvangar, he is taken to the **College of Saint Jerome** in **Geneva** where he is interrogated by the President of the **Consistorial Court of Discipline** [AS, 6]. Dr Cooper later delivers the bomb that the **Church** hopes will destroy **Lyra**, preventing the second **Fall** of Man. The bomb is based on the

Barnard–Stokes' 'many-worlds' heresy [AS, 24]. He has a rabbit **dæmon** [AS, 69]. He is called Dr Sargent in the stage play.

COOPER, MRS – **Will**'s elderly piano teacher who takes care of **Mrs Parry** in Will's absence. Prior to this visit, Mrs Cooper hadn't seen Will in over one year. She has a daughter in Australia [SK, 1].

CORAM, FARDER – An elderly, respected member of the **gyptians**. By the time **Lyra** meets him, Farder is weak and old, unable to walk without two sticks and constantly trembling. His mind, however, is as sharp as ever and his voice is 'rich and musical' [NL, 7]. Forty years previously, Farder had been 'young and strong and full of pride and beauty'. At that time, he rescued **Serafina Pekkala** from an assault from a great red bird in the **Fens** of **Eastern Anglia**. Pekkala falls in love with him at once and stays with him long enough to bear him a child, although the boy dies in a great epidemic from the East not long after birth. Serafina leaves Coram when she is recalled to her clan to become Clan-Queen on the death of her mother. Though she cannot get away, Serafina continues to look out for Farder, sending him herbs and spells to help him recover when he is wounded by the poisoned arrow of a **Skraeling** [NL, 10, 18]. Farder continues to love Serafina though he knows it cannot be fully requited. During his younger years, Coram also travelled to **Heidelberg** where he saw a book that detailed the symbols of the **alethiometer** and how to read it [NL, 9]. He had also travelled to Africa and visited Morocco where he saw a **spy-fly** [NL, 9]. In his latter years, Farder Coram acted as the wise, principled adviser to **John Faa** and helped advise and plan the gyptian rescue of the children from **Bolvangar** [NL, 7]. His **dæmon** is an elegant autumn-coloured cat, twice the size of an ordinary cat, called Sophonax [NL, 9]. Sophonax is derived from Sophia, the Greek word for wisdom.

COSTA, BILLY – One of the children kidnapped by the **Gobblers** and taken to **Bolvangar** [NL, 15].

COSTA, MA – Head of a **gyptian** family and mother of **Tony** and **Billy Costa**. **Lyra** knows that Ma Costa is the fearsome owner of a grand and sumptuous boat that she once hijacked with **Roger**, Simon and Hugh from **Oxford** [NL, 3; AS, 23]. In fact, Lyra has a long history with Ma Costa. It is she who nurses Lyra as a child at **Lord Asriel**'s Oxfordshire estate and who hides Lyra from the vehemence of **Edward Coulter**, who tries to kill her. When Lyra is ordered into the care of the **Sisters of Obedience** at Watlington, Ma Costa pleads with the court to become Lyra's guardian but this is not granted. Nevertheless, she continues to keep an eye on Lyra and receives regular reports of her movements from **Bernie Johansen**, the gyptian's spy in the kitchens of **Jordan College** [NL, 7]. Ma Costa has a hawk **dæmon** with fierce yellow eyes [NL, 3].

COSTA, TONY – The eldest son of **Ma Costa** and brother of **Billy Costa**. Tony rescues Lyra from the Turk traders in London [NL, 6]. Like his mother, Tony has a hawk **dæmon** [NL, 8].

COULTER, EDWARD – **Marisa Coulter**'s husband at the time of her affair with **Lord Asriel**. Edward Coulter is a politician, a member of the King's party and one of his closest advisers. When Marisa becomes pregnant, Edward believes the child to be his but after the birth it is apparent that **Lyra** is not his child as she looks like Asriel. Marisa lets Asriel take Lyra to his Oxfordshire estate and claims that Lyra is dead. However, Edward is told the truth and ransacks Asriel's house for the child. Lord Asriel arrives in time and they fight, which results in Edward's death [NL, 7].

COULTER, MARISA MRS – **Lyra**'s mother. Mrs Coulter is the principal antagonist of the *His Dark Materials* trilogy. Her appearance – her incandescent beauty, sleek black hair and intoxicating voice – disguises a corrupt, power-hungry and ruthless nature [NL, 3; SK, 9]. This immorality is matched only by a guile and ingenuity that keeps her ahead of her enemies.

Her **dæmon** is the vile and impish **golden monkey** that remains nameless throughout the trilogy [NL, 3].

Clever and insightful, Marisa Coulter becomes a scholar at **Saint Sophia's** and one of the very few members of the **Royal Arctic Institute** [NL, 4]. She doesn't just explore in the frozen north: Africa seems to occupy her time also. She is also the author of *The Bronze Clocks of Benin* [NL, 9; LO]. But the pursuit of knowledge is not her prime goal. Marisa has an insatiable craving for power that she first sought to satisfy through marriage. Her husband, **Edward Coulter,** is a powerful member of the King's party and is destined for high office. But she jeopardises it all when she meets **Lord Asriel.**

As soon as they meet, Lord Asriel and Mrs Coulter fall in love. They begin a clandestine affair and soon Marisa becomes pregnant. She keeps the parentage of the baby secret from Edward. However, after the birth it is clear that Edward is not the father. Marisa sends the baby, Lyra, to Asriel's Oxfordshire estates and pretends to Edward that the baby died in childbirth. The deception does not hold: Edward is informed of the baby's existence and goes to Oxfordshire, perhaps to confront Asriel, or perhaps to retrieve the baby. In the event, Edward is overpowered by Asriel and killed [NL, 7].

The most disturbing aspect of the trial that follows is Marisa's actions. With nothing to gain from having the child, and Edward gone, she turns her back on Lyra completely. When Asriel deposits Lyra with the **Master of Jordan College,** he stipulates only one condition: that Mrs Coulter should never be allowed to see her daughter [NL, 7].

Now, Marisa is free to seek power in other ways. She continues to consort with the powerful, becoming **Lord Boreal**'s mistress [NL, 23]. The most logical route is to ally herself with the **Church.** As she cannot become a priest, her only option is to establish her own order. Asriel later notes that she was clever to specialise in **Dust** as everyone is so frightened of it that they readily give her money and resources to investigate further. Marisa is the person who makes the connection between Dust settling and the fixing of one's dæmon at puberty. Using the precedent of circumcision, she obtains a licence to experiment with cutting. And so the **General Oblation Board** is born and Mrs Coulter gains her own channels of influence [NL, 21].

It is never made clear what Mrs Coulter's own religious beliefs are. She is certainly well versed in religious doctrine, as one would expect, and has a personal and 'ghoulish' interest in **intercision** which could imply a firm belief in **original sin** [NL, 21]. However, she is initially dismissive of the notion of **angels**, believing them to be 'an invention of the Middle Age' [AS, 16]. There is always the suspicion that any religious piety is simply a show for advancement.

The General Oblation Board seems to have come into existence some two or three years before Lyra's adventure as this is when the children began to disappear. Marisa seems to have spent some time in the Arctic, securing the support, or at least the non-interference of the **witch** clans, for the establishment of **Bolvangar**. Then news starts to reach her of Asriel's activities: his investigation into the **Barnard–Stokes** hypothesis, his profoundly heretical view of Dust and his intention to create a **bridge** to another world through the **Aurora**. Now, Mrs Coulter visits **Svalbard** with the intention of gaining the support of the armoured bears. She soon finds an ambitious bear-prince, **Iofur Raknison**, and plays on his vanity and affectations. She asks that Iofur capture and imprison Lord Asriel, and seems to moot the notion of another research station, more terrible than Bolvangar and beyond human laws. Iofur's price is simple: help him to become king of the bears. To that end, Mrs Coulter provides Iofur with the drug he needs to make his plan succeed. She also promises to have him baptised in the Church, although he does not have a dæmon [NL, 19, 20].

With Asriel safely contained in Svalbard, the Oblation Board continues its work. It is then that Marisa enters Lyra's life. Mrs Coulter later claims that she took Lyra away from **Jordan College** to protect her from the **Gobblers**. She again saves Lyra when the doctors at Bolvangar threaten to sever her from **Pantalaimon** using the **silver guillotine**. And she claims to be protecting Lyra from the Church when she kidnaps her and holds her an unconscious prisoner in the Himalayan cave [AS, 16]. Lord Asriel, of course, regards all as bare-faced lies, noting with disgust that 'she lied in the very marrow of her bones' [AS, 16]. But what is the truth? Did the horrors of intercision remind her of her duties as a mother? Asriel certainly seemed to think that Lyra had drawn Marisa's poison [AS, 16].

Whatever the motivation, Mrs Coulter does help Lyra but is only able to do so by calling on those qualities that have made her such a powerful opponent. She is able to beguile **Metatron**, using her body and charm as she had done with so many others, but not before Metratron undertakes a searching examination of her soul. No better summary of Mrs Coulter's nature can be found. Before him he sees a being of profound corruption and lust for power; a person who has killed, tortured and betrayed without regret. 'You have never from your earliest years shown a shred of compassion or sympathy or kindness without calculating how it would return to your advantage'. Above all, she is 'pure, poisonous toxic malice . . . A cesspit of moral filth' [AS, 30]. But for all that, perhaps because of it, Metatron still falls for her charms. She leads him to Asriel where, together, they make the ultimate sacrifice and fall into the **abyss** to fall for eternity [AS, 31].

Mrs Coulter is a fascinating character, every bit a match for Cruella D'Evil or the White Witch of Narnia. What makes her all the more interesting, however, is her guile and cunning. Mrs Coulter thinks on her feet, adapts, manipulates, and all because of a profound understanding of human weaknesses. She plays on ambition, fear and desire, whether they are those of individuals like Lord Boreal or Metatron, or institutions like the Church. She can even command the **Spectres** it seems by simply persuading them that she can lead them to more souls [SK, 9, 10]. And like all good foes, she's never quite clear-cut. Just how much poison has been drawn by Lyra and, if little, why does she seek to protect her child? Has she some sense of Lyra's importance? The third book certainly presents a different kind of Mrs Coulter, although her final confrontation with Metatron reveals that she has lost none of the dexterity that allowed her to reach her position of power in the Church.

Nicole Kidman plays the role in *The Golden Compass* movie. In the film she is blonde, rather than having black hair.

COUSINS – The manservant of the **Master of Jordan College**. He and **Lyra** have been enemies as long as she can remember. However, on her return to **Jordan College**, she is surprised to be greeted affectionately by Cousins [AS, 38].

CREATOR, THE – *See* **Authority**.

D

DÆMONS – Philip Pullman claims that the dæmons are the best idea he's ever had. In **Lyra's** world, every person has a dæmon, a creature like an animal that sticks close to them. Children's dæmons shift their shape, but adults' dæmons are fixed in form, according to the true character of that person. While it's never quite said in the novels, as the radio series puts it, 'a dæmon's what you have if you're alive, it's your soul'.

For the people of Lyra's world, dæmons are both taken for granted and deeply mysterious. An elaborate etiquette has developed around them. Once your dæmon is fixed you, and everyone else, knows what kind of person you are. Most servants have dog dæmons [NL, 1]. At puberty, they can go from being great playmates to troublesome and confusing dæmons. People can disagree with their dæmons, argue with them and force them to follow them. Daemons can't stray more than a few yards from their hosts without feeling great pain, although the distance they can travel varies from person to person – **Mrs Coulter's gold monkey** can go further than most, and **witches** can send their dæmons great distances. Daemons fade away when their hosts die. It's harder and rarer for a dæmon to be killed, but when it happens, the host dies instantly, too. Daemons rarely talk to anyone but their host, but it is possible [NL, 9]. Their voices are 'a tiny buzz'. There's a hint that people can hear what their dæmons can hear [NL, 11]. **Lee Scoresby** suggests that if he's asleep, so is his dæmon, but **Pantalaimon** is often awake before Lyra. Cedarwood has a soporific effect on dæmons. [NL, 7] People from other worlds, like **Dr Mary Malone**, **Will** and **Major John Parry** gain a dæmon on entering Lyra's world, but need help to perceive it.

The energy that links humans and their dæmons is immensely powerful. It is this that powers **Asriel**'s experiments into crossing to parallel worlds, and the **quantum entanglement bomb** of the **Church**.

Pullman notes that many portraits of people include animals, often ones that represent the character of the person being portrayed. There is also the legend of the **witch**'s familiar, an animal servant. Another possible influence is that of the Native American spirit guide – animals that can answer questions on quests, provide insight into your true character, and which are often said to be able to shift their form.

In *Northern Lights*, Lyra reviews the brass plaques naming the dæmons of former **Masters of Jordan College**. They include a serpent, a monkey, a basilisk (a mythical creature) and a fair woman. In the American editions of *Northern Lights*, the 'fair woman' dæmon is deleted. However, Philip Pullman, in his interview for Radio 4's *Devout* Sceptics on 9 August 2001, said that dæmons were 'not always' animals.

It's pronounced as the word 'demon' (dee-mon), not day-mon.

In 2004, Cadburys ran a series of commercials that took the dæmons as their inspiration, with people's 'Happiness' portrayed as animals that urged them to give in to temptation and eat chocolate. The creatures were stylised puppets . . . and the advertising campaign was baffling to anyone who hadn't read *His Dark Materials*. The official movie website www.golden-compassmovie.com allows its visitors to find out the identity of their daemon by completing a short personality quiz.

DEAN – One of the scholars at **Jordan College**.

DEATH – 'Pale unremarkable creatures' that take their hosts to the **land of the dead**. Everyone has a personal death from the moment they are born to the time of their death. According to Magda's death, some people, like **Will** and **Lyra**, keep their deaths at bay and are unable to see them, although they are forever present: 'wherever you look, they hide'. Magda's death entreats all to live in friendship with their deaths [AS, 19].

The notion of death as a sentient entity draws on a long tradition in world mythology. The Grim Reaper of modern European folklore is perhaps the most familiar depiction of death in this way. Philip Pullman's unique twist is to give each person a death, unique to them, and to make them companionable.

DEE, DR – In **Lyra's** world, a great magician who lives at Mortlake [NL, 3]. In reality, Dr John Dee (1527–1608) was a prominent **alchemist** and mathematician who earned a reputation as a sorcerer. In 1571, he purchased a mansion at Mortlake, where he died in poverty. There are a number of interesting connections between the life of Dr Dee and *His Dark Materials*. John first gained public notoriety when he created a mechanical flying beetle for a stage play, not unlike the **spy-fly** that pursues Lyra. Dee also claims to be able to speak to **angels** through a process of divination using crystals. Perhaps most interestingly, Dee claims to have discovered a quantity of the Elixir of Life at Glastonbury. It is not clear from the description in *Northern Lights* whether Dee still resides at Mortlake.

DICK – A sixteen-year-old acquaintance of **Lyra** whom she admired for his spitting [NL, 3].

DOCKER, PROFESSOR – A middle-aged scholar who attends **Mrs Coulter's** cocktail party in London. Docker is particularly knowledgeable on **Dust** and the researches into it. Docker is the person who reveals to **Lyra** that the **Gobblers** are the **General Oblation Board** (from the initials) and that Mrs Coulter is its prime agent. He has a cat **dæmon** [NL, 5].

DRAGONFLIES – The steeds of the **Gallivespians**, larger than the dragonflies of **Will's** world. Each Gallivespian clan has its own breed of dragonflies: **Chevalier Tialys**'s clans are powerful red and yellow creatures with brutal appetites while **Salmakia**'s clans are fast and slender electric-blue dragonflies that can glow in the dark. The Gallivespians use oil and honey to either keep the larvae in suspended animation or hatch them. Salmakia and Chevalier are able to hatch their dragonflies in 36 hours [AS, 9]. After hatching, each dragonfly is fitted with a harness consisting of spider-silk reins, stirrups of titanium, and a saddle of hummingbird skin, which it wears for the rest of its life [AS, 11].

While the Gallivespian dragonflies are larger than those that Will has seen, our world has been home to species of giant dragonfly in the past. The largest species found, Protodonata, had a wingspan of 75 centimetres and is estimated to have lived over 250 million years ago.

E

EISARSON, SØREN – An old bear counsellor who suffers under the reign of **Iofur Raknison**. Eisarson is involved in negotiating with **Lord Asriel** the terms of his imprisonment at **Svalbard** [NL, 20, 21].

ENOCH – *See* **Metatron**.

EVE – The name for **Lyra** in the **witches**' prophecy. *See* **Fall**.

EVERETT, HUGH III – Originator of the 'many-worlds' thesis in c.1957, referenced by **Sir Charles Latrom**. Charles believes that the researches of **Dr Mary Malone** and **Dr Oliver Payne** will in some way advance this theory [SK, 12].

As one might expect, the reference to Hugh is accurate. In 1956–57, he first put forward the theory that the universe we see is only part of a number of universes that make up a 'multiverse'. His theory is contained in his Princeton thesis, 'The Theory of Universal Wavefunction' but was popularised in the 1970s by Bryce DeWitt as the 'many-worlds' theory.

F

FAA, LORD JOHN – 'Lord of the western gypsies' [NL, 7]. By the time of **Bolvangar**, John was in his seventies but still tall, bull-necked and powerful. It is John who orders the Roping and leads the **gyptians** to Bolvangar to rescue the children from the **Oblation Board**. John feels a tremendous sense of loyalty to **Lord Asriel** for his services to the gyptian people and continues to keep watch over **Lyra** in her days at **Jordan College**. He is also a tremendous fighter and famously slays the **Tartar** champion on the steppes of Kazakhstan [NL, 8]. In the days after the second **Fall** of Man, John transports **Will** and **Lyra** back to **Cittàgazze** [AS, 38]. He has a crow **dæmon**.

FELDT, LENA – A **witch** from **Serafina Pekkala**'s clan who helps to rescue the children from **Bolvangar**. Shortly after she witnesses **Lord Boreal**'s death, she is captured and interrogated by **Mrs Coulter** who has the witch's snow-bunting **dæmon** enveloped by a **Spectre**. In terrible agony, Lena Feldt reveals to Mrs Coulter that **Lyra** is known to the witches as **Eve**. A spectre kills her [AS, 23].

FIORELLI, JOHNNY – A man at the Horse Fair at the **Jericho** waterfront in **Lyra**'s world. One **gyptian** child claims to have last seen **Billy Costa** holding Johnny's old horse [NL, 3].

FLYING SPIRITS – *See* **spy-fly** [NL, 9].

G

GALLIVESPIANS – A proud and somewhat haughty race of people who would be conspicuous but for their exceptional smallness [AS, 5]. The Gallivespians are slender people of no more than a hand's span in height and are consequently excellent spies. They live to only nine or ten years [AS, 6]. Their world developed along a different path to that of **Lyra** and our own. On their world, two kinds of conscious beings developed: humans and the Gallivespians. The humans were mostly servants of the **Authority** and, believing the Gallivespians to be 'diabolic' had sought to exterminate them for as long as anyone could remember. As a result, the Gallivespians found it difficult to trust humans and earned respect in part through the poisonous stings in the spurs on their heels. These stings could deliver enough poison to kill a man, but became weaker and weaker with each sting. It took a full day for each sting to reach its full potency once again [AS, 25]. Gallivespian society is divided into clans who each breed their own **dragonflies** for steeds. Each clan has dragonflies of specific hues and characteristics [AS, 9]. Given their long battle with the followers of the Authority on their own world, the Gallivespians are a natural ally for **Lord Asriel**. Under the leadership of **Lord Roke**, and later **Madame Oxentiel**, they prove to be fearless and effective spies. Roke is able to keep in contact with his spies, **Chevalier Tialys** and **Lady Salmakia**, through the **lodestone resonator**, a communications device that uses quantum theory. The Gallivespians are able to keep watch over **Will** and Lyra on their long journey from the **Himalayas** to **the Battle on the Plain**, where they help the children reunite with their **dæmons** and escape **Metatron**.

The Gallivespians may well be a nod to the Lilliputians of Jonathan Swift's *Gulliver's Travels*. Lilliputian society is petty and small-minded but, on the whole, morally upright and noble. There are two political parties, the High-Heels and the Low-Heels, perhaps the inspiration for the peculiar heel stings of the Gallivespian spies. Among the many areas satirised by Swift, including the British sense of morality, Empire and academia, there is a critique of the differences between the Anglican and Catholic faiths.

GERRITT, RAYMOND VAN – A **gyptian** at the Ropings. He is reprimanded by **John Faa** for questioning the sacrifice the gyptians are proposing to make for **Lyra** [NL, 7, 8].

GHOSTS – That part of a human being which, after death, passes to **the land of the dead**. In **Lyra's** world, each person consists of 'body and ghost and **dæmon** together' – much as Saint Paul described people as spirit and soul and body [AS, 30, 33]. **Will** and Lyra deduce that ghosts are human consciousness, that is that part of the human being that is capable of conceiving body and dæmon as separate parts [AS, 13]. At the moment of death, one's ghost is compelled to the land of the dead, a prison camp for the spirits of the departed established by the **Authority** in the early ages [AS, 2]. This may be the same '**spirit world**' referred to by the **Tartars** [SK, 10]. On their way to the land of the dead, the ghosts forget their own land and material existence, as Will and Lyra witness in the case of **Dirk Jansen** [AS, 18]. Once in the land of the dead, ghosts have no substance and can only whisper [AS, 22]. Lyra and Will are able to release the ghosts, and therefore strike a blow at the Authority, by cutting a window through to the world of the **Mulefa**, which releases the ghosts to dissipate and become part of what is alive again [AS, 23]. It is intimated that ghosts can occasionally be seen by the living: **Pantalaimon** claims to have seen an old ghost in **Godstow**, although Lyra hasn't [NL, 9].

In Greek mythology, ghosts are usually 'shades'. On their way to the land of the dead, shades are forced to drink from the Lethe, one of the rivers that flows through Hades. The Lethe is sometimes called the River of Oblivion since all who drink from it forget their past lives on earth.

GOLDEN MONKEY, THE – **Marisa Coulter's dæmon**. The monkey has long, silky fur 'of the most deep and lustrous gold', and small black hands with horny claws [NL, 3]. Like its host, the golden monkey has a vicious, almost predatory character – in the Himalayan cave it seems to take great pleasure in idly tearing the wings off bats.

The golden monkey is one of the most memorable characters in the entire trilogy although it is never named in the books. In the radio adaptation it was called Ozymandias.

GOMEZ, FATHER LUIS – The youngest member of the **Consistorial Court of Discipline**, 'pale and trembling with zealotry' [AS, 6]. Father Gomez does pre-emptive penance every day of his adult life and is therefore chosen by the President of the **Consistorial Court of Discipline** for the task of killing **Lyra** and granting **pre-emptive absolution**. He pursues **Dr Mary Malone** to the land of the **Mulefa** where he soon exerts dominion over the **Tualapi**. After finding Mary's camp, Gomez tracks Lyra and **Will** to the grove where the second **Fall** of Man takes place. He is prevented from carrying out his task by **Balthamos** who, after a short struggle, drowns the priest [AS, 35]. Gomez's **dæmon** is a large and iridescent green-backed beetle [AS, 6].

GRACIOUS WINGS – *See* **Harpies**.

GRAZING CREATURES – The cattle in the world of the **Mulefa**. The creatures are about the size of a deer or antelope, with the same colouring, but legs that have evolved in a diamond formation [NL, 5].

GREENWOOD, MISS – A historian at **Saint Sophia's**. She tells **Lyra** something of the history of **alchemy**. Although forgetful, her marmoset **dæmon** remembers what she cannot [LO].

GRUMMAN, STANISLAUS – *See* **Major John Parry**. Grumman is pronounced 'Grew-man' according to the radio adaptation.

GYPSIES – *See* **gyptians**.

GYPTIANS – aka **gypsies**. Boat-dwellers who travel around the **Fens** and surrounding area of **Eastern Anglia**. The gyptians have an ancient right of free movement in and out of the Fens which assures their dominance of the area [NL, 3]. Gyptian society is extremely tightly-knit, being built around the bloodlines and family ties of six principal families. At the time of *His Dark Materials*, the families were headed by **Nicholas Rokeby, Adam Stefanski, Roger van Poppel, Simon Hartmann, Benjamin de Ruyter** and **Michael Canzona**. Individual families would be offshoots of these six: for example, the Costas were part of the Stefanski family [NL, 8]. When **Lyra** finds herself adopting gyptian ways, **Ma Costa** warns her that she cannot become a gyptian: 'There's deeps in us and strong currents' [NL, 7].

In times of great need, the gyptian leader calls all gyptians to a special meeting called a Byanroping. On these occasions, gyptian families moor their boats around the **Byanplats** in the Fens. It is said that you can walk for miles over the Fens on the decks of the moored canal boats. The meeting takes place in an ancient wooden meeting hall, the **Zaal**. The heads of the six families are called upon to raise a levy and provide men and hold key positions of responsibility under the service of the gyptian leader [NL, 7]. **Tony Costa** refers to the leaders as the 'council' [NL, 8]. The leader of the western gypsies is **John Faa**, who is assisted by his seer, **Farder Coram**. They are 'precious and extravagantly loved' in their community [NL, 3]. Between the arrival of the gyptians in **Oxford** for the spring fair and their departure after the autumn fair, the **Collegers** and the gyptian children are at war [NL, 3]. During one memorable summer, Lyra and her friends hijack the grand and sumptuous boat belonging to the Costa family and set it free of its moorings [NL, 3; AS, 18].

Had she known the intimate connection between her family and the gyptians Lyra would have thought twice. The gyptians recognise a debt of honour to **Lord Asriel** who allows them free passage across his Oxfordshire estate and fights for their rights in Parliament [NL, 8]. When Lyra is put into care, Ma Costa pleads unsuccessfully to become her guardian. Since then, the gyptians maintain an interest in Lyra and her well-being, placing a spy in **Jordan College, Bernie Johansen** the pastry cook, to keep watch over her and to visit Oxford every year for the latest news [NL, 7].

It is unsurprising, then, that the gyptians were the first to come to Lyra's aid after her escape from **Mrs Coulter**'s London residence. Around two to three years previously, the gyptians had heard of the **Gobblers** and had learned that they took children north for experimentation [NL, 3]. Soon, their children are also taken. They catch a Gobbler and discover the nature of the experiments [NL, 6]. At the Roping, the gyptians agree to travel north to rescue Lord Asriel and the children from **Bolvangar**. Their ferocious attack on the research complex assures its complete destruction. The gyptians then take the children back to England, but come to Lyra's aid once more when they collect her from the world of the **Mulefa** and take her back to **Cittàgazze**.

The gyptians are explicitly the nomadic people known as Roma or more commonly (and pejoratively) as gypsies. The name 'gyptian' is a direct allusion to the inaccurate belief that the Roma people originated in Egypt. Pullman is careful to explore the mistrust and demonisation of these people in *Northern Lights*. Our first view of the gyptians is Lyra's, tainted as it is by summers of warfare with the gyptian children. Once she is aboard the Costa's canal boat, however, Lyra comes to understand the gyptians more and to admire their culture. In particular, she delights in the gyptians' tradition of storytelling, with their tales of the **Fen**-dwellers, **Nälkäinens**, **Windsuckers** and **Breathless Ones** [NL, 6, 7]. Philip Pullman presents the gyptians as proud and noble spirits, steeped in ancient practices and folklore, and driven by an unswerving loyalty to family. If anything, the depiction is rather overly romanticised but serves to make the gyptians some of the most memorable characters in the books.

H

HARPIES – Malevolent shrieking creatures, half-bird half-woman, that torment the **ghosts** in the **land of the dead**. Harpies are about the size of a vulture with the head and breasts of a woman. Though their faces are smooth and unwrinkled, their hair is filthy, their lips crusted and their eye-sockets filled with slime [AS, 21]. When the **Authority** created the land of the dead, He gave the harpies the power to see the worst in everyone and to feed on this negativity. The harpies torment each ghost with all the horrible things they did in their life [AS, 23]. When **Will** and **Lyra** arrive in the land of the dead, they are pursued by a harpy called No-Name. Lyra discovers that the harpies can just as easily feed on the truth and persuade them to let the ghosts of the dead pass through their domain in return for their life stories. When No-Name saves Lyra from the **abyss**, Lyra renames her **Gracious Wings** [AS, 29].

The harpies are taken from Greek mythology. Originally, they appeared as the beautiful winged daughters of Electra and Thaumus but they are more popularly remembered in the form in which we see them in *The Amber Spyglass*. The harpies feature in the story of Jason and the Argonauts, in which the three harpies, Aello, Celaeno, and Ocypete, steal food from Phineus, the prophet king of Thrace, as a punishment from Zeus. They are chased away by the Argonauts. Scholars believe the harpies to have been the personification of storm winds.

HARTMANN, SIMON – A senior **gyptian**; presumably one of the heads of families. He is the treasurer of the gyptian expedition to **Bolvangar** and is accountable to all for the proper use of the gyptians' gold [NL, 8].

HAWKER, PETER – A **gyptian** who brings back **Jacob Huismans** to **Farder Coram** after **Benjamin de Ruyter**'s disastrous raid on the **Ministry of Theology** [NL, 9].

HEADMAN – An aged leader of the **Yenesei Pakhtar** tribe of Siberian **Tartars** that have **Stanislaus Grumman** as their shaman. He has a wolverine **dæmon** [SK, 10].

HEYST, FATHER – The plump, elderly Intercessor at **Jordan College**, who is responsible for leading all college services, conducts prayers and hears confessions. In **Lyra's** early years he took an interest in her spiritual wellbeing but decided that she was not spiritually promising. Heyst admonishes Lyra and **Roger Parslow** for playing in the catacombs beneath the Oratory. He has a lizard **dæmon** [NL, 3].

HIGH COMMANDERS – **Lord Asriel's** military advisers in the world of his **fortress**. They include the **Gallivespian** spy-captain **Lord Roke** and later **Madame Oxentiel**, the African **King Ogunwe** and the rebel angel **Xaphania** [AS, 16].

HJALMURSON, HJALMUR – An **armoured bear** who fights **Iorek Byrnison** over a she-bear. Hjalmur is under the influence of a drug which **Iofur Raknison** gives him, and supplied by **Mrs Coulter**, that prevents him from backing down in the face of Iorek's superior strength. Iorek loses control and kills Hjalmur, which leads to his exile [NL, 20].

HOOK, GERARD – **Benjamin de Ruyter** leads the raid on the **Ministry of Theology** and captures Gerard, a **gyptian** [NL, 9].

HOUSEKEEPER – *See* **Mrs Lonsdale**.

HUDSON, CAPTAIN – An explorer who undertook a famous voyage to **Van Tieren's Land**. It was during this expedition that he used a fire-striker that was on display in the library of the **Royal Arctic Institute** [NL, 4].

HUISMANS, JACOB – Jacob, a **gyptian,** is a member of the party that **Benjamin de Ruyter** leads to investigate the **Ministry of Theology** at **White Hall**. Jacob is mortally wounded with an arrow but makes it back to **Farder Coram** to recount de Ruyter's death and the capture of **Gerard Hook**. He has a ferret **dæmon** [NL, 9].

I

INQUIRER – One of the twelve members of the **Consistorial Court of Discipline**. He leads the Court's inquiry into **Lyra** that lasted eight days [AS, 6].

INTERCESSOR – *See* **Heyst, Father**.

J

JANSEN, DIRK – A middle-aged man who has his throat cut by an angry mob. Jansen is the first **ghost Lyra** and **Will** encounter on their journey to the **land of the dead** [AS, 18].

JAXER – A **gyptian** who helps **Tony Costa** and **Kerim** save **Lyra** from the Turk traders in London [NL, 6].

JERRY – A 'stout and placid' able-seaman who teaches **Lyra** the ways of life on board ship. He and Lyra talk about **dæmons** fixing. Jerry knows a sailor who has a dolphin dæmon and is therefore unable to live away from the sea. Jerry believes that the compensation for fixing is knowing what kind of person you are. He has a seagull dæmon called **Belisaria** [NL, 10].

JOHANSEN, BERNIE – A kindly, solitary pastry cook in **Jordan College**'s kitchens who comforts **Lyra** when **Roger** is taken by the **Gobblers** [NL, 3]. Bernie is in fact half-**gyptian** and is sent to Oxford to look after Lyra while she's there. He is one of those rare people whose **dæmon** is the same sex as himself [NL, 7].

JOPARI – *See* **Parry, Major John**.

K

KAISA – **Serafina Pekkala**'s snow goose **dæmon**. Kaisa helps **Lyra** to find the dæmon cages. He seems to be able to perform magic [NL, 15]. Kaisa is a Finnish name meaning 'pure'.

KAMAINEN, JUTA – A headstrong young **witch** (just over one hundred years old) who falls in love with **Stanislaus Grumman**. When her love is unrequited, she vows to kill him. Juta kills Stanilaus with an arrow just at the moment when he reveals to **Will** that he is his missing father, **Major John Parry**. Juta is horrified by the revelation and kills herself [SK, 2, 13, 15].

K'ANG-PO, EMPEROR – **Lord Asriel** visits the palace of the Emperor K'ang-Po and sees the billions of blue starlings that whirl around it at sunset [AS, 28].

KAROSSA – The name of the **dæmon** of one of the children at **Bolvangar** [NL, 16].

KASKU, IEVA – A **Witch**-Queen who **Ruta Skadi** consults over the war against the **Authority** [SK, 13].

KERIM – A **gyptian** who helps **Tony Costa** and **Jaxer** save **Lyra** from the Turk traders in London [NL, 6].

KHUNRATH, PAVEL – According to the stage play programme, the creator of the **alethiometer** was Pavel Khunrath, a scholar working in Prague during the reign of Rudolf II (1552–1612). Khunrath tried to record the influences of planets using a method combining astrology and memory theatre. He discovered an alloy of two rare metals that had the mysterious property of pointing to the truth (the alloy is presumably titanium and magnesium, the same alloy used for the **window**-cutting edge of the **subtle knife** and the blade of the **silver guillotine**). Khunrath adapted the technique of memory theatre to generate symbols. He had begun work on recording the meanings of each when, in 1612, Rudolf II was succeeded by Frederick, a fanatical opponent of occult philosophy, and Khunrath was burned at the stake. A few of his devices and a copy of his book of readings survived to be taken up by later scholars. It was only after his death that the name 'alethiometer' was adopted. Khunrath is not mentioned in the novels.

KIGALIK, MATT – An Eskimo friend of **Jake Peterson**. **Major John Parry** meets Kigalik on his expedition to **Lookout Ridge**. Kigalik reveals that the **Soviet Union** is investigating the **anomaly**, which John Parry later discovers to be a **window** to **Cittàgazze** [SK, 5].

KIRJAVA – **Will's dæmon**, named by **Serafina Pekkala**. Kirjava does not know she exists until she is torn from his heart on Will's passage to the **land of the dead**. As a result of the separation of Will and Kirjava at the land of the dead, Kirjava can travel far from her human like a witch's dæmon. She and **Pantalaimon** travel through many worlds, including that of the **Gallivespians**, and talk to **angels**, but agree to say nothing of what they do together until they know the time is right. Kirjava fixes as a cat 'of no ordinary size' with lustrous rich fur of blacks, blues, greys and purples [AS, 36, 37, 38].

On naming Kirjava, Serafina tells the dæmon that it will know the meaning of its name soon enough. In Finnish, Kirjava means 'multi-coloured'.

KOOPMAN, NELLIE AND RUUD – **Gyptians** saved by **Lord Asriel** in the **floods of '53**.

KULANG – **Ama's dæmon**, not yet fixed [AS, 4].

KYRILLION – **Annie's dæmon**, not yet fixed [NL, 16].

L

LANSELIUS, DR MARTIN – The **Witch-Consul** at **Trollesund**. Martin is a fat man with a florid face with witchlike intense green eyes. It is his duty to keep contact with the non-witch inhabitants of the north. When **Lyra** reveals her ability to read the **alethiometer** without a book of symbols, he suspects that she is the subject of a witch prophecy and confirms this fact by testing her to pick a spray of **cloud pine**, which **Serafina Pekkala** uses [NL, 10]. Martin also assists Serafina when she seeks to understand **Lord Asriel**'s intentions after the creation of the **bridge** [SK, 2]. Although not a witch, Martin is one of those men who serve the **witches**. Some men are also kept as husbands and lovers but their relatively short lives cause great pain to the witches [NL, 18]. It is claimed that Martin visits **Sebastian Makepeace** and knows of his gold elixir that could save the lives of witches who succumb to a new and deadly disease [LO].

LATROM, SIR CHARLES – *See* **Lord Carlo Boreal**. Latrom is pronounced Lat-rom, not Lay-trom, in both audio versions of the story.

LE CLERC, SIMON – **Master** of **Jordan College** between 1765 and 1789. His **dæmon** is called **Cerebaton** [NL, 3].

LIBRARIAN – One of the Scholars at **Jordan College**. He is an old friend of the **Master of Jordan College**, who takes the Librarian into his confidence about the plan to poison **Lord Asriel**. The Librarian's first name is Charles [NL, 2].

LISTER, DR – An academic working on the third floor of **Dr Mary Malone**'s building in **Oxford**. **Lyra** pretends to be delivering a parcel to Dr Lister to get past the porter [SK, 4].

LONSDALE, MRS – A housekeeper at **Jordan College** responsible for **Lyra**'s quarters. She is a member of the Parslow family. **Roger Parslow**'s father is her second cousin. Mrs Lonsdale tries to teach Lyra how to sew but she is resistant until shown how by **Jerry** the able-seaman on her voyage to the north [NL, 10]. She has a stolid retriever **dæmon** [NL, 3].

LORENZ, JOACHIM – A horseman in the world of **Cittàgazze** who flees from his party of adults and children when **Spectres** attack. Lorenz tells the **witches** about the history of his world, the **Philosophers' Guild** and the coming of the Spectres [SK, 6].

LOUIS, BROTHER – Convenor of the Secretariat of the **Consistorial Court of Discipline**, based at the **College of Saint Jerome** in **Geneva**. He is a 'fresh-faced' young priest with a rabbit **dæmon** [AS, 24].

LOVAT, HUGH – A kitchen boy from Saint Michael's in **Lyra's Oxford**. He is with Lyra and **Simon Parslow** when **Ma Costa** discovers her son **Billy Costa** has been taken by the **Gobblers** [NL, 3].

LYALL, FRANCIS – **Master of Jordan College** between 1748 and 1765. His **dæmon** is called **Zohariel** [NL, 3].

LYRA – aka Lyra Belacqua, Lyra Silvertongue, Mother Eve. The principal character of the *His Dark Materials* trilogy. 'Lyra' is the word that opens *Northern Lights* and the word that closes *The Amber Spyglass*. Lyra's story is one of growing up, of moving from a state of innocence to a state of experience, of travelling the path to wisdom.

Lyra, perhaps as her name suggests, was born into a lie. She was the illegitimate daughter of **Lord Asriel** and **Mrs Marisa Coulter**, illegitimate as Marisa was already married to another. When Lyra was born it was obvious that **Edward Coulter**, Marisa's husband, was not the father. Mrs Coulter deposited Lyra with Asriel, claiming that the baby died in childbirth. Edward discovered the truth and confronted Asriel. In the ensuing fight, Asriel killed Edward. Mrs Coulter abandoned Lyra to the court who rejected an appeal from Lyra's **gyptian** nurse, **Ma Costa**, for custody. Instead, Lyra was placed with the **Sisters of Obedience** at **Watlington**. Asriel would not countenance the **Church** raising his child and took her to **Jordan College** where he placed her in the care of the **Master**, demanding only that Mrs Coulter never be allowed to see her daughter. The gyptian, owing a debt of gratitude to Lord Asriel, took it on himself to look out for Lyra, visiting **Oxford** every year [NL, 7]. Lyra grew up thinking that Lord Asriel was her uncle and that her mother and father, the Count and Countess Belacqua, died in an aëronautical accident in the north [NL, 5].

When we meet Lyra, she is thirteen years old, although she looks young for her age [NL, 14; AS, 31]. She had been in the care of the Master of Jordan College for ten years or more [NL, 7]. There, among the splendid decaying grandeur of the College, Lyra lived an innocent life, a 'half-wild, half-civilised girl, left among [the scholars] by chance'. She was a reluctant student, though a succession of **scholars** persisted to make her learn and she did gain some knowledge of atoms, elementary particles, anbarology and **experimental theology** among other things [NL, 5]. Instead, she preferred to live an unfettered life of play. From her quarters, a narrow room at the top of Staircase Twelve, to the crypt beneath the Oratory, she had explored much of Jordan College and the city [NL, 3]. She felt utterly at home on the streets of Oxford and built around her a group of friends of similar age, the children of servants and tradesmen employed by the Colleges. Among them all, her 'particular' friend was **Roger Parslow**.

Although a prankster, Lyra was well-liked. The Master saw in her a lot of goodness and sweetness, but also determination in her character [NL, 4]. She was 'a sanguine and practical child', not one to brood and was lacking in imagination [NL, 15]. But she was also quick-thinking. It was this that gave Lyra her principal skill – lying. Lyra was such a prodigious and effective liar, she could talk with almost irresistible conviction about seemingly anything. The skill certainly came in useful, whether she was facing off Mrs Coulter or tricking the king of the bears, a race supposedly immune to human deception. It was in honour of this skill that she earned the name Silvertongue from **Iorek Byrnison** [NL, 20]. Ma Costa complemented Lyra on this ability, saying that she had witch-oil in her soul and was deceptive like marsh-fire [NL, 7]. Others were critical: **Chevalier Tialys** said that fantasy came so easily to Lyra that 'your whole nature is riddled with dishonesty, and you don't even admit the truth when it stares you in the face' [AS, 19].

It seems odd, therefore, that such a typical, healthy child should be the subject of prophecy. The **witches** of the north had heard 'immortal whispers' from behind the **Aurora** that told of one child with a great destiny that could only be fulfilled in another world. The witches had talked of her for centuries and knew how to recognise her when she picked a spray of cloud pine used by a witch from a pile of similar sprays [NL, 10; SK, 2]. **Fra Pavel Rašek** also believed that her ability to read the **alethiometer** without books was a sign [SK, 2]. The details of this prophecy related to her 'true name', the name of her destiny: 'she will be the mother . . . she will be life . . . she will disobey . . . Eve, again! Mother Eve!' [SK, 15]. More specifically, **Serafina Pekkala** knew that Lyra would carry something of immense value to Lord Asriel: 'the fates are using her as a messenger' [NL, 18]. Nevertheless, her precise role was still unclear to the witches: Serafina wondered if Lyra was the weapon Æsahættr of which the ancient **cliff-ghast** spoke [SK, 13]. The gyptians too spoke of Lyra in this way, talking of her in terms of witch-oil and marsh-fire [SK, 2]. Even the Master of Jordan College observed that Lyra had a part to play 'and a major one' in the unfolding events and the interests of the **Oblation Board** [NL, 2].

The Master also had another, altogether more disturbing prophecy: that Lyra would commit a great betrayal and must do so in ignorance [NL, 2]. In *Northern Lights* we are perhaps meant to believe that delivering Roger to Asriel is the great betrayal. However, in *The Amber Spyglass*, Lyra chooses to travel to the land of the dead without her dæmon, **Pantalaimon** [AS, 21]. This, it seems, is the betrayal although it results in a profound new ability, that of being able to separate from her dæmon for some distance while staying as one.

The prophecy of course recounts Lyra's destiny to become **Eve** and to persuade her Adam, **Will**, to taste the tree of knowledge of good and evil. Lyra's relationship with Will is one that grows quite quickly, with them being together less than two months. But it is nevertheless convincingly handled. Our first indication comes in *The Subtle Knife* when, while Lyra is supposedly sleeping, Will tells Pan that Lyra is the best friend he has ever had. Lyra's heart beats hard at the news [SK, 13]. Thrown together by circumstances, the emotional bond is forged quickly and hard. The final moments as Lyra and Will part are utterly heart-rending. And yet everyone knows that, although it is all we want, for them to meet again would undermine the story.

On her return to Oxford, Lyra is accompanied by her dæmon, Pantalaimon, now fixed in the form of a pine marten. The Master sees how Lyra's unconscious grace has been replaced by an awkward awareness of her own body. The Master takes her back in, pretending that Asriel has set up an endowment for Lyra [AS, 38], and she is placed under the tutelage of **Dame Hannah Relf**, the principal scholar of the alethiometer, at **Saint Sophia's** [AS, 38].

It's been stated in a couple of books that the name Lyra comes from **William Blake**'s 'The Little Girl Lost' in his *Songs of Innocence*. In fact, the name of the girl is Lyca, although in Blake's hand it can look like Lyra. Philip Pullman has said in interviews that the name was a play on 'liar', Lyra's principal gift, a point made all the more obvious by the cawing of the harpies [AS, 21]. Lyra is also the Greek word for lyre, revealing another likely inspiration, the legend of Orpheus. The lyre was created by Apollo and given to Orpheus who was able to move all to emotion with his music. When Orpheus' wife, Eurydice, was killed, Orpheus descended into the underworld to retrieve her. Persephone asked him to walk out of the **land of the dead** and take it on trust that Eurydice was following him. When he exited, he turned to see but Eurydice had not yet passed the gates of Hades and she vanished forever. Zeus placed the lyre in the sky as a constellation of stars as a tribute to lost love – a fitting metaphor for Lyra's relationship with Will.

M

MACPHAIL, FATHER HUGH – The Scottish President of the **Consistorial Court of Discipline**. MacPhail is dark-featured, tall and imposing with wiry grey hair. He only eats bread, fruit and water and trains for one hour per day with a trainer of champion athletes. He is in his forties and, as the Presidency of the Consistorial Court is a lifetime appointment, he is expected to mould the Court and the **Church** for a significant time to come [AS, 6]. It is MacPhail who directed the Church's attempts to kill **Lyra,** temporarily breaking down the rivalry between the Court and the **Society of the Work of the Holy Spirit** for mutual benefit, and ultimately granting **Father Gomez** pre-emptive absolution for the murder of Lyra. Mac-Phail severs himself from his lizard **dæmon** to power the **bomb** intended to kill Lyra that actually opens the **abyss.**

MAGNUSSON, CAPTAIN – **Mrs Coulter** hires the stout Captain Magnusson to transport children, who are captured by the **Oblation Board,** from a **Limehouse** wharf to the north [NL, 3]. He skippers a steam launch.

MAKARIOS, TONY – A nine-year-old child who is captured and severed by the **Oblation Board.** Tony lives in Clarice Walk, Limehouse, with his mother who is of Irish, **Skraeling** and Lascar descent. As a result, Tony looks more Chinese than Greek [NL, 3]. **Mrs Coulter** takes him from that part of London to the warehouse near **Hangman's Wharf** where he and a dozen other children are held before being taken to the north. In **Bolvangar,** a nurse takes him for **intercision** because she thinks that his **dæmon** has fixed. In fact, Tony's dæmon, Ratter, *does* change but not very much because 'Tony hisself never thought much about anything' [NL, 15]. After he is severed from his dæmon, Tony escapes from Bolvangar and finds his way to a fish-house in a village north of **Trollesund.** It is here that **Lyra** discovers him and brings him back to the **gyptians.** Tony Makarios cannot settle without his dæmon and dies [NL, 13].

MAKEPEACE, SEBASTIAN – A scholar of Merton College, with a reputation for violence and madness, who first appears in 'Lyra and the Birds'. He is thought to be the first person to study **alchemy** for 250 years, and rumours have it that he talks to himself and was once tried (and acquitted) of manslaughter. He is believed to have a gold elixir capable of saving **witches** from a new and deadly disease. **Dr Martin Lanselius** is said to have visited him. Makepeace's **dæmon** is a black cat. Lyra tracks him down to a house on Juxon Street, and he tells her that he and **Yelana Pazhets** were once lovers, who have a son. This son dies fighting for **Lord Asriel**. His mother, fighting on the other side, is driven mad by the idea that she might have killed him in the heat of battle. It becomes clear to Lyra that he is only pretending to be an alchemist, but won't tell her what he's really up to [LO, 'Lyra and the Birds'].

MAKEPWE, FATHER – The eldest of the twelve members of the **Consistorial Court of Discipline**, who is described as 'ancient and rheumy-eyed' [AS, 5].

MALONE, DR MARY – A particle physicist who 'plays the serpent' to effect the second **Fall** of Man. Mary is in her late thirties, with short black hair and red cheeks, when **Lyra** barges into her office at an **Oxford** College. She establishes the **Dark Matter Research Unit** with **Dr Oliver Payne** to investigate '**Shadow Particles**'. Together, they make the radical discovery that these particles are conscious. Ironically, the truth is so far-fetched that it makes their chances of obtaining funding to continue their research unlikely. To that end, Oliver attends a job interview in **Geneva**, leaving Mary to worry about the outcome of their proposal to a funding committee [SK, 4]. **Sir Charles Latrom**, better known to Lyra as **Lord Boreal**, recognises that their research is potentially ground-breaking and offers to help, although secretly his mind is bent on Lyra, the **alethiometer** and the **subtle knife**.

With Lyra's help, Mary learns how to communicate with the Shadow Particles, also known as **Dust**. She discovers that these particles are **angels** and is told that she should 'play the serpent' [SK, 12]. Mary follows the angels' directions and passes through the **window** beneath the hornbeam trees into **Cittàgazze** [AS, 7] and then to the world of the **Mulefa**. Mary learns to communicate with the Mulefa, befriending a **zalif** called **Atal**. The Mulefa appeal to Mary to stop the loss of Dust from their worlds. Mary is able to view the movement of Dust by creating the **amber spyglass**. Mary is informed in a dream to expect **Will** and Lyra and to take care of them, which she does until the second Fall of Man [AS, 32].

While she studies to become a scientist, Mary is also a nun. The order allows her to keep up her university career and to complete her doctorate. Mary intended to teach at university and continue research into particle physics while remaining a nun. But, seven years prior to her encounter with Will and Lyra, she met **Alfredo Montale** at a conference in Lisbon. The encounter reminded her of her first love, **Tim**, a boy she danced with at a disco when she was twelve. Mary realised at that moment that no one would benefit from her self-denial and turned her back on the **Church**. It is this tender story that helps Lyra to recognise her love for Will [AS, 33].

Thereafter, Mary's relationship with the Church is more confrontational. She sees that there is no God and decries the Christian religion as 'a very powerful and convincing mistake' [AS, 33]. Mary also comes to see that good and evil are what people do, not what they *are*: good and evil do not exist independently of people [AS, 33]. Nevertheless, she remains a very spiritual person. On her travels through other worlds, Mary uses the **Book of Changes**, given to her by her grandfather, and the **yarrow stalks** method of divination for guidance [AS, 7].

After leaving the convent, Mary continues her researches. She attends a high-energy physics conference in California where she meets a mathematician who teaches her how to climb the great redwoods. She lives with him for four years although they never marry, scandalising her family [AS, 7, 20, 33].

After her adventure in the world of the Mulefa, Mary returns to England with Will and Lyra. **Serafina Pekkala** teaches Mary how to be able to view her own **dæmon**: an Alpine chough. Before parting, Mary promises Lyra that she will look after Will [AS, 36].

MARGARET – A **gyptian** at second Roping who entreats **John Faa** to take vengeance against the **Gobblers** [NL, 8].

MARTHA – A 'subdued-looking' child with a rabbit **dæmon** who is held at **Bolvangar** [NL, 14].

MASTER OF JORDAN COLLEGE – An aged scholar, well over the age of seventy, who is in charge of **Jordan College** [NL, 1]. The Master was once a powerful man: he had been a member of the **Council of State** and both **Lord Asriel** and **Lord Boreal** counted him as a friend. However, by the time of **Lyra's** adventure he had started to 'slow down'. The Master had promised Lord Asriel that he would look after Lyra when she was brought to the College by Asriel from the **Sisters of Obedience** at Watlington, and kept the **alethiometer** safe for her. When Lyra returned from her adventure, he allowed her to stay at Jordan College in her old lodgings and to attend **Saint Sophia's** to study alethiometry under **Dame Hannah Relf**. He lived in the Master's lodgings, a grand and slightly gloomy house that opened into the Yaxley Quadrangle. His man-servant, **Cousins**, was an old enemy of Lyra's [NL, 3]. The Master had a raven **dæmon**, unnamed in the books but called Lenore in the radio version (after the poem 'The Raven', by Edgar Allan Poe).

The prime action of the Master of Jordan College is to attempt to poison Lord Asriel at the beginning of *Northern Lights*. His reasons for doing so are open to speculation. The Master said that the alethiometer warned of appalling consequences if Lord Asriel was to pursue his research, consequences that would draw Lyra in when he sought to keep her safe for as long as possible [NL, 2]. The most detailed explanation comes from **John Faa**. John suggests that the Master is a man of complex and competing loyalties: his promise to Lord Asriel to protect Lyra; his duty to the College in the face of the **Church**; his own morals and scruples particularly about the **Barnard–Stokes** heresy. John's suggestion is that the Master had tried for ten years or more to keep the balance between **Mrs Coulter** and Lord Asriel but that the Church's increasing power, and the threat posed by Asriel's investigation, put him in a situation where Lyra was safer with Mrs Coulter than with Asriel or the College. 'I see the Master as a man having terrible choices to make; whatever he chooses will do harm; but maybe if he does the right thing, a little less harm will come about than if he chooses wrong.' [NL, 7].

MATAPAN – The name of the **dæmon** that once belonged to one of the **ghosts** in the **land of the dead** [AS, 22].

MCGINN, BRIDGET – One of the children at **Bolvangar**. She witnesses **Tony Makarios** being taken away for **intercision**. She hears one nurse describe the operation as one cut to fix the **dæmon** in one form and make the children grown-up [NL, 15].

MCKAY – A research student at **Bolvangar** who is responsible for the section that includes the **dæmon** cages [NL, 16].

METATRON – aka, **Regent, Lord**. *De facto* ruler of the **Kingdom of Heaven**. Metatron feels that the Churches of the world concede the will of God too readily [AS, 5] and sets about subduing Man's independence and restoring the dominance of the **Authority** by intervening directly in human affairs. **Asriel**'s forces and the **ghosts** of the dead are able to prevent Metatron from finding and killing **Will** and **Lyra** during the **Battle on the Plain**, by throwing him, and themselves, into the **abyss**.

Metatron is described as being 'exactly like a man in early middle age, tall, powerful and commanding'. He is fiercely bright, so bright that **Mrs Coulter** is uncertain whether he has wings [AS, 30]. When Metatron attacks Will, he is seen to be larger and stronger than **Balthamos** and **Baruch**, and armed with a spear [AS, 2].

Metatron is no ordinary **angel**. Unlike the majority of angels, he was originally a man – **Enoch**, 'the son of Jared, the son of Mahalalel, the son of Kenan, the son of Enosh, the son of Set, the son of Adam' [AS, 30]. Enoch had many wives and empathised with the fallen angels and their love of human women [AS, 30]. Four thousand years before the events of *The Amber Spyglass*, the Authority took Enoch into the Kingdom of Heaven to be his Regent and together they plan a permanent Inquisition. Enoch was Baruch's brother but cast him out for undeclared reasons [AS, 5].

The story of Metatron is based on a mixture of biblical sources, both canonical and apocryphal. Enoch's passage into Heaven is recounted in Genesis 5:24, at the age of 365, and not 65 as indicated in *His Dark Materials* [AS, 30]. For Enoch's transformation into an angel, however, we must read the *Book of Enoch*, a pseudepigraphal work rejected by Western Christianity but nevertheless officially recognised by the Ethiopian Church. In this work, Enoch fails to effect a reconciliation between God and the fallen angels but is taken by God, given great wisdom and knowledge and transformed into a fiery angel to work at God's side. In *His Dark Materials*, Metatron makes a direct reference to his failed attempt to plead the case of the fallen angels [AS, 31]. Asriel notes that Metatron is talked of as Enoch in the 'apocryphal scriptures' [AS, 28]. Interestingly, Asriel implies that defining the Book of Enoch as apocrypha was a deliberate act on the part of Metatron to conceal himself.

MITI, REINA – the Queen of a **witch** clan. Reina, **Ruta Skadi** and half-a-dozen other witch clans fly against the **angels** from the **Clouded Mountain** with pitch-pine dipped in bitumen and are set alight [AS, 29].

MONICA, SISTER – One of the stenographers at the **Consistorial Court of Discipline**. She is from the order of **Saint Philomel** and has sworn an oath of silence [AS, 6].

MONTALE, ALFREDO – A man who **Dr Mary Malone** meets at a physics conference in Lisbon [AS, 33].

MOXIE – **Will**'s pet tabby cat. It trips up the burglar in Will's house, resulting in the man's death [SK, 1].

MULEFA – Creatures from a parallel world, where they appear to be the dominant, intelligent species. They are the size of deer or antelope but with legs in a diamond formation – two in the centre, one under the head and one under the tail. They move with a rocking motion. They use seed-pods as wheels, grabbing them in their clawed front and rear legs, propelling themselves with their middle legs [AS, 7]. They use stone, wood, cord, shell and horn more than they use metals. The overall effect is that of an antelope crossed with a motorbike, although they also have short trunks. They have fire, society and buildings [AS, 10]. Individuals are known as zalif. They live in a symbiotic relationship with their surroundings, very respectful of their environment ... but also vulnerable to changes. They evolved around 33,000 years ago, the same time as modern man on other worlds. Most importantly, they possess the ability to see **Dust**, giving them a great natural insight into the phenomenon. **Mary Malone** lives among the Mulefa, and researches Dust with them. The word is pronounced 'moo-leff-ah', and might be a nod to the Moomin stories of Tove Jannson, admired by Philip Pullman.

MUSCA – The dæmon of **Ignatius Cole**, a former **Master of Jordan College** [NL, 3]. Musca is Latin for fly.

MUSK-OX – Creatures that live in the frozen north. In the calamity that followed the opening of **Lord Asriel**'s **bridge**, the creatures galloped south, then west or north again [SK, 2].

N

NÄLKÄINENS – According to the **gyptians**, Nälkäinens are headless **ghosts** that inhabit the forests of the north and attack people in their sleep [NL, 6]. Nälkäinen is Finnish for hungry.

NELL – A **gyptian** at second Roping who asks **John Faa** to consider taking women on the expedition to **Bolvangar** to look after the rescued children [NL, 8].

NELSON – A physicist who is part of the **Nuniatak dig** that hires **John Parry** as a guide for their expedition to **Lookout Ridge**. Although regarded by John as a 'genial dimwi', Nelson is employed by the Ministry of Defence to investigate the '**anomaly**' under the guise of a study of high-level atmospheric particles in the **Aurora Borealis**. He disguises his radiation suit as weather balloons [SK, 4, 5].

NORTHLANDERS – A term used by **Dr Martin Lanselius**, the **Witch-Consul** at **Trollesund**, to describe the non-witch inhabitants of the north [NL, 10].

O

OGUNWE, KING – An African king from **Lyra**'s world and one of **Lord Asriel**'s high commanders [AS, 5]. Ogunwe leads the squadron of **gyropters** that battle the forces of the **Church** while Lyra, **Will** and the **Gallivespian** spies escape from the Himalayan cave where Lyra is held captive [AS, 9]. He is not immune to **Mrs Coulter**'s charms but does not betray Asriel. He has a cheetah **dæmon** [AS, 16].

ORDERLY – A man in the service of **Lord Asriel** in the **Adamant Tower**. He has a terrier **dæmon** [AS, 16].

OXENTIEL, MADAME – A **Gallivespian** second-in-command who takes over from **Lord Roke** on his death. She has steely grey hair and uses Lord Roke's blue hawk as a steed [AS, 28]. Madame Oxentiel comes to the aid of **Will** and **Lyra** when they search for their **dæmons** at the **Battle on the Plain**.

OZYMANDIAS – *See* **Golden monkey**.

P

PAGDZIN *TULKU* – A great healer and monk who resides in a Tibetan monastery along the **Cho-Lung-Se** trail. The Pagdzin *tulku* is famed for curing an outbreak of the white fever a year before **Lyra** is held captive in a Himalayan cave. He provides **Ama** with a potion that counteracts **Mrs Coulter**'s sleeping draft. He has a bat **dæmon** [AS, 4]. In Tibetan Buddhism, a *tulku* is a reincarnated Lama, for example the Dalai Lama who has existed in fourteen reincarnations since the late fourteenth century. Steven Seagal, an advocate for Tibetan causes, was proclaimed a *tulku* in 1997.

PALMERIAN PROFESSOR – *See* **Trelawnay**.

PANSERBØRNE – *See* **Bears** (the word is pronounced pan-sir-bee-your-knee).

PANTALAIMON – **Lyra's dæmon**, Pan for short. At the start of *His Dark Materials*, Pan's form has not fixed and he is able to use his various forms to support Lyra in her endeavours. His keen eyesight as a wild cat helps Lyra at night [NL, 6]. When she is lying, he adopts his most inexpressive form, a dark-brown moth, to hide her feelings and not betray her [NL, 1, 5]. When she prepares to battle with the **gyptian** children, Pan turns into a dragon the size of a deer-hound [NL, 3]. He reserves his polecat shape, the most ugly and vicious of all his forms, for expressing Lyra's bitter hatred [NL, 17]. He also turns into an ermine for politeness when dining at the Master's lodgings [NL, 3]. The ermine is also his favourite sleeping form [NL, 2].

But, in the peculiar dualism of dæmon and human, where they are elements of the same person and yet consciously different, Pan is also capable of separate emotions. He can feel fear where Lyra can't, turning into an agitated bat when Lyra casually plays with the coins in the Oratory. By contrast, he turns into a lion to scare away the **night-ghasts** that subsequently terrorised Lyra [NL, 3]. When she is nervous, he becomes as big as he can and adopts the form of a panther to reassure her [NL, 7]. He even feels seasick when Lyra doesn't [NL, 9]. Pan also consciously uses his shape to toy with Lyra, becoming a hedgehog in her bed when she complains that he is her awake [NL, 4], or imitating the golden monkey [NL, 4].

This 'separateness' could also be an underlying instinct that Lyra has but does not consciously act on. When **Will's** fingers were severed, Pan licked the wounds clean, breaking the great taboo. Lyra was shocked as Pan had acted on his own initiative, yet afterwards she recognised that it was the right thing to do [SK, 8]. Both of them were experiencing a closeness with Will although they had not openly discussed it. When Pan and Lyra met up with **Tony Makarios**, the severed boy, only days before, Pan wanted to comfort the child but the great taboo prevented him [NL, 13].

Pan soon comes to experience a more profound form of separateness. At the **land of the dead**, Lyra chooses to travel with the **boatman**, knowing that she will be separated from Pan [AS, 21]. It is something that they had tried before on the journey to the Arctic [NL, 9]. This deliberate separation was 'the cruellest thing she had ever done' and arguably the great betrayal that the **Master of Jordan College** had said she was destined to perform [NL, 2]. Unbeknown to Lyra, however, she and Will undergo a rite-of-passage that is undertaken by all would-be witches; a process of painful, deliberate separation that nevertheless results in the ability to be apart from one's dæmon for great distances and periods of time [AS, 36]. Pan and Will's dæmon, subsequently named **Kirjava** by **Serafina Pekkala**, then travel the many worlds, including that of the **Gallivespians** and talk to **angels**. Before they return to their separate worlds, the dæmons promise each other only to reveal what they had seen when they feel that the time is right. Lyra suspects the suspense is punishment for their actions at the land of the dead [AS, 38].

In the land of the **Mulefa**, Pantalaimon fixed in the form of a pine marten, 'a large and powerful ferret, red-gold in colour, lithe and sinuous and full of grace' [AS, 37]. His name is pronounced 'pant-a-lie-mun'.

PAOLO – A young boy of **Cittàgazze**. He has an older sister, **Angelica**, and an older brother, **Tullio** [SK, 3].

PARADISI, GIACOMO – The bearer of the **subtle knife** prior to **Will**. He was the last in a long line of philosophers, alchemists and men of learning who formed the **Philosophers'**

Guild of the **Torre degli Angeli** in **Cittàgazze**. In his time, Giacomo had explored other worlds: he was familiar with **Lyra**'s world and had cut the **window** beneath the hornbeam trees to try to lure **Sir Charles Latrom** through to his death at the hands of the **Spectres**. He lamented that, with 'unforgivable forgetfulness', he had forgotten to close this window, the same one through which Will first entered another world. Giacomo was rescued by Will and Lyra from **Tullio**, an adolescent boy who stole the knife. In his fight with Tullio, Will lost two fingers, revealing himself to be the true **bearer**. Giacomo instructed Will on using the knife to open and close windows before poisoning himself to escape being killed by the Spectres [SK, 8].

PARKER, MISS – A teacher at **Saint Sophia's** who **Lyra** claims is the best teacher in the world – though she is probably lying [LO].

PARRY, ELAINE – **Major John Parry**'s wife and mother of **Will**. She suffers from some kind of paranoia, partly induced by real persecution from those interested in the '**anomaly**' that her husband is investigating when he disappears. Will leaves his mother in the care of **Mrs Cooper**, his former piano teacher [SK, 1, 5, 13].

PARRY, MAJOR JOHN – aka **Dr Stanislaus Grumman**, **Jopari**. The Father of **Will** Parry and prime mover in many of the events in *His Dark Materials*. John was originally a commissioned officer in the Royal Marines where he rose to the rank of Major. He left the army to become a professional explorer and led geographical and scientific expeditions to remote parts of the world [SK, 1, 4, 5]. He was married to **Elaine Parry** and they had a son, Will.

In 1985, the year of Will's birth, John accompanied a team of six scientists and geographers to the north of Alaska. The **Nuniatak dig**, as it became known, was a preliminary survey of the area for the remains of early human settlements and was sponsored by the **Institute of Archaeology** at **Oxford** University

[SK, 4]. Although he was hired to assist the expedition, he had his own reasons for going along. He had heard old legends of a strange **anomaly**, 'a rent in the fabric of the world' that constituted a gateway between this universe and another. The anomaly was known to the Eskimo who believed it to be a gateway to the spirit world. However, John was not the only one aware of the anomaly. A physicist called **Nelson** had been hired by the Ministry of Defence to investigate the anomaly. John discovered that the **Soviet Union** had also been searching for the anomaly which, he learned from the Eskimo **Matt Kigalik**, was a kind of gap in the air [SK, 5]. During the expedition some of John's companions got lost in a blizzard. In searching for them, John and two others walked through the **window** by accident. They only realised their situation when they came upon a town and realised that they had passed into another world. Try as they could, they were unable to find the window again. Worse, they discovered that this world was haunted by apparitions John later came to know as **Spectres**. John's two companions died at their hands [SK, 10].

John could not wait to leave this new world but was unable to find the window back to his own. With a little more searching, he found another window to **Lyra's** world. Soon after, he discovered that he had a **dæmon**, a beautiful osprey (sometimes termed a fish-eagle) called **Sayan Kötör** [SK, 6]. Over time, they learned to stay connected some 40 feet apart, more than regular humans in Lyra's world [SK, 14]. Together, they explored the northern lands and John began to see the answers to many mysteries. It was at this time that he befriended the **Tartars** of the **Yenesei Pakhtar** tribe.

Around nine years before his death, John adopted the name **Dr Stanislaus Grumman** and made his way to Berlin [SK, 6]. He presented a thesis to the **Berlin Academy** and gained membership by defending it in debate. He believed that there was evidence of human civilisations 35,000 years ago, earlier than previously thought. He argued that the earth's magnetic field had changed dramatically at various times in the past, and that the earth's axis had shifted so that temperate zones became ice-bound. Evidence of these civilisations was hidden under the ice, he claimed. 'Stanislaus' made a name for himself by publishing on the variations on the magnetic pole. About two years later, he met the Director of the **Imperial Muscovite Academy**'s astronomical observatory north of **Nova Zembla**. The Director was perplexed by Stanislaus' past – no one knew him as a student, or knew of his previous work. Stanislaus appeared to have come out of nowhere [SK, 6].

Meanwhile, John searched for other forms of knowledge. At least five years before his death, he returned to the Yenesei Pakhtar tribe and was initiated into the skull-cult. The trepanning, witnessed by an old **seal-hunter**, lasted two nights and a day and was undertaken with a bow-drill [SK, 6, 10]. The Tartars called him **Jopari**, a corruption of his real name. He became a shaman and made lots of useful discoveries, including an ointment made from bloodmoss that he used to heal his leg when he fell foul of a trap laid by **Yakovlev** at the northern end of the Urals [SK, 6]. It was around this time that he rejected the love of a **witch, Juta Kamainen**. It was a mistake that would haunt him [SK, 6].

Although now an adopted Tartar and shaman, John's academic and scholarly pursuits continued. The Academy sponsored some of Stanislaus' expeditions and he became a celebrated academic. At some point, he became a scholar at **Jordan College** [NL, 2]. Eighteen months prior to his death, the Berlin Academy sent John as far north as the magnetic pole to make various celestial observations. The expedition vanished shortly after but not before, in one of his last messages to the Academy, Stanislaus reported 'certain natural phenomenon only seen in the lands of the north' [NL, 2].

Rumours were rife of Stanislaus' death, but it was not the first time. The scholars of Jordan College believed that he had been the victim of an accident and had fallen down a crevasse. The Arctic drifters of the north had far more fanciful versions of his death: some said he was shot outright in the **Skraeling** wars; others said that he was killed in an avalanche at **Sakhalin** [SK, 6]. A more grisly proposition was to be put forward.

Six months after Grumman's disappearance, **Lord Asriel** went to the north supposedly on a diplomatic mission to the

King of Lapland. In fact, his intention was to find out what happened to Stanislaus' expedition and to delve deeper into the phenomenon he reported. Asriel took photographs of the **Aurora Borealis** using a special emulsion. The **photograms** showed both **Dust** and a city beyond the Northern Lights. This was the phenomenon Stanislaus had reported – proof of the **Barnard–Stokes** hypothesis that Asriel sought. Asriel presented these photograms to the scholars at Jordan College on his return from the north twelve months later. He also brought with him the head of Stanislaus, recovered from the ice near **Svalbard**. Stanislaus had apparently been murdered by Tartars or **bears**. The horrible artefact was enough to convince the scholars to fund another expedition for Asriel to the north [NL, 2].

In fact, Stanislaus had not been murdered but what exactly happened to him after the loss of his expedition remains a mystery. It is likely, however, that he returned to the Yenesei Pakhtars and developed his skills as a shaman. He discovered Asriel's plans and regarded it as the greatest undertaking in 35,000 years of human civilisation. In his spirit body, he explored the world of **Cittàgazze** and learned of the **subtle knife**. He also learned how to recognise the **bearer** and what that person must do in Asriel's cause. It was at this time that he called **Lee Scoresby** to him to take him northward to Asriel's world where he would instruct the bearer on his task [SK, 2, 10].

Lee took John north but they were pursued by the **Church**. Although John was able to call up a storm that destroyed most of the pursuing **zeppelins**, one party of the elite **Swiss Guard** survived. At **Alamo Gulch**, Lee bravely fought and died to give John enough time to escape to safety. Shortly after, John found the knife-bearer, Will, and told him to take the knife to Asriel. Then came a flicker of recognition and each realised who the other was. At that precise moment, John was killed by the arrow of Juta, the witch he had scorned. She had taken her own life [SK, 15].

This was not the end for John, or Lee. Will and Lyra were reunited with them both in the **land of the dead**. John and Lee led a charge of the **ghosts** of the dead onto the **Battle on the**

Plain where they were able to hold off the Spectres long enough to let Lyra and Will escape with their dæmons to safety. Their work finished, John and Lee dissipated into the air, rejoining the world of the living [AS, 26].

John is one of the most influential characters in *His Dark Materials* although his actual 'screen time' is short-lived. As Stanislaus, it is John who provides Asriel with the impetus to investigate the **Aurora**. It is John who discovers the purpose of the knife and who instructs its bearer. And it is John who brings the **angels** to Will's side to guide him to the conclusion. His role is very much that of the wise man/wizard in Joseph Campbell's typology of archetypes and, like *Star Wars'* Ben Kenobi or *The Lord of the Rings'* Gandalf the wizard, his role is to dispense wisdom and die, passing on the torch.

John is also one of the few characters who grasps the enormity and totality of Asriel's plan. 'We've had nothing but lies and propaganda and cruelty and deceit for all the thousands of years of human history. It's time we started again, but properly this time' [SK, 15]. John rightly sees Asriel's intent as the greatest in human civilisation. And he is prepared to put that first: Parry consciously breaks his oath to Lee and instructs Will to take the knife to Asriel, knowing that in so doing he will jeopardise Lyra [SK, 15].

PARRY, WILLIAM – *See* **Will**.

PARSLOW, ROGER – **Lyra**'s 'particular friend' in **Oxford**, with whom she gets up to mischief, whether on the roof of **Jordan College**, in the **crypt** below the Oratory or at war with the **gyptian** children. Roger is one of the kitchen boys at Jordan College [NL, 3]. His family are stonemasons and scaffolders who keep the fabric of Jordan College together for five generations [NL, 3]. He has a brother, **Simon Parslow**, and his father is **Mrs Lonsdale**'s cousin. Roger is captured by the **Oblation Board** in Oxford and is taken to **Bolvangar**. Lyra pursues and rescues him only to take him to **Lord Asriel** who seeks a child to create his **bridge** to the stars. In an attempt to escape, Roger and his **dæmon**, Salcilia, are separated [NL, 15].

Roger dies and, as a **ghost**, travels to the **land of the dead**. It is here that he appears to Lyra in a dream and asks for her help [AS, 1]. Lyra is reunited with Roger in the land of the dead where, with **Will**'s help, they are able to release the ghosts from their torment. Roger is the first ghost to leave the land of the dead [AS, 26].

PARSLOW, SIMON – One of **Lyra**'s companions from **Oxford** who was with her when **Ma Costa** discovers that her son **Billy** has been taken by the **Gobblers**. The Parslow family includes **Roger**, Lyra's best friend, and **Mrs Lonsdale**, Lyra's housekeeper [NL, 3].

PAVEL, FRA – *See* **Fra Pavel Rašek**.

PAYNE, DR OLIVER – A particle physicist and colleague of **Dr Mary Malone**. Oliver and Mary establish the **Dark Matter Research Unit** to investigate 'Shadow Particles'. It is Oliver, 'an all-round intellectual' and amateur archaeologist, who discovers **Shadows** around trepanned skulls and who names **the Cave** after the works of Plato. Although they make the radical discovery that Shadows are conscious, Oliver feels that the discovery is too far-fetched to secure future funding for their research. He attends a job interview in **Geneva**, leaving Mary to worry about the outcome of their proposal to a funding committee [SK, 4]. On his return, however, he is seduced by **Sir Charles Latrom**'s offer of support for their application. Mary resists and later destroys the Cave [SK, 12].

PAZHETS, YELANA – A 600-year-old witch, the former lover of **Sebastian Makepeace**, and the mother of his child, who she kills in the battle between **Asriel** and **Metatron**. She is part of a **witch** clan, past the Urals, that is allied to that of **Serafina Pekkala**'s through the birch-oath. Her bird **dæmon** is called **Ragi** ['Lyra and the Birds'].

PEKKALA, SERAFINA – The Queen of the **witch** clan in the region of **Lake Enara**. Although appearing younger than **Mrs**

Coulter, Serafina is at least 300 years old. Forty years before she met Lyra, she had been saved from an assault from a great red bird in the **Fens** of **Eastern Anglia** by **Farder Coram**. Serafina falls in love with Farder immediately and stays with him long enough to bear him a child. The boy dies in a great epidemic which came from the East not long after birth. Serafina leaves Farder when she is recalled to her clan to become Queen on the death of her mother. Though she cannot get away, she continues to look out for Farder, sending him herbs and spells to help him recover when he is wounded by the poisoned arrow of a **Skraeling** [NL, 10, 15]. Serafina helps the children escape from **Bolvangar** and later, having learnt of **Lord Asriel**'s plan, brings her clan into battle against the **Authority**. She gives **Lee Scoresby** a little red flower from a chain of flowers around her neck so that he can call for her in time of need: Lee remembers the flower too late. She is fair with bright green eyes and wears the traditional **witches'** dress of strips of black silk [NL, 17]. **Dr Mary Malone** has never seen a human form so slender and graceful [AS, 36]. Serafina teaches Mary how to see **dæmons** in her world [AS, 36]. Her own dæmon, **Kaisa,** is a beautiful grey goose with a head crowned with a flash of pure white [NL, 11].

PERKINS, ALAN – Lawyer in **Oxford** who is ordered by **Major John Parry** to pay money into **Will**'s mother's bank account every three months until told otherwise. Perkins hasn't seen Parry since the day he left the instruction, prior to the **Nuniatak dig** [SK, 4].

PETER – Man awaiting his **Death** in the holding area on the outskirts of the **land of the dead**. **Will** and **Lyra** are the first people he and his family have seen without a Death for a long time. His mother is called Magda [AS, 19].

PETERSON, JAKE – Old gold-miner residing in **Fairbanks**, Alaska, in June 1985. He tells **Major John Parry** that the Eskimo knows of the '**anomaly**' and believes it to be a doorway to the **spirit world**. Jake provides John with rough co-ordinates for the **window** that are sufficient for John to be able to locate it. He is a friend of the Eskimo, **Matt Kigalik** [SK, 5].

POLSTEAD, DR – One of the young scholars at **Jordan College** whose quarters lay just under the roof. He is an affable stout young man with ginger hair and a ginger cat **dæmon** to match. He had been **Lyra**'s unwilling teacher some two to three years previously ['Lyra and the Birds'].

POPPEL, ROGER VAN – Head of one of the six **gyptian** families. He is responsible for all non-military stores, such as food and cold-weather clothing, for the expedition to **Bolvangar** [NL, 8].

PORTER – *See* **Shuter**.

POSTNIKOVA, PRINCESS – One of the guests **Mrs Coulter** considers inviting to her cocktail party [NL, 5].

PRIEST – A priest at **Trollesund** who holds **Iorek Byrnison**'s armour for the townspeople. In his cellar, he tries to tempt evil spirits out of it. His house is virtually destroyed when Iorek smashes through it to retrieve his armour. He has a maidservant with a hen **dæmon**. The priest has a pelican dæmon [NL, 11].

R

RAGI – The bird **dæmon** of **Yelena Pazhets**. He and his human visit **Trollesund** where they learn to read the time in **Lyra**'s manner ['Lyra and the Birds'].

RAKNISON, IOFUR – Deceitful, self-appointed king of the **Svalbard bears**. Iofur Raknison is a high-born among the bears although, unlike **Iorek Byrnison**, he is not expected to become king. Taller and bulkier than Iorek, Iofur is also more 'human', or aspires to be so. His face is more mobile and expressive, and he possesses a political skill and cunning to rival humans. His deceitfulness runs deep: on his first hunting expedition he fights and kills a lone bear, only to discover and cover up that the bear is his father [NL, 19]. Above all, however, he wants a **dæmon**. When **Mrs Coulter**, seeking to establish another station like **Bolvangar** only worse, offers Iofur baptism into the **Church** in return for his support for her activities, Iofur cannot resist [NL, 20]. He successfully engineers the exile of Iorek by ensuring a fight breaks out between Iorek and **Hjalmur Hjalmurson**. With Iorek in exile, Iofur sets about creating a new order in Svalbard. The ice palace is abandoned in favour of marble, new alliances and treaties are established and Iofur sets about exploiting the natural resources of the Arctic with the help of human engineers. He supports Mrs Coulter's experiments, or at least overlooks them, and imprisons **Lord Asriel** for the **Magisterium**. Little do they know that Iofur is seeking to play both sides, giving Asriel access to equipment to continue his heretical experiments. Iofur's reign reaches its end when Lyra, claiming to be Iorek's dæmon, encourages Iofur to fight Iorek for the right to become her new master [NL, 19]. Despite his size advantage, Iofur is unable to withstand the onslaught from Iorek and is killed.

An obvious model for Iofur is King Louie in *The Jungle Book*, an ape who wants to be a man, and takes on the airs and graces of a human monarch. The character was renamed Ragnar Sturlusson for the movie.

RANSOM, MARK AND LISA – Names adopted by **Will** and **Lyra** in Will's **Oxford**. Mark and Lisa are supposed to live at 26 Bourne Road. Lyra prefers to use the name Lizzie as she has used it before as **Lizzie Brooks** in **Bolvangar** [NL, 14; SK, 3].

RAŠEK, FRA PAVEL – **Alethiometrist** working for the **Consistorial Court of Discipline**. He is known by **Lord Asriel** to be thorough but slow. When the **Church** needs to find **Lyra** quickly, the President of the Consistorial Court join forces with the **Society of the Work of the Holy Spirit** whose alethiometrist works faster than Rašek. He is a thin-faced man with a frog **dæmon** [SK, 2; AS, 6, 16].

REGENT, LORD – *See* **Metatron**.

RELF, DAME HANNAH – Head of **Saint Sophia's**, one of the women's colleges in **Lyra's Oxford** [NL, 3]. She is an elderly grey-haired lady whom Lyra initially finds to be dull and frumpy – and smells of cabbage! On her return to **Jordan College**, however, Lyra comes to see Relf as an altogether more clever, kind and interesting person. According to the **Master of Jordan College**, Relf's scholarship in the field of **alethiometry** is unmatched: it is logical that Lyra is put in Relf's hands. Lyra agrees to study at Saint Sophia's in the north of the city while continuing to live in her quarters at Jordan College [AS, 38]. She has a marmoset **dæmon** [NL, 3].

REYNOLDS, JESSIE – A child from the saddler's in the market of **Lyra's Oxford** who went missing the day before **Billy Costa**'s abduction [NL, 3].

ROGER – *See* **Parslow, Roger**.

ROKE, LORD – The leader of the **Gallivespians** and one of **Lord Asriel**'s high commanders. He has a small blue hawk as a steed. Lord Roke dies when he kills a **witch** serving the **Church** at **Saint-Jean-les-Eaux**. **Madame Oxentiel** succeeds him as leader of the Gallivespians [AS, 25].

ROKEBY, NICHOLAS – A stout, black-bearded **gyptian** and head of one of the six gyptian families. He raises gold and 38 men for the expedition to **Bolvangar**. Rokeby was put in charge of finding a vessel to transport the gyptians to the north [NL, 8].

RUKH, LORD – An arctic explorer who freezes to death on one expedition. He is found holding a stone carved with an inscription in an unknown language. The stone is on display in the library of the **Royal Arctic Institute** [NL, 4].

RUSAKOV, BORIS MIKHAILOVITCH – A Muscovite scientist who discovers an elementary particle subsequently known to the **Church** as **Dust**. The **Rusakov particle** is difficult to detect and does not interact with other fundamental particles in the expected way. Most peculiarly, they are attracted to adults and children whose **dæmons** are fixed, but are less concentrated around pre-pubescent children. Rusakov's discovery is announced through the **Magisterium**. An Inspector from the **Consistorial Court of Discipline**, sent to check the discovery for heresy, suspects Rusakov of 'diabolic possession', exorcises his laboratory, and interrogates him under the rules of the Inquisition. In the end, the Magisterium accept that the Rusakov particle really exists. It became known as Dust later [NL, 5, 21].

RUTH – A girl at the head of the school at **Saint Sophia's**. She is four years older than Lyra [LO].

RUYTER, BENJAMIN DE – The head of one of the six **gyptian** families. He is put in charge of spying. Benjamin leads a party of gyptians to **Clerkenwell** where they capture three **Gobblers**. The Gobblers reveal connections to the **Ministry of Theology** and **Lord Boreal**. Benjamin sends Frans Broekman and Tom Mendham to investigate Lord Boreal while he, **Jacob Huismans** and **Gerard Hook** investigate the Ministry of Theology in **White Hall**. Benjamin and Hook meet stiff resistance inside the Ministry: Hook is captured, Jacob is mortally wounded and Benjamin is killed when he falls from a high staircase during a fight. He has a bird **dæmon** [NL, 8].

S

SALMAKIA, LADY – A **Gallivespian** spy who infiltrates the **Society of the Work of the Holy Spirit** on the orders of **Lord Roke**. She convinces a priest in the Society that she is the spirit of wisdom [AS, 5]. Salmakia is present when the **Consistorial Court of Discipline** and the Society put aside their differences in order to find **Lyra** and prevent the second **Fall** of Man [AS, 9]. Salmakia wears a loose skirt of silver material, a green sleeveless top and the familiar poisonous spurs [AS, 13]. Her face is not beautiful but calm and kindly and her voice is low and expressive [AS, 21]. Salmakia and her companion **Chevalier Tialys** die after they help **Will** and Lyra escape from the **land of the dead**.

SAMOYED – A race of people who live and hunt in the Arctic. Samoyed hunters attack the **gyptians** and capture **Lyra** to sell to the **experimental theologians** at **Bolvangar**. They have Asiatic features and powerful limbs suited to the hostile conditions [NL, 12].

SANDLING – The name of the **dæmon** that was once part of a **ghost** girl **Lyra** and **Will** encountered in the **land of the dead** [AS, 22].

SANTELIA, PROFESSOR JOTHAM – Regius Professor of Cosmology at the University of Gloucester and a prisoner of **Iofur Raknison**. By the time **Lyra** shared a cell with **Jotham**, the professor, aged with a grey beard and tattered hair, had gone mad and his lizard **dæmon** was weary-looking and listless. Jotham claims that he had been invited to **Svalbard** by Raknison who intended to establish a University and to make Jotham its first Vice-Chancellor. Jotham's arch rival, **Trelawnay**, the **Palmerian Professor** at **Jordan College**, was also supposedly present. Jotham told Lyra that he had discovered final proof of the **Barnard–Stokes** hypothesis and suggested that a jealous Trelawnay had lied about Jotham to Raknison, prompting the bear king to throw Jotham in prison. Aside from Trelawnay, Jotham also railed against the Publications Committee of the **Royal Arctic Society** who had apparently spurned his contributions. While Jotham's mental state means that one should take his story with care, Trelawnay was certainly aware of Raknison's intention to establish a University [NL, 2, 19]. Jotham was freed once Iofur was overthrown and wrote 'A Prisoner of the Bears' [LO].

SATTAMAX – The oldest zalif and Dr Mary Malone meet in the world of the Mulefa. He has white hair and moves stiffly. Nevertheless, through the amber spyglass she sees him bathed in a very rich and complex Shadow cloud [AS, 13].

SAYAN KÖTÖR – Major John Parry's dæmon that he discovers shortly after he enters Lyra's world. She is a beautiful osprey and can fly up to 40 feet away from John [SK, 6]. Sayan is most likely a reference to the Sayan mountains, not far from the Yenesei where John joins a tribe of Tartars.

SCORESBY, LEE – A Texan aeronaut who fights and dies to help Will and Lyra on their adventure. Lee is a tall and lean man with 'a thin black moustache, narrow blue eyes and a perpetual expression of distant and sardonic amusement' [NL, 10]. A New Dane from Texas, he buys a balloon and becomes an aeronaut, taking commissions as he finds them. At the time he was hired by John Faa, Scoresby was stranded at the quayside of Trollesund, having hoped to join an expedition that had run out of funds even before it left Amsterdam [NL, 10]. In the radio dramatisation, he claims to be six foot five.

Scoresby's business is his balloon. The main balloon can take six people [NL, 13]. He also has a second, smaller balloon for surveillance [NL, 14]. As one would expect, he knows many ways to inflate the balloon: hydrogen from iron filings and sulphuric acid, gas made from rock-oil or, for speed, ground-gas vented from a fire-mine, which could fill the main balloon in an hour [NL, 13]. Inside the basket, Lee carries furs, bottled air and racks of philosophical instruments, plus his trusty long-barrelled pistol [NL, 17]. The pistol provides ample protection from the cliff-ghasts and unfriendly witches [NL, 19, 20].

Lee is an old hand in the Arctic and a great asset to the gyptian expedition and to Lyra. He is well acquainted with the lands of the north and has many contacts, not least Sam Cansino and the other Arctic drifters of the Samirsky Hotel at Nova Zembla [SK, 6]. He has flown over the lands of the Yenesei Pakhtar tribe, the tribe who had Major John Parry as its shaman, some years before [SK, 10]. He also speaks half-a-dozen languages [SK, 10].

Lee is also an old friend of **Iorek Byrnison;** they fought together in the **Tunguska campaign** [NL, 11]. It was during this campaign that Lee rescued Iorek from the Tartars who had surrounded his ice-fort and were starving him out. He had to guess Iorek's weight, including armour, and hoped that there was ground-gas beneath the ice-fort Iorek had built [NL, 13]. Lee is one of only three non-**bears** for whom Iorek ever expressed any regard (the others are **Serafina Pekkala** and Lyra) [AS, 9].

After helping the gyptians to **Bolvangar,** and fighting off cliff-ghasts, Lee is caught in the disturbance created by **Lord Asriel's bridge.** He is honoured to share his thoughts at the Witch-Council at **Lake Enara** where he takes it upon himself to 'postpone his retirement' to help Lyra by searching for the explorer **Stanislaus Grumman** whom he believes knows something of an object that could protect its holder [SK, 2]. Thereafter, his search takes him to **Nova Zembla** and then to the **Imperial Muscovite** Observatory where he is attacked by a **Skraeling** representative of the **Magisterium.** Lee kills the Skraeling, but killing does not come easy to him: Lee had had to kill three times before that time, and can remember the horror of a man pulled apart from his **dæmon** as his balloon rose [SK, 6, 10]. Eventually, he reaches the Yenesei Pakhtar tribe only to discover that he had been called there all along by Stanislaus who possesses Scoresby's mother's ring, a ring he hasn't seen in 40 years [SK, 10]. Lee transports Grumman to Asriel's world, pursued relentlessly by the forces of the Church. At **Alamo Gulch,** Scoresby bravely fights a regiment of **Swiss Guards,** buying Stanislaus enough time to escape. He is mortally wounded and dies soon after [SK, 14]. Later, Iorek pays Lee the honour of eating his flesh as bear tradition dictates [AS, 3].

It is a sad end. Lee said that he wanted to end his days in comfort. After every job he used to send some gold back to the Wells Fargo Bank, with the hope that one day he would have enough savings to buy a little farm, a few head of cattle, some horses. He pictured himself at rest, just the evening wind over the sage, a cigar and a bottle of bourbon. At that time, he planned to book passage on a steamer to Port Galverston and never to leave the ground again [NL, 18].

But this was not the end. Lyra meets Lee again in the **land of the dead**, where he and Stanislaus, better known as John Parry, lead an army of **ghosts** against the **Spectres**. Their effort helps Lyra and Will reunite with their dæmons and escape to safety. His task over, Lee Scoresby allows his consciousness to dissipate, travelling upwards to join his beloved dæmon, a shabby, thin but tough-looking hare called Hester [AS, 26, 31]. He never married [SK, 10].

Philip Pullman's main influence may well be Han Solo from the *Star Wars* films. Like Han, Lee is a practical rogue, who demands a great deal of money for the use of his ship and has no time for revolutions or hokey religions. His former partnership with Iorek is perhaps reminiscent of Han's relationship with Chewbacca the Wookiee.

SEAL-HUNTER – An old seal-hunter, temporarily resident at the **Samirsky Hotel** in **Nova Zembla**, who was present at the initiation of **Stanislaus Grumman** into the tribe of the **Yenesei Pakhtar Tartars**. He believes that Stanislaus has got caught up in the Skraeling wars over towards **Beringland** and that he's been shot outright [SK, 6].

SERGI – **Ruta Skadi**'s bluethroat **dæmon** [SK, 6].

SHUTER – An elderly porter at **Jordan College**. **Lord Asriel** neatly blames Shuter for spilling the **Tokay** that the **Master of Jordan College** poisons. Shuter tries, unsuccessfully, to keep **Lyra** in the College on the night of the **Gobblers'** visit to **Oxford** [NL, 1, 3]. After she returns to Oxford, Shuter gives Lyra a key to climb on to the roof of the College from the Lodge Tower [LO].

SIMON – A boy at **Bolvangar** who puts the word around that the **Gobblers** kill children while **Mrs Coulter** watches [NL, 14].

SKADI, RUTA – A 'beautiful, proud and pitiless' Queen of the Latvian **witches** [SK, 2]. Ruta is as beautiful as **Mrs Coulter**; vivid and passionate with large black eyes and an extra air of the mysterious and uncanny. She and **Lord Asriel** had been lovers. Her curly hair is ringed with the teeth of snow tigers that she had had to kill to punish the **Tartars** who worship them (the Tartars had then tried to worship the Witch-Queen but she scorned them). In the aftermath of the creation of Asriel's **bridge**, Ruta argues forcefully that the witch clans should join together. She and **Serafina Pekkala**'s clan fly into the world of **Cittàgazze** where Skadi joins a flight of **angels** and makes her way to the **Adamant Tower**. There she learns from Asriel the wickedness of the **Magisterium**. She returns to inform Serafina of her discoveries before returning to her own world to consult with **Ieva Kasku**, **Reina Miti** and the other Witch-Queens. Skadi succeeds in rallying some of the witch clans against the **Authority** and flies, with Reina Miti's clan, against the **Clouded Mountain**. She is 416 years old. She has a bluethroat **dæmon** called Sergi [SK, 6].

SKRAELINGS – A race of people in the north, not dissimilar from the **Tartars**. The Skraelings had been separating human and **dæmon** by hand for centuries [NL, 16]. At the time of **Stanislaus Grumman**'s disappearance, the Skraelings had been involved in wars over by **Beringland** [SK, 6]. The representative of the **Magisterium** at the **Imperial Muscovite Academy**'s observatory near **Nova Zembla** is a Skraeling with a snowy owl dæmon [SK, 6].

The term Skraeling was used by Vikings in the tenth century to describe indigenous peoples they found on their forays into North America. Scholars now believe that the Skraelings they referred to were most likely members of the Micmac or Beothuk tribes of Indians in what is today Newfoundland in north-east America. Interestingly, the Beothuk people were famed for covering their bodies in a red ochre paint, giving rise to the term 'redskins'. If the Beothuk are the Skraelings, then they were significantly more expansionist in **Lyra**'s world than our own, since Beringland, where they fought, was most likely Alaska – the other side of the North American continent.

SPECTRES – aka Spectres of indifference [SK, 6]. Spectral forms that feast on the souls of adults, but not children, enveloping them in 'a transparent shimmer' [SK, 6]. Each time the **subtle knife** cuts a window, a Spectre is created: 'it's like a little bit of the **abyss** that floats out and enters the world' [AS, 37]. The **Philosophers' Guild** of the **Torre degli Angeli** in **Cittàgazze**, who created the knife to cut the smallest bonds between particles, are unaware of this hidden consequence of using the knife. In cutting windows intensively and carelessly, they unwittingly unleash the Spectres into their own and other worlds, destroying their livelihoods and reducing their city to decay [SK, 9]. The people of Cittàgazze resort to stealing from other worlds, and preserving adults at all costs, in order to survive [SK, 6]. Only the Philosophers' Guild know for sure their error and even they do not understand the reasons. Some of the inhabitants of Cittàgazze believe that the Spectres came from the stars [SK, 7].

But what sustains the Spectres? In the books, Spectres are compared to vampires, undead creatures who feed on the blood of the living. **Serafina Pekkala** heard the legend of the '**vampyre**' from travellers in her own world and sees a similarity in the Spectres' malice and feasting on souls [SK, 6]. **Major John Parry** makes the connection but observes that, where the vampire feasts on blood, the Spectres' food is attention, 'a conscious and informed interest in the world'. The immaturity of children did not sustain them and so they were protected: with their parents gone, many lived in Cittàgazze as 'Spectre-orphans' [SK, 14]. Spectres grew and fed on **Dust** [AS, 37].

Nevertheless, some adults are immune to their powers. **Mrs Coulter** evidently commands the Spectres by promising to lead them to more souls [SK, 11]. The **angels** tell **Mary Malone** that she will not be touched by the Spectres [SK, 12]. **Father Gomez** believes that he is able to traverse Cittàgazze as the Spectres sense his 'sacred task to perform' [AS, 10]. The **bearer** of the knife is also protected, hence the interest of the adolescent **Tullio** in the knife [SK, 8]. Towards the end of *The Amber Spyglass*, **Will** and **Lyra** begin to see the Spectres faintly. Will is able to kill one by plunging the knife into it [AS, 29, 31].

Interestingly, Will at one point believes that the Spectres may be from his world, reasoning that his mother's paranoia and compulsive actions are in some part based on seeing, and attempting to distract herself from, the Spectres [SK, 11, 13].

SPIRITS – *See* **Ghosts.**

SPY-FLY – A flying clockwork beetle sent by **Mrs Coulter** to find **Lyra**. They are about the length of Lyra's thumb, with a green body, six legs and powerful wings. According to **Farder Coram**, although the spy-fly is mechanical, there is 'a bad spirit with a spell through its heart' pinned to the spring. The spy-fly never stops while the spirit is within it and the spirit kills instantly if it is ever released. Coram last saw a spy-fly in Morocco. He sealed it in a smokeleaf tin, intending to drop it into a fire-mine [NL, 13].

Pullman's spy-fly may be based on the actual creation of **Dr Dee**, a sixteenth-century alchemist referred to in *The Northern Lights*.

STARMINSTER, ADÈLE – A journalist who attends **Mrs Coulter**'s cocktail party in London without permission. Mrs Coulter ejects her and threatens to see that she never works in journalism again. Adèle has a butterfly **dæmon** [NL, 5].

STEFANSKI, ADAM – Head of one of the six **gyptian** families that include the **Costas**. Stefanski raised gold and 23 men for the expedition to **Bolvangar**. He is put in charge of arms and munitions and commands the fighting [NL, 8].

STEWARD – *See* **Cawson.**

STURLUSSON, RAGNAR – The new name for the character **Iofur** in *The Golden Compass* movie.

STURROCK, CARDINAL – A senior member of the **Church** who questions **Mrs Coulter** about **Lyra**. A witch reveals the prophecy about Lyra to him under torture. **Serafina Pekkala** kills Sturrock in her escape from Mrs Coulter's launch. He has a macaw **dæmon** [SK, 2].

SYSSELMAN – The term used for the governor at **Trollesund**. He refuses to help **John Faa** and **Farder Coram** retrieve **Iorek Byrnison**'s armour [NL, 11].

T

TARTARS – Feared people of the north and renowned fighters. The region of **Ob** near **Nova Zembla** is home to the Tartars [SK, 6]. The regiment of 60 **Sibirsk** Tartars that guard **Bolvangar** is the fiercest that **John Faa** has ever seen. Armoured in padded mail, with only snow-slits in their helmets allowing them to see, and predatory wolf **dæmons** with piercing yellow eyes they are a terrifying sight [NL, 17]. In the years prior to **Lyra**'s adventure, the Tartars had been seeking to expand their territories, and were keen to move north for coal-spirit and fire-mines. At the time of Lyra's visit to the **Witch-Consul** at **Trollesund**, the Tartars appeared to be ready to attack the gold-rich area of **Kamchatka**. In fact, it was too far away from their position and would stretch them too far [NL, 10]. Their reputation was fearsome: some of the **gyptian** people believed that the **Gobblers** had been buying off the Tartars by giving them children, which they then baked and ate [NL, 6].

But the Tartars are also a spiritual people. At least one tribe worshipped snow tigers, which **Ruta Skadi** kills as punishment [SK, 2]. The Tartars are famous for trepanning – boring holes in the skull – although the meaning of the act is often misunderstood. According to **Lee Scoresby**, the Tartars have been doing this for thousands of years as a great privilege, not a punishment: the Tartars believe that trepanning allowed people to hear the gods [NL, 13]. One of the children at

Bolvangar hears that the Tartars believe the holes allow **Dust** to enter [NL, 14]. **Major John Parry** is initiated into the skull-cult by the Tartars of the **Yenesei Pakhtar** tribe and becomes their shaman.

Tartar, also spelled Tatar, is a name given to a number of Turkic-speaking peoples that live in west-central Russia along the course of the Volga River and east into the Ural Mountains. The Tartars also settled in Kazakhstan and in western Siberia. The most famous Tartar was Ghengis Khan.

TAYMYR – The tern **dæmon** of a **witch** who is captured by **Mrs Coulter**. His witch's clan had allied with the 'child-cutters' until they realised the true nature of the experiments at **Bolvangar**. Taymyr's witch is tortured by Mrs Coulter. The witch is released from her torment by **Serafina Pekkala** who kills her with an arrow [SK, 2]. The Taymyr peninsula is on the north coast of Siberia, near the **Yenesei** river.

THOROLD – **Lord Asriel**'s manservant, who has a pinscher **dæmon** called **Anfang**. He serves Lord Asriel at **Svalbard** but does not join his master in the new world. Instead, Thorold stays to guard the house at Svalbard until told otherwise, or until he dies. He is known to **Dr Martin Lanselius**, the **Witch-Consul** at **Trollesund** [NL, 21; SK, 2]. In the books he serves Lord Asriel for 40 years but only 20 years in the radio series.

TIALYS, CHEVALIER – A proud and haughty **Gallivespian** spy. He is ordered to spy on the **Consistorial Court of Discipline** by **Lord Roke** [AS, 5]. Tialys keeps in contact with Lord Roke daily by means of the **lodestone resonator**. Tialys and his companion the **Lady Salmakia** are reluctantly persuaded by **Will** and **Lyra** to accompany them on their journey to the **land of the dead**. They help the two children until their deaths at the **Battle on the Plain**. Reflecting on Tialys' fearsome character, Lyra believes that his **dæmon** would be a tigress [AS, 14].

TIM – The first boy **Dr Mary Malone** loved. He gave her marzipan at a party when she was twelve. It was this, and the story of Mary's decision to leave the **Church**, that inspired **Lyra** [AS, 33].

TRELAWNAY, PROFESSOR P. – The Palmerian Professor at **Jordan College**. He was supposedly present in **Svalbard** when **Iofur Raknison** considered establishing a University. **Jotham Santelia** claimed that Trelawnay was responsible for having him thrown into prison by the bear-king. While Jotham's words should be taken with care, Trelawnay certainly knew of Iofur's intention to establish a university [NL, 2, 19]. Trelawnay is the author of 'Fraud: an Exposure of a Scientific Imposture' and a member of the **Royal Arctic Institute** [LO].

TUALAPI – Gigantic birds and enemies of the **Mulefa**. They have necks like swans, beaks as long as a forearm, powerful legs and wings twice as tall as a man. The Tualapi travel on the water by holding their wings upright, fore and aft, as sails. They are vicious scavengers that raid Mulefa settlements and take the precious **seed-pods** [AS, 10]. **Father Gomez** exercises dominion over them by terrifying them with his rifle.

TULLIO – The elder brother of **Angelica** and **Paolo** in **Cittàgazze** [SK, 3]. Tullio breaks into the **Torre degli Angeli** to steal the **subtle knife** from its **bearer, Giacomo Paradisi**, for protection from the **Spectres**. When **Will** fights Tullio and retrieves the knife, the boy flees from the tower and is killed by the Spectres [SK, 8]. Angelica vows to have Will and **Lyra** killed in retaliation and gladly gives **Father Gomez** information on their whereabouts [AS, 10].

U

UMAQ – **Tartar** – A guide who takes **Lee Scoresby** to the **Imperial Muscovite Academy**'s astronomical observatory near

Nova Zembla. Umaq states that the break between the **worlds** caused by the creation of **Lord Asriel**'s **bridge** has happened before, many thousands of generations ago. The **spirits** that moved between the worlds sealed it up after a while but the barrier between worlds remained thin behind the Northern Lights. Umaq believes that the barrier will be sealed again after 'big trouble, big war. Spirit war' [SK, 6]. He has an arctic fox-**dæmon**.

V

VAMPYRE – **Serafina Pekkala** hears from travellers in her own world the legend of the 'vampyre' and sees in them a similarity with the **Spectres** [SK, 6]. **Lee Scoresby** has also heard of them in tales [SK, 14].

VERHOEVEN, JACK – A **gyptian** who is shot and his boat sunk by the authorities in search of **Lyra** [NL, 9].

VRIES, DIRK – A **gyptian** present at the second Roping [NL, 8].

W

WALTERS, INSPECTOR – A police inspector who claims to be from Special Branch. He and **Sergeant Clifford** question **Dr Mary Malone** about **Will** [SK, 7, 12]. He probably works for **Sir Charles Latrom**.

WATCHERS – *See* **Angels**.

WILL – Will Parry. The son of **Elaine** and **John Parry**, aka **Dr Stanislaus Grumman**. Will is one of the principal characters of the *His Dark Materials* trilogy. When he is introduced in *The Subtle Knife*, Will is twelve years old [SK, 1]. When he is one year old, his father goes missing while on the **Nuniatak dig** to the Arctic. In fact, John Parry is investigating, and succeeds in finding, a **window** to another world. John is not alone in his interest in the window: evidently the British secret service is interested in the '**anomaly**' and the Soviets send a spy to search for the window. John Parry disappears from Will's life in the summer of 1985.

Will and his mother, Elaine, live in Winchester, in a Close on a modern estate. He may have gone to a school called Saint Peter's in Hampshire [SK, 4]. When Will is seven, he realises that his mother is not well. She has moments of great fear and anxiety, paranoia that she disguises as games to play with her son. Over the next months, Will realises that his mother's fears are in her head and that he has to look after her. She has occasional moments of lucidity but these do not seem to be the norm. He becomes adept at blending in, fearful that making himself obvious would prompt the authorities to take his mother away and leave him with strangers. They have no family, only themselves and a tabby called **Moxie** [SK, 1].

In fact, Elaine's paranoia is not entirely in her head. Will overhears men questioning his mother about his father, enquiring whether he has contact with foreign embassies. They are evidently interested in John Parry's investigations. Will suspects they are seeking a green leather wallet containing John's final letters to Elaine, which Elaine occasionally reads and weeps over. Will becomes convinced that his father is alive and in trouble somewhere. Will takes matters into his own hands and places Elaine in the care of his former piano teacher, **Mrs Cooper**, while he tries to find out more about his father's whereabouts. Shortly after, on the outskirts of **Oxford**, he discovers a 'window' in the air and enters another world.

Will's story deliberately parallels that of **Lyra**. Both have a mysterious explorer for a father-figure, one that they have never really known. Lyra and Will both glamorise **Lord Asriel** and John Parry in their dreams. Will too is the subject of prophecy. His mother tells him that one day, he too will follow in his father's footsteps [SK, 1]. John Parry too discovered the destiny of the **bearer** and seeks him out to instruct him [SK, 15]. Even the **witches** sense in Will greatness: **Ruta Skadi** sees in Will's eyes the same kind as Lord Asriel, but **Serafina Pekkala** doesn't dare to look [SK, 13].

Although younger than Lyra, circumstances forced Will to mature earlier. From the moment he meets Lyra in **Cittàgazze**, Will is the confident and capable one, determined and resolute, while Lyra is quick to anger and acts on instinct. Together, they are formidable and yet both are vulnerable. Will tells **Pantailamon** that Lyra, a girl he has known barely days, is the best friend he has ever had [SK, 13]. The news secretly delights Lyra who is growing closer to Will all the time.

Will's name is a reference to the notion of free will; a running theme in the books. Will insists throughout that he, and other characters, have a choice, although he is aware of the duty of the knife and the destiny of the **bearer**. Once he has cut the window out of the world of the dead, Will pointedly tells his father that he has completed his duty and will now choose what he does: 'And I will choose, because now I'm free' [AS, 31].

WINDSUCKERS – Creatures of the north that float in the air and sap ones strength on contact. **Lyra** is told their story by the **gyptians** [NL, 6]. In the radio dramatisation of *Northern Lights* it is implied that the windsuckers are **spectres**.

WITCHES – Magical inhabitants of the north-lands [NL, 4]. Witches are known to the men and woman of the north but lived apart from them in the hostile tundra. Witches maintain contact with the 'Northlanders' through **Dr Martin Lanselius**, the **Witch-Consul** at **Trollesund**. The **gyptians** seek the aid (or at least the neutrality) of witches when setting out to retrieve the children from **Bolvangar**. **Serafina Pekkala**'s clan in particular comes to the aid of the gyptians and **Lyra** and thereafter supports Lyra, **Will** and their companions in the battle against the **Authority**.

Most of the people of Lyra's world are wary of witches, largely because of a lack of knowledge about them. **Father Semyon Borisovitch** describes them as 'daughters of evil, determined to seduce and kill' [AS, 8]. Yet, **Farder Coram** more wisely observes that all sorts of things play on the lives of witches that are unknown or invisible to others [NL, 13]. They are certainly far different from most of the people of Lyra's world. For a start, witches look different: piercing green eyes and slender forms wrapped in robes made from strips of black silk. Witches are possessed of great old age: the oldest witch-mother is nearly one thousand years old [NL, 18], while **Juta Kamainen** is young by witch standards at just over one hundred years old [SK, 2]. Their society is uniquely female: while men can serve witches, like the Witch-Consul at Trollesund, or can be taken as lovers or husbands, there are no male witches. As Serafina explains, 'men pass in front of our eyes like butterflies, creatures of a brief season . . . They die so soon that our hearts are continually racked with pain' [NL, 18]. It is believed to be wise not to refuse a witch's love, as **John Parry** finds to his cost [SK, 6, 15].

Witch society is also different. Witches belong to clans, probably based around family and location: Serafina succeeds her mother as Clan-Queen of the **Lapland** witches of **Lake Enara**. Other Witch-Queens include **Ieva Kasku**, **Reina Miti** and **Ruta Skadi** who were Clan-Queens of the Latvian witches [SK, 2, 13]. The stage play gives the names of some other witches: Pipistreelee, Caitlin, Grimhild and Grendella. Their society is democratic, but only to a point: all witches can speak at the witch council but men are not allowed to speak and only the Queen can make decisions [SK, 2]. It is only in exceptional circumstances that **Lee Scoresby** is allowed to speak at a witch council [SK, 2]. Witches own nothing and have no means of exchange other than mutual aid. As a result, cost is not a factor in deciding to go to war, only reason. Pride is not a concern either: 'Nor do we have any notion of honour, as bears do . . .' explained Serafina. 'How could you insult a witch? What would it matter if you did?' [NL, 18].

Yet the community of witches is just as divided as the world of man. There exists a complex web of alliances and enmities of witch clans pitted against witch clans. Some witches, for example, are engaged in a war between 'various other forces, some in the spirit world', in which possession of **Lord Asriel**'s

bridge would be an advantage. Serafina's clan is not yet part of an alliance but is under pressure to declare for one side or another [NL, 11]. Equally, some witches support and work for the Authority, despite the fact that witches worship gods other than the Authority [SK, 2]: Serafina is surprised to learn that some witches continue to work for the **Oblation Board** even after learning the nature of the experiments at Bolvangar. One witch is even in the service of the President of the **Consistorial Court of Discipline** [AS, 25]. Apart from **Yambe-Akka**, the goddess of death [NL, 18], the nature of the gods that the witches worship is unclear: when **Joachim Lorenz** asks Serafina if she 'treats with the devil', she gives a neatly inconclusive answer [SK, 6]. They certainly commit animal sacrifice [SK, 13].

Witches are also possessed of magical abilities. Most obviously, witches are able to fly by using any branch of **cloud pine** [NL, 10, 15]. 'To fly is to be perfectly ourselves,' observes Serafina [NL, 18]. They can perform a kind of mental-magic where they become 'unnoticed' [SK, 2]. Witches also have a range of healing spells: Serafina sends Farder spells and herbs to heal his poisoned wound [NL, 18] and they try, albeit unsuccessfully, to stop the bleeding when Will's fingers are severed [SK, 11]. Serafina gives Lee a little red flower from a chain of flowers around her neck so that he can call for her in time of need [SK, 2]. Witches also seem capable of appearing in other people's dreams, as Serafina appeared in **Dr Mary Malone**'s dream [AS, 36].

Witches also have a different perception of the world around them. They possess a kind of sight that others have not got: witches sense an air of hatred and fear around Bolvangar that is shared by animals [NL, 11]. It implies that they can experience using different senses: they can feel the light of the stars or the 'silky feeling' of the moonlight, or hear the music of the Northern Lights [NL, 13]. Witches are even able to see people's **dæmons** in Will's world: Serafina finds it strange to think that Mary cannot see them as she can [AS, 36]. Seeing them requires the same use of **negative capability** as the **alethiometer, the Cave** and the **subtle knife**. Yet, despite this, they cannot see **Dust** without the aid of the **amber spyglass** [AS, 36].

One of their most disconcerting abilities is that of separating themselves from their dæmons for great distances. Farder says that witches can send their dæmons far abroad or down below the ocean. He believes that the great red bird he shoots when saving Serafina is probably a witch's dæmon [NL, 10]. Learning to do this is a rite of passage for all witches. Serafina explains how a girl must leave behind her dæmon and cross a desolate wasteland in the north-lands, 'where a great catastrophe happened in the childhood of the world, and where nothing has lived since'. After, the child realises that she and her dæmon are whole; she is accepted as a witch. Will and Lyra unwittingly do something of the same when passing through the **land of the dead,** making them as witches but for the ability to fly [AS, 36].

The witches also have the power of prophecy, although it is not clear whether this is an ability that they themselves possess. Martin reveals that the prophecy about Lyra has been passed on to the witches by the 'immortal whispers' of those who pass between worlds, that is **angels** [NL, 10]. Serafina explains that 'there are powers who speak to us, and there are powers above them; and there are secrets even from the most high' [NL, 18]. Serafina explains to Scoresby that witches cannot read the darkness [NL, 18]. It seems that witches communicate with angels where the veil between **worlds** is thin. They are certainly aware of other worlds, noting that 'millions of other universes exist, unaware of one another' [NL, 11].

The reference to a place of desolation may also have its origins in history. In the seventeenth century and before, it was believed by some that the entrance to Hell lay somewhere in northern Europe, particularly the Finnmark, a county in the north of Norway. Because of this purported connection to Satan, the Finnmark was believed to be a place where witches thrived and the indigenous people, the Sami, were labelled sorcerers. The Sami, sometimes called the Lapps, also believed in a goddess of the underworld called Yambe-Akka. **Milton** mentions witches in Finland in Book II of *Paradise Lost.*

WREN – A plump butler at **Jordan College** who has a long-standing rivalry with the **Steward**. **Lyra** once saw him steal some leaf from the smoking mill [NL, 1]. According to the radio series, his red setter **dæmon** is called Fidolia.

X

XAPHANIA – The female leader of the angelic forces and one of **Lord Asriel's high commanders**. Xaphania is tall, naked and winged, with a curious old–young face [AS, 16, 36] and an austere but compassionate expression [AS, 37]. The shimmering light that suffuses her body indicates her high rank among the **angels** [AS, 16]. It may have been Xaphania who appeared to **Dr Mary Malone** in a dream and told her to expect **Will** and **Lyra** and take care of them [AS, 32].

In fact, Xaphania is probably the oldest and most significant angel featured in *His Dark Materials*, save for the **Authority** Himself. According to **Balthamos**, it was Xaphania who first unmasked the Authority's lie [AS, 2] and by implication led the rebellion that resulted in her exile. Seeking 'vengeance', the rebel angels intervened in human evolution, engineering the first **Fall** [SK, 12]. Xaphania tells Will and Lyra that the rebel angels tried to open minds, while the Authority and the **Church** sought to keep them closed. 'All the history of human life [has] been a struggle between wisdom and stupidity', she explains [AS, 36]. For Xaphania, the Authority's great tyranny was in seeking to keep man in ignorance and fear, dutifully earning a place in Heaven after death rather than working to create Heaven on earth during their lives.

It would therefore follow that Xaphania is the Satan of Christian theology. Indeed, her statement that she has been 'wandering between many worlds' since the rebellion against the Authority mirrors Satan's comment to God that he has been 'roaming through the earth and going back and forth in it' since his banishment [AS, 16; Job 1:7]. However, according to Collin de Plancy's *Dictionnaire Infernal* (1818), 'Xaphan' was one of the second order of fallen angels who joined Satan.

So who is she? Leaving Christian theology aside for one moment, the gnostic tradition provides an interesting slant. The gnostics believed in a goddess of wisdom called Sophia who, through the serpent, brought knowledge to humankind. This was enough to enrage the false God who had created the physical world who proceeded to cast Adam and Eve out of the Garden of Eden. In another gnostic tradition, Sophia breathes knowledge into humankind, giving consciousness to add to their physical bodies and their souls – self-consciousness to add to body and **dæmon**. The name Sophia, which is Greek for 'wisdom', is derived from the Hebrew *SephanyAh* – remarkably close to Xaphania in *His Dark Materials*. *See* the **Fall** for more information.

Y

YAKOVLEV – A hunter who lives in the frozen north. Five years before **Lyra's** adventure, he had been to the northern end of the Urals where he laid a trap of which **Dr Stanislaus Grumman** fell foul. Yakovlev was regarded as a fool by **Sam Cansino** [SK, 6].

YAMBE-AKKA – The goddess of the dead who comes to a **witch** at the end of their life. According to **Serafina Pekkala**, 'she comes to you smiling and kindly and you know it is time to die' [NL, 18]. This description is similar to that of the **Deaths** that **Will** and **Lyra** encounter in the suburbs of the **land of the dead** [AS, 18, 19]. The witch, who is captured by **Mrs Coulter** after the creation of **Lord Asriel's** **bridge**, cries to Yambe-Akka for release, which is granted when Serafina kills her with an arrow [SK, 2].

According to the indigenous Lapp people of northern Scandinavia, Yambe-Akka, sometimes known as Jabme-akko, is the goddess of the underworld. Her name means 'the old woman of the dead'. The Lapp underworld is a mirror of the land of the living.

YENESEI PAKHTARS – The tribe of **Tartars** who **Major John Parry** befriends. He is later initiated into the skull-cult and becomes their shaman. The Yenesei Pakhtars are located at the foot of the **Semyonov** range, near a fork of the **Yenesei River** and a river that comes down from the hills. A large rock marks the landing stage [SK, 6].

Z

ZOHARIEL – The **dæmon** of **Francis Lyall**, a former **Master of Jordan College** [NL, 3].

ZOMBI – **Lord Asriel** states that the Africans have a way of making a slave called a *zombi* that has no will of its own. **Lyra** sees in his words the description of a person without a **dæmon**. **Dr Martin Lanselius** says that an entire regiment of warriors has been severed and are now fearless *zombi*. The authorities are hiding a regiment of *zombi* in **Trollesund** [SK, 2].

2. THE WORLDS

This chapter contains A–Z entries on all the places, organisa-
tions, objects and worlds that appear in Pullman's *His Dark
Materials* novels – from the Abyss to Zeppelins. Here you can
explore the fascinating differences between our world and the
worlds of *His Dark Materials*.

A

ABYSS, THE – Oblivion. The abyss was 'created' when the
Consistorial Court of Discipline detonated their **quantum
entanglement bomb** intending to kill **Lyra**. The explosion
opened a vast bottomless pit and sent fissures throughout the
worlds through which **Dust** was pulled at an increasingly faster
rate. **Will** notes that the edge of the abyss is the same as the
edge of a **window** [AS, 26] through which Dust also escapes.
In fact, the abyss is a vast nothingness that exists outside the
worlds. When **Metatron**, **Asriel** and **Mrs Coulter** fall into the
abyss they are doomed for eternity as their physical bodies will
die but their spirits continue to fall [AS, 26, 31]. It is the duty
of the angels, in the wake of the second **Fall** of Man, to close
all the windows, Asriel's **bridge** and the abyss to prevent Dust

from escaping the universe [AS, 37]. The abyss can be seen as the void that existed before creation, when Dust became conscious of itself.

ADAMANT TOWER – **Lord Asriel**'s chambers in his **basalt fortress**. The Adamant Tower is situated on the highest rampart of the fortress, with windows allowing views north, south, east and west [AS, 5]. It is here that Asriel consults with his **high commanders** and holds **Mrs Coulter** prisoner.

AËRODOCK – A **zeppelin** station where **Lord Asriel** lands for his visit to **Jordan College** [NL, 1].

AESAHÆTTR – *See* **Subtle knife**. The word is pronounced as-hat-ter in the audiobook, ess-het-air in the radio version.

ALAMO GULCH – The site of **Lee Scoresby**'s last stand. It is here that he ably fights off a party of Swiss Guards, giving **Major John Parry** enough time to escape, at the cost of his own life [SK, 14].

ALCHEMY – An obsolete form of science focused on turning base metals into gold. According to **Miss Greenwood**, alchemists discovered many things about acids but their world view fell apart and chemistry provided a more stable conceptual framework. In Lyra's day, alchemists are mocked and there hasn't been any serious alchemists for 250 years, although **Sebastian Makepeace** claims to be one ['Lyra and the Birds'].

ALETHIOMETER – aka '**golden compass**', '**symbol reader**', '**truth measure**'. A device that can be used to read the truth of the past, present or even the future, although it does not forecast in the true sense [AS, 6]. The name comes from the Greek 'alethia' (αληθεια), meaning 'truth' and 'meter' meaning 'measure'. It is pronounced ah-leeth-ee-om-eater. At the start of the first book, **Lyra** is given the alethiometer by the **Master of Jordan College**. Some years before, the device had been donated to the College by **Lord Asriel** [NL, 4]. Lyra uses the device many times to avoid and escape trouble over the course of her adventures, and her mastery of the alethiometer is an early sign that she has an important role to play.

Lyra's alethiometer is made of brass (not gold as one might think from the US title, *The Golden Compass*, or as stated in the Radio 4 dramatisations) and crystal, with a face that looks like it is made of ivory. Although it is very important to the story, its exact size is never specified – we are told it is 'like a large watch or small clock' and that it is 'a thick disc of brass and crystal' [NL, 4]. On the covers of some of the foreign editions it's as small as a pocket watch, on others (and in the stage play) it looks to be about the size of a side plate. Sometimes it is depicted with a cover, like some pocket watches or compasses have, but this doesn't seem to be the case, as Lyra keeps hers in a velvet cloth, and can see its face as soon as it's unwrapped [NL, 4]. Lyra wears it in a pouch around her waist, but it can also fit into a coat pocket. Lyra is surprised how heavy it is. Some foreign editions of the book make the mistake of showing a normal compass, not an alethiometer, on their covers. In the movie, the alethiometer is a little larger than the palm of Lyra's hand and has a flip-open cover.

The alternative name for the device, the 'symbol reader', is a telling description of how it works. There are 36 delicately painted pictures where the numbers would appear on a clock face. In the books, we are told about 25 of these pictures: anchor, hourglass surmounted by a skull, bull, beehive, angel, helmet, dolphin, globe, lute, compasses, candle, thunderbolt, horse [NL, 4]; serpent, crucible [NL, 9]; camel, cornucopia, ant [NL, 10]; infant, elephant, chameleon [NL, 9]; griffin [NL, 12]; alpha and omega [SK, 4]; puppet, loaf of bread [AS, 2]. When Lyra uses **the Cave** she sees an additional two symbols – garden and moon – which are presumably also on the alethiometer's face [SK, 4]. The alethiometer as featured on the cover of *Northern Lights* also includes: the sun, Madonna, apple, bird, sword, crocodile, tree, owl and wild man. Each picture could mean a whole series of things: **Farder Coram** explains how the Anchor's first meaning is hope, but it also means steadfastness, snag or prevention and the sea; Coram believes each symbol had 'ten, twelve, maybe a never-ending series of meanings' [NL, 7]. Coram notes that the meanings are sometimes hidden in the pictures, if one looks closely [NL, 9]. Lyra says that there are 'thousands' of meanings [AS, 38].

The face resembles a watch with four hands: three small ones that can be turned to specific points by dials on the side, and a larger fourth hand. Left alone, the fourth hand, duller and more slender than the others, twitches and never quite settles [NL, 5]. Once the owner has adjusted the smaller hands to point at three of these, they ask a question, keeping in mind the meanings of the symbols they have selected. The fourth hand moves around to point at a fourth symbol or sequence of symbols. The reader could not press or fret, but just watch the hand move [NL, 7]. Lyra came to realise that a certain state of mind was required to read the alethiometer – the same state of mind that was required to use the Cave, for **Will** to use the **subtle knife** and for **Dr Mary Malone** to see her own **dæmon**. The poet Keats called it **negative capability** [SK, 4].

But the alethiometer is far from a passive device, capable only of prompted responses. Lyra quickly suspects that a spirit was moving the hand and that 'it knew things like an intelligent being' [NL, 9]. She equates the experience to talking to someone [NL, 9] and at one point even feels rebuked by the alethiometer for asking it the same question twice [NL, 20]. Increasingly, she came to attribute to it moods and she sensed when it had more to say. It would even give her instruction: 'Do not lie to the scholar,' she is told firmly [SK, 4]. In fact, the device is guided by **Dust** – the same mysterious **Shadow Particles** or **angels** with whom Mary is able to communicate using the Cave [NL, 11]. If angels are providing the answers, it is not a talent known to all angels: **Balthamos** does not know how the alethiometer works and even suspects that Lyra makes up her readings [AS, 2].

Rather like Tarot cards, the set of symbols must be read; the alethiometer doesn't give a straight answer. Traditionally, this means memorising the meanings of all the symbols beforehand, and referring to the books of reading. Mary Malone uses the **I-Ching** to do much the same thing, and it is not an exact science. However, Lyra has an (apparently) instinctive ability to come up with accurate interpretations of the readings, using the alethiometer 'as naturally as her muscles moved her limbs' [NL, 19]. **Xaphania** explains that Lyra could read it by 'grace'. It is not clear whether this meant that she was granted the ability by angels. Lyra loses this gift at the end of *The Amber Spyglass*, and vows to study the traditional method which will take a lifetime. Xaphania tells her that 'after a lifetime of thought and effort', Lyra's abilities will be better than before because they have come from a process of conscious understanding [AS, 37].

According to the Master of Jordan College, only six alethiometers were ever made [NL, 4]. They were said to originate in the city of Prague in the seventeenth century. The scholar who created it was trying to discover a way of measuring the influences of the planets according to the ideas of astrology. He sought to create a device that would respond to Mars or Venus as a compass responds to magnetic north. Although he failed in his task, the alethiometer appeared to be responding to something. The symbols appear to have been added subsequently but were commonly symbols of the time with readily understood meanings [NL, 10]. By the time of Lyra's adventure, **Mrs Coulter** believed there to be only two or three [NL, 17]. **Fra Pavel**, the alethiometrist of the **Consistorial Court of Discipline**, said that there were only two – all others had been acquired and destroyed by the **Magisterium** [SK, 2]. Farder Coram had seen one used by a wise man in **Uppsala** [NL, 17] and **Dr Lanselius** had seen one once before but noted it was not as fine as Lyra's [NL, 10]. We also learn that there are several copies of books of reading, including copies at the **Abbey of Saint Johann** in **Heidelberg** [NL, 9, 10] and at **Bodley's Library** in **Oxford** [AS, 38]. **Dame Hannah Relf**'s scholarship of the alethiometer was unmatched [AS, 38].

Some of the material in the programme of the stage play written by Philip Pullman offers a more detailed history of the alethiometer. It was created by **Pavel Khunrath**, a scholar working in Prague during the reign of Rudolf II (1552–1612). Khunrath tried to record the influences of planets using a method combining astrology and memory theatre. He discovered an alloy of two rare metals that had the mysterious property of pointing to the truth (the alloy is presumably titanium and magnesium, the same alloy used for the **window**-cutting edge of the subtle knife and the blade of the **silver guillotine**). Khunrath adapted the technique of memory theatre to generate symbols. He had begun work on recording the meanings of each when, in 1612, Rudolf II was succeeded by Frederick, a fanatical opponent of occult philosophy, who had Khunrath burned at the stake. A few of his devices and a copy of his book of readings survived to be taken up by later scholars. It was only after his death that the name 'alethiometer' was adopted.

The programme material states that each symbol has 'potentially infinite' meanings. Each subsidiary meaning is related to the primary meaning, so subsidiary meanings of sun always relate to the principal meaning, day. Alethiometrists sometimes think of meanings as a ladder, with the number of times a symbol is touched indicating the rung of the ladder. Some ranges of meaning have been explored to the depth of a thousand or so but no one has ever reached the end. The programme material also makes it clear that although some meanings appear to coincide with others, for example, the sea appears in both the dolphin and the anchor, each symbol has a different interpretation.

The programme also includes a picture of the alethiometer with an explanation of the most important meanings attributed to each symbol. The picture is a mirror image of that on the cover of *Northern Lights* and so we don't know the order in which they are supposed to appear on the alethiometer's surface. The following table lists the meanings attributed to each symbol in the novels and in the programme of the stage play.

Symbol	Meanings given by Lyra in the novels	Meanings given in the NT programme (Primary meaning, *Subsidiary meanings*)
Alpha and Omega	Language [SK, 4]	Finality; *process, inevitability*
Anchor	Stretched out, tight as anchor rope [NL, 10]; according to Farder Coram it meant (1) hope, (2) steadfastness, (3) snag or prevention, (4) the sea [NL, 7]	Hope; *steadfastness, prevention*
Angel	Messages [SK, 4]	Messenger; *hierarchy, disobedience*
Ant	Activity, purpose and intention [NL, 10]; diligence [SK, 4]	Mechanical work; *diligence, tedium*
Apple	None given	Sin; *knowledge, vanity*
Baby	Difficult [NL, 10]; Lyra [NL, 9]	The future; *malleability, helplessness*
Beehive	Hard work [NL, 9]	Productive work; *sweetness, light*
Bird	Dæmon [NL, 13]	The soul (the dæmon); *spring, marriage*
Camel	Asia, Tartars [NL, 10]	Asia; *summer, perseverance*
Candle	Understanding [SK, 4]	Fire; *faith, learning*
Chameleon	Air [NL, 9]	Air; *greed, patience*
Compass	Careful figuring with numbers [SK, 4]	Measurement; *mathematics, science*
Cornucopia	Gold [NL, 10]	Wealth; *autumn, hospitality*
Crocodile (caiman)	None given	America; *rapacity, enterprise*
Crucible (cauldron)	Knowledge [NL, 9]	Alchemy; *craft, achieved wisdom*

Dolphin	Playful ('one of its deep-down meanings') [NL, 10]	Water; *resurrection, succour*
Elephant	Africa [NL, 9]	Africa; *charity, continence*
Helmet	War [NL, 10]	War; *protection, narrow vision*
Hourglass	Time (primary); death (secondary) [NL, 9]	Time; *death, change*
Madonna	None given	Motherhood; *the feminine, worship*
Owl	None given	Night; *winter, fear*
Serpent	Cunning [NL, 9]	Evil; *guile, natural wisdom*
Sword	None given	Justice; *fortitude, the Church*
Sun	None given	Day; *Authority, truth, kingship, a particular king, rationality and intellect, archery, power of administering punishment from a distance, plague, the creative arts, the laurel, honour, divination, pastoral husbandry, a particular farm, a particular beast, homosexual love, gold*
Thunderbolt	Anger [NL, 9]; electricity [SK, 4]	Inspiration; *fate, chance*
Tree	None given	Firmness; *shelter, fertility*
Wild man	None given	Wild man; *the masculine, lust*

The phrase 'The Golden Compass', the American title of the book, isn't a reference to the alethiometer. It's taken from **John Milton**'s *Paradise Lost*, Book VII, and was the original name for the trilogy: '. . . in his hand / He took the golden compasses, prepared / In God's eternal store, to circumscribe / This universe, and all created things: / One foot he centred, and the other turned / Round through the vast profundity obscure; /

And said, Thus far extend, thus far thy bounds, / This be thy just circumference, O World! / Thus God the Heaven created, thus the Earth, / Matter unformed and void . . .'

ALETHIOMETRIST – A person skilled in the use of an **alethiometer**. In the course of *His Dark Materials* we encounter several alethiometrists: **Fra Pavel Rašek**, **Teukros Basilides**, and of course **Lyra**. **Dame Hannah Relf** is presumably also capable of using the alethiometer.

AMBER SPYGLASS – A telescope of sorts made by **Dr Mary Malone** from the sap-lacquer produced by the **Mulefa** from the **seed-pod** trees. Mary theorises that **Shadow Particles**, when acting like light waves, can be polarised. By creating two polished sheets of translucent 'glass' from the sap-lacquer, coating one with the oil from the Mulefa's seed-pods, and holding them a distance apart, Mary is able to produce a device through which she can see **Shadows**, or **Dust**, as clearly as the Mulefa. With the amber spyglass, Mary is able to witness the rapid loss of Dust into the **abyss**, and its return following the second **Fall** of Man [AS, 17].

ANBARIC POWER – The name for 'electricity' in **Lyra**'s world. The Common Room and the Library at **Jordan College** are lit by anbaric lights [NL, 1]. There is an 'Anbaric Park' on the way to **Yarnton**, near **Oxford** [NL, 2]. London has tramcars powered by overhead anbaric wires [NL, 6]. It is in the capital that **Mrs Coulter** teaches Lyra about the anbaromagnetic charges in atoms [NL, 5]. **Bolvangar** is surrounded by an anbaric fence [NL, 11]. The **Maystadt anbaric scalpel** is used in early **intercision** experiments [NL, 16]. **Lord Asriel**'s **Adamant Tower** has anbaric forges and an anbaric locomotive [AS, 15, 16]. **Saint-Jean-Les-Eaux** is home to a hydro-anbaric generating station to be used for **Dr Cooper**'s bomb [AS, 24].

Although there are many 'anbaric' devices in Lyra's world, energy seems to be created by an array of means. The projecting lantern at Jordan College is powered by oil. Lord

Asriel travels to London after his meeting with the **scholars** by steam-driven locomotive [NL, 2] and the unfortunate children captured by the **Gobblers** are transported to the Arctic in a steam launch. Yet, Lyra's world also uses hydroelectric and nuclear power, which they call atomcraft.

The word 'anbaric' is derived from the Arabic word 'anbar' meaning amber. The ancient Greeks discovered that rubbing amber could create static electricity. It is one of several examples in *His Dark Materials* where the Greek root of a word is used where we would use the Latin, creating an 'otherworldly' equivalent, for example 'chthonic' for underground as in **Chthonic Railway** [NL, 6].

'ANOMALY' – *See* **Windows**.

APOCALYPSE OF SAINT JOHN – Biblical passage, more commonly known as the Book of Revelation, referenced by the Russian priest **Father Semyon Borisovitch**. Semyon believes that the changes to the Siberian landscape, following the creation of **Lord Asriel**'s **bridge**, are the first signs of the coming apocalypse [AS, 8].

ARCHAEOLOGY, INSTITUTE OF – Oxford-based organisation that sponsors the ill-fated scientific expedition to the north of Alaska that hires **Major John Parry** as a guide [SK, 4].

ASTRONOMY – According to **Mrs Coulter**, there are only six planets in the solar system, including Mars, Venus and the Earth, each orbiting the sun [NL, 5, 10]. In the stage play, we learn that the Church has only recently acknowledged that the Earth goes round the Sun, and that the known planets are named after the Greek gods, not the Roman ones. They are Hermes, Aphrodite, Earth, Ares, Zeus and Poseidon (with the peculiar implication that they have discovered Neptune but not Saturn or Uranus). In the books, the planets are named after the Roman gods [NL, 10].

We should perhaps not be surprised that astronomical understanding is not so advanced in **Lyra**'s world as in ours.

The **Church** would doubtless have the same scepticism to early astronomical enquiry that was experienced by Copernicus (1473–1543) and Galileo (1564–1642), both of whom suffered persecution at the hands of organised religion. Copernican thinking was denounced as heresy and Galileo, a supporter of Copernicus, was sentenced to a life of imprisonment under the Inquisition. Indeed, it was only in 1992 that Pope John Paul II lifted the edict of Inquisition against Galileo, some 350 years after his death. Nevertheless, Coulter's comments indicate that the Copernican view – that the planets revolve around the Sun – is held to be true.

ATOMCRAFT – Presumably the process of creating nuclear power in **Lyra**'s world. Some atomcraft-works are built on **Jordan College** land and they pay rent to the college [NL, 3]. Lyra naively believes that children could be taken to the Arctic to work as slaves in Uranium mines for atomcraft [NL, 3]. 'Atomkraft' is German for nuclear power.

AURORA BOREALIS – aka the Aurora, Northern Lights. A breathtaking natural phenomenon occurring at the magnetic North Pole; a curtain of shimmering multi-coloured light. **Lord Asriel** takes a 'photogram' of the Aurora using a new emulsion which reveals a city in the sky, consisting of towers, domes, and buildings suspended in the air [NL, 2]. According to **Kaisa**, the charged particles of the Aurora have the property of 'making the matter of this world thin, so that we can see through it for a brief time.' This has always been known to the **witches** but they seldom speak of it [NL, 11].

The Aurora Borealis – and its southern counterpart, the Aurora Australis – is a naturally occurring phenomenon in our world. Lord Asriel's explanation of the phenomenon as 'storms of charged particles and solar rays' [NL, 2] is largely accurate: the Aurora is the result of the interaction of charged electrons from solar winds and oxygen and nitrogen in the earth's atmosphere at the magnetic pole. The colour of the Aurora depends on which element is struck and at what altitude. The

Aurora was so named by French philosopher and scientist Pierre Gassendi (1592–1655) after the Roman goddess of the dawn.

B

BANBURY ROAD – A location in **Will**'s **Oxford** [SK, 7].

BARNARD–STOKES – Barnard and Stokes are two theologians from **Lyra**'s world who propose the existence of numerous worlds, 'material and sinful', in parallel to their own. 'They are there, close by, but invisible and unreachable' [NL, 2]. The **Cassington scholar** at **Jordan College** believes that there are sound mathematical arguments for their theory. The **Church**, however, denounce it as heresy, seeing the hypothesis as a threat to their own view that only two worlds exist, the earth and the spiritual world of Heaven and Hell. **Lord Asriel**'s photogram of the **Aurora** and the other world behind it, apparently add credence to the theory. Asriel approaches the scholars of Jordan College for funding to test the Barnard–Stokes hypothesis [NL, 2]. In fact, it is Asriel's intention to create a **bridge** to this other world.

BATTLE ON THE PLAIN, THE – The great confrontation between the forces of **Metatron** and **Lord Asriel**. Each side seems to have brought together a wide range of troops drawn from different times and worlds. Metatron's forces include 'flying machines', riflemen, **Centaurs**, troops with flame-throwers, poison-spraying cannons and 'weapons such as none of the watchers had ever seen'. Asriel's forces include 'armed vehicles,' **gyropters**, **intention craft**, **witches** and **Gallivespians** on **dragonflies**. Both sides have humans and **angels**. Metatron's greatest force, the **Spectres**, are held fast by the **ghosts** of the dead, led by **Lee Scoresby** and **John Parry**, until **Lyra** and **Will** can find their **dæmons** and escape [AS, 29]. The outcome of the battle is not seen in the books, but in the stage play both sides have destroyed themselves utterly.

BEARER – The name given to the holder of the **subtle knife**. When **Will** arrives in **Cittàgazze**, the rightful bearer is **Giacomo Paradisi**. The knife indicates time to leave one bearer and settle with another by severing the little finger and the finger next to it on the left hand – the sign of the bearer. It is the old bearer's duty to instruct the new bearer in use of the knife and to relay the rules for its use laid down by the **Philosophers' Guild** [SK, 8].

BELVEDERE – A classical villa and temple situated in parkland in the world of **Cittàgazze**. It is here that **Will** and **Lyra** rest after retrieving the **alethiometer** from **Lord Boreal**, and where **Angelica** and the children of Cittàgazze attack them [SK, 11].

BENIN – A land known to the people of **Cittàgazze** [SK, 6].

BERGAMO – A place in the world of **Cittàgazze** that has **commedia players** [SK, 6].

BERINGLAND – A location in the north to which the **Skraeling** wars extend. An old **seal-hunter** believes **Stanislaus Grumman** was shot and killed here [SK, 6].

Beringland is most likely a reference to the area of the Bering Straits, the narrow passage that separates Alaska and Siberia. Centuries ago this area was called Beringia and provided the first route for the peoples of Asia into North America. The Bering Land National Preserve in Alaska protects the last vestiges of the original land bridge that existed 13,000 years ago.

BERLIN ACADEMY – aka Imperial German Academy. On passing into **Lyra**'s world, **Major John Parry** travels to Berlin under the name of **Stanislaus Grumman**; he presents a thesis and gains membership to the Academy [SK, 10]. It is here that he meets the Director of the **Imperial Muscovite Academy**'s astronomical observatory north of **Nova Zembla** [SK, 6]. The Academy sponsors some of Grumman's expeditions including his last ill-fated journey north of Lapland and on to the ice, over one year before the events of *Northern Lights* [SK, 6]. In one of his last messages to the Academy, Grumman reports 'certain natural phenomenon only seen in the lands of the north', which prompts **Lord Asriel** to investigate further [NL, 2].

BODLEY'S LIBRARY – *See* **Oxford.**

BOLVANGAR – aka the Station, the **Experimental Station.** A research base built by the **General Oblation Board** at which **experimental theologians** study **Dust** in young children. The station, which is a four-day trek north-east of **Trollesund**, is surrounded by a high **anbaric** perimeter fence and is well defended by a company of Northern **Tartars** [NL, 11]. The base may be part of a complex that extends to hostels to the south where, it is believed, children are taken after **intercision** [NL, 15]. The **dæmons** of severed children are kept in cages in a squat, square building kept apart from the low structures that make up the main building [NL, 15]. According to **Kaisa**, the station is surrrounded by an air of hatred and fear that keeps all living creatures away, giving rise to the name Bolvangar, meaning 'the fields of evil' [NL, 11]. After rescuing the children, the **gyptians** completely destroy the station [NL, 17].

BOTANIC GARDENS – Gardens in **Oxford** that are remarkably similar in both **Will** and **Lyra**'s worlds. At the end of the garden is a wooden seat under a low-branched tree where the young lovers promise to sit, once a year at midday on Midsummer's Day, to be together [AS, 38].

BRANTWIJN – A drink taken by the **Master of Jordan College** and the **Librarian** to drown their sorrows after 'difficult episodes' [NL, 2, 3]. Brantwijn is the Middle Dutch name for distilled wine, more commonly named brandy.

BRASIL – A land known to the people of **Cittàgazze** [SK, 6]. There is a **High Brazil** in **Lyra**'s world.

BRIDGE, THE – aka Bridge to the Stars. Vast **window** between **Lyra's** world and the world of **Cittàgazze** created by **Lord Asriel**. It is supposedly Asriel's intention to prove the **Barnard–Stokes** hypothesis but it enables him to begin his war against the **Authority**. Asriel's experiment requires the power from **intercision**, which is provided when **Roger** falls to his death. The resulting explosion blows **Serafina Pekkala** and the **witches** out to sea, which creates the window [SK, 2]. In truth, the bridge has more alarming consequences than cutting a window with the **subtle knife**. The explosion results in profound disturbances in the earth's magnetic field, ultimately leading to climatic changes that force the **armoured bears** to leave **Svalbard**. It also shifts the alignment of the parallel worlds, so that Lyra's **Oxford** and **Will's** Oxford no longer exist side by side. The bridge also means that **Dust** is lost into the **abyss** at an increasing rate. **Xaphania** and the **angels** make it their duty to close all windows, including the bridge to the stars, after the second **Fall** of Man.

BRYTAIN – The name for Britain in **Lyra's** world [NL, 3].

BURGUNDY – A type of wine stored in the cellars of **Jordan College** [NL, 3].

BYANPLATS – The only patch of slightly higher ground in the hundreds of square miles of the **Fens** [NL, 7]. It was here that the Byanroping took place.

C

CABINET COUNCIL, THE – In **Lyra's** world, the Prime Minister's special advisory body that usually meet in the Palace. **Lord Asriel** and the **Master of Jordan College** are both members of the Cabinet Council [NL, 1]. This seems to be distinct from the **Council of State** which advises the King.

CAHUCHUC – The name in **Lyra's** world for rubber. It is used to cover cables [NL, 6]. It is probably from the word 'caoutchouc', meaning an unvulcanised natural rubber, obtained from tropical plants to produce latex.

CANARY – A type of wine stored in the cellars of **Jordan College** [NL, 3]. It is a type of sweet wine similar to Madeira.

CAVE, THE – The name given by **Dr Oliver Payne** to the computer used by himself and **Dr Mary Malone** to measure **Shadows** in the **Dark Matter Research Unit**. The name is an explicit reference to the allegory of the cave contained in Book VII of **Plato**'s *The Republic*, in which Plato records the philosophy of Socrates. In the allegory, Socrates describes a scenario in which a number of prisoners are only able to experience reality by seeing Shadows projected on to the cave wall in front of them. The prisoners believe the Shadows to be reality, played out in front of them. It is only when one prisoner is able to move outside the cave that the reality of the world is truly experienced.

There are three ways in which the allegory has relevance to the events of *His Dark Materials*. Most superficially, the computer allows the scientists to 'see' Shadows. This is the explicit reason given in the book as to why Payne calls the computer The Cave [SK, 4]. However, the allegory can also be understood to be an illustration of the imperfect way in which we perceive the world around us – how we can confuse names for things with the actual things themselves. When Mary finds a way to communicate with Shadows, she discovers that they can also be understood as **angels** [SK, 12]. In fact, **Dust, spirit**, angels, **Shadow Particles** – all are imperfect names for what 'Shadows' actually are. This seems to support the view of Platonic realism that certain universals are conceived in the mind and do not exist in time and space.

More fundamentally, the allegory is a statement on wisdom and ignorance. Socrates says that we all live in a world of ignorance and many of us are comfortable not to know reality. When we start to face reality, it is an uncomfortable process: some people hide, some thrive and some (whom Socrates might term 'philosophers') seek to convince others of the truth. Socrates argues that once we have tasted the truth, we cannot return to ignorance. In this way, the allegory of The Cave is another allusion to the **Fall** of Man, and to the theme of pursuing understanding and intellect over close-mindedness and ignorance.

CHANGES, BOOK OF – *See* **I-Ching.**

CHAPEL OF THE HOLY PENITENCE – A building in **Geneva** with a belfry that overlooks the **College of Saint Jerome** [AS, 24].

CHARIOT, THE – *See* **Clouded Mountain.**

CHÂTEAU-VERT – A wood to the east of **Lyra's Oxford** [NL, 3].

CHOCOLATL – Chocolate in **Lyra's** world. **Mrs Coulter** abducts **Tony Makarios** with a form of drinking 'chocolatl' [NL, 3]. Chocolatl was the name given by the Aztecs to drinking chocolate, although theirs was a spicy mixture of ground cocoa beans and chillies. The Spanish conquistador Hernando Cortez reputedly drank chocolatl at the court of Montezuma in Mexico.

CHO-LUNG-SE – The trail that leads from **Ama's** village to the monastery of the **Pagdzin** *tulku*. The journey takes Ama three hours [AS, 4].

CHTHONIC RAILWAY – In **Lyra's** London, the equivalent of our underground railway or tube. **Mrs Coulter** tells Lyra that it is not really intended for people of their class [NL, 6]. 'Chthonic' comes from 'khthón', the Greek word for 'earth' and is sometimes used to describe the underworld.

CHURCH, THE – aka the **Magisterium**. A religious organisation that exerts absolute power over the lives of individuals in

Lyra's world. The Church's dominance seems to have been established in the sixteenth century when Pope John Calvin moved the seat of the Papacy to **Geneva** and established the **Consistorial Court of Discipline**. The Consistorial Court was based at the **College of Saint Jerome** in Geneva and ruled by a President. After John Calvin's death, the Papacy itself was abolished and replaced by a collection of courts, colleges and councils known as the Magisterium.

The Magisterium, however, was not always a united body. There was a great deal of factionalism and in-fighting: for a large part of the nineteenth century. The **College of Bishops** had been the most powerful part of the Magisterium but it had given way in more recent times to the Consistorial Court of Discipline. Nevertheless, it was still possible for independent agencies to be established under the auspices of different parts of the Magisterium, the **General Oblation Board** being one of them [NL, 2]. Another part of the Church was the **Society of the Work of the Holy Spirit**, a rival to the Consistorial Court at the time of Lyra's adventures [AS, 9].

While this factionalism suited the leaders of the Magisterium, who could play one agency off against another, it could also be a threat. When a clear and present danger emerged in the form of Lyra, the second Eve, there was much disagreement and secrecy in the Magisterium as one branch sought to keep its discoveries from the others [AS, 5]. It was only when the two most active branches of the Magisterium, the Consistorial Court of Discipline and the Society of the Work of the Holy Spirit, joined forces, that a serious attempt was made to capture and kill Lyra.

The Church's power over every aspect of life was absolute. **Experimental theology** fell within the purview of the Church as its leaders sought to control knowledge itself. The Magisterium insisted that every philosophical research establishment had to include a representative of the Magisterium on its staff to suppress any heretical discoveries [SK, 6]. The Magisterium also imposed its will through military power: it trained and financed the **Imperial Guard of Muscovy**, the best-trained soldiers in Lyra's world, and gained their fierce loyalty [SK, 6].

In the years preceding Lyra's adventures, the Church had become more commanding. There was even talk of reviving the Office of Inquisition [NL, 7].

On her return to Oxford after her adventures, Lyra discovered that the power of the Church had greatly increased for a while and then waned just as quickly. Upheavals in the Magisterium had brought more liberal factions to power, the Oblation Board had been dissolved and the Consistorial Court was leaderless [AS, 38].

Material in the programme of the stage play provided by Philip Pullman provides further information in the form of 'History of the Magisterium', an article from the *Encyclopaedia Europaica*. It tells how Jacques Calvin, a French Bishop, was elected Pope in 1555 after a difficult convocation. He set about dismantling the Papacy, hoping to return to the early days of faith with 'every man his own priest'. However, the consequence was the emergence of rival factions, one of whom, the Madre di Fede in Antichità, better known as the Mafia, was suppressed by all other bodies and confined to Sicily. Since then, other factions have fought for dominance.

CITTÀGAZZE – aka Ci'gazze, the City of Magpies. A city where the **subtle knife** is forged. The world in which Cittàgazze is located was once an idyllic place of spacious cities, bounteous harvests and forests of game. The great cities of this world were centres of trade, diplomacy and culture, where ambassadors from **Brasil**, **Benin**, **Eireland** and **Corea** mixed with tradesman and entertainers. Cittàgazze itself is a coastal city at the foot of verdant hills. **Will** estimates that Cittàgazze is most likely located in either the Mediterranean or the Caribbean as the city can support palm trees and has the customary wide commercial boulevards. The city is also home to the **Philosophers' Guild** who work from the **Torre degli Angeli**, the **Tower of the Angels**. Then, 300 years prior to the events of *The Subtle Knife*, the city falls prey to the **Spectres** [SK, 6]. Life in Cittàgazze collapses. It becomes impossible for the inhabitants to trade or live as they had and the city falls to ruin. **Joachim Lorenz** knows it as the city of magpies, so called because the residents can no longer build but can only steal from other **worlds** [SK, 6]. In fact the coming of the Spectres was the result of the actions of the Philosophers' Guild whose creation and careless use of the subtle knife made Cittàgazze a cross-road between worlds, and consequently the place where the largest number of Spectres would congregate [SK, 9]. By the time of Will and **Lyra**'s first visit, Cittàgazze was deserted, save for pre-pubescent children who were safe from the Spectres. The people of this world do not have visible **dæmons** [SK, 3].

It is pronounced Chee-tar-gart-sea in the audiobook version, but Chitter-gart-sea in the radio adaptation. The name is Italian; Citta meaning city and gazza meaning magpie and therefore one presumes it is located on the Italian peninsula. Fortunately for Will and Lyra, the children speak English.

CLAYBEDS – A place in **Lyra's Oxford** where the brick-burners' children live [NL, 3].

CLERKENWELL – An area of London where **Benjamin de Ruyter** and his fellow **gyptian** spy three **Gobblers**. The Gobblers reveal their connections to the **Ministry of Theology** and **Lord Boreal** [NL, 8].

CLOUDED MOUNTAIN, THE – aka the **Chariot**. The seat of the **Authority**'s power. When the Authority was young it was not surrounded by clouds but over the centuries he gathered more and more cloud to it. The summit had not been seen for thousnds of years. **Metatron** sought to take the Clouded Mountain into the worlds of consciousness from which he could lead his new Inquisition. The Authority Himself dwells at the heart of the mountain. [AS, 2]. In fact, on closer inspection, the Mountain is barely such at all. **Mrs Coulter** discovers it to be an enormous structure of terraces, chambers, colonnades and watch-towers apparently made of light, air and vapour. The cloud is apparently flights of **angels** loyal to the Authority [AS, 30].

CLOUD PINE – Sprays of cloud pine are used by the witches of **Lyra**'s world to fly. **Dr Martin Lanselius**, the **Witch-Consul at Trollesund**, asks Lyra to pick out a spray of cloud pine touched by **Serafina Pekkala** from those that have not been. In succeeding, Lyra proves herself to be one that 'the witches have talked about . . . for centuries past', namely the second Eve [NL, 10].

COAL-SPIRIT – A type of fuel in **Lyra**'s world [NL, 6].

COLA – Coke exists in **Will**'s world, but not **Lyra**'s [SK, 1]. It comes in cartons, rather than cans in the world of **Cittàgazze**, according to the stage play, but comes in cans in the books and the radio version.

COLBY – The last place in **Eastern Anglia** before the **German Ocean**. There is a Smokemarket and refinery nearby [NL, 9].

COLBY WATER – The estuary of the River Cole and the last stretch of inland water in the **Fens** before reaching the **German Ocean** [NL, 9].

COLLEGE OF BISHOPS – A branch of the **Church**. The College of Bishops had been the most powerful arm of the Church in the nineteenth century but, in recent years before *Northern Lights*, it had been superseded by the **Consistorial Court of Discipline** [NL, 2; AS, 6].

COLLEGE OF SAINT JEROME – The ancient high-towered building in **Geneva**, complete with spire, cloisters and tower, serves as the chamber of the President of the **Consistorial Court of Discipline**. **Mrs Coulter** visited the College three times before the events of *The Amber Spyglass*. The College is overlooked by the belfry of the **Chapel of the Holy Penitence** which is located nearby. The guard at the College gatehouse has a pinscher **dæmon** [AS, 6, 24].

COLVILLE RIVER – A landmark in Alaska that **Major John Parry** says is a mile or so south of the **window** [SK, 5].

CONCILIUM – A part of **Jordan College** that manages the institution's finances [NL, 2].

CONSISTORIAL COURT OF DISCIPLINE – Dominant part of the **Church** in the time of **Lyra**'s adventure. The Consistorial Court was created by **Pope John Calvin** after he moved the seat of the Papacy to **Geneva**. Following his death, the Papacy was abolished and replaced by the **Magisterium** [NL, 2]. The Consistorial Court was based at the **College of Saint Jerome** in Geneva and ruled by a President who was elected for life. In Lyra's day this was **Father Hugh MacPhail**, a dark-featured Scot with a lizard **dæmon** [AS, 6]. It was under the auspices of the Consistorial Court that the **General Oblation Board** was established. The Consistorial Court was the most determined in the search for Lyra: MacPhail made a truce with the rival **Society of the Work of the Holy Spirit**, granted **Father Luis Gomez** pre-emptive absolution and commissioned the **quantum entanglement bomb** from **Dr Cooper** [AS, 9]. After MacPhail's death and the second **Fall**, more liberal factions came to power in the Magisterium, the Oblation Board was dissolved and the Consistorial Court found itself broken and leaderless [AS, 38]. In its recent past, the Consistorial Court had investigated **Boris Mikhailovitch Rusakov** for diabolic heresy under the rules of the Inquisition.

The Consistorial Court of Discipline was the central agency of John Calvin's theocracy in Geneva in the 1540s and 1550s.

COREA – A country in **Lyra**'s world. The **gyptians** have enamelled dishes from **Corea** [AS, 38]. There is also a Corea in the world of **Cittàgazze** [SK, 6].

CORONA – A form of currency used by the inhabitants of **Cittàgazze** [SK, 1].

COUNCIL OF STATE – The ruling elite in **Lyra**'s world, of which **Lord Boreal** is a member. The King holds the Council of State weekly at **White Hall Palace** [NL, 3; SK, 9].

CRYPT – *See* **Jordan College**.

D

DARK MATTER – *See* **Dust.**

DARK MATTER RESEARCH UNIT – The **Oxford** college home for the research project of **Dr Mary Malone** and **Dr Oliver Payne**. Mary and Oliver are investigating the existence of **Dark Matter** – matter that exists in the universe but cannot be detected. Their hypothesis is that Dark Matter is a kind of elementary particle that is difficult to see. To that end, they create a detector that filters out unwanted materials, then amplifiy the signal through a computer nicknamed **The Cave**. They discover the existence of Shadow Particles, or **Shadows**, that appear to be conscious and drawn to human consciousness [SK, 4].

Dark Matter is a real phenomenon and the focus of a great deal of cosmological research. It was first hypothesised in 1933 when Swiss astrophysicist Fritz Zwicky calculated that there was insufficient visible mass in the universe to account for the gravity that kept the galaxy together. He concluded that around 95 per cent of the universe must consist of unobservable 'Dark Matter'. His thesis is sometimes known as the 'missing mass problem'. Currently, cosmologists believe that there are two forms of Dark Matter: baryonic Dark Matter termed MACHO (Massive Compact Halo Objects); and non-baryonic subatomic particles termed WIMPs (Weakly Interacting Massive Particles). The latter is believed to be an elementary particle, like an electron, neutron or proton, but one that does not interact with the electromagnetic spectrum and is therefore difficult to detect. These particles are sometimes called 'Shadow Particles' and are the focus of Dr Mary Malone's researches.

DOLLARS – A currency in **Lyra's** England. **Lord Asriel** gives Lyra five gold dollars when he leaves **Jordan College** [NL, 3]. A smaller denomination is the shilling [NL, 6]; a larger is the sovereign [NL, 7].

In the radio version of *The Subtle Knife*, but no other, Lyra has never seen paper money before **Will** shows her banknotes from his world. Gold dollars are also used in the stage play: Lyra offers **Iorek Byrnison** two gold dollars to join her quest, and later **Lee Scoresby** wants a 'ridiculous' one hundred gold dollars for the hire of his balloon.

DUST – aka *sraf*, **Shadows, Dark Matter, angels, original sin.** Described as 'a distant theological riddle' by the **Librarian** of **Jordan College** [NL, 2], Dust is nevertheless the prime preoccupation of most of the major characters in the trilogy. The **Church** seeks to destroy it, **Lord Asriel** seeks to preserve it, the **Mulefa** seeks to keep and treasure it. Yet the reader is never entirely clear what *it* is, as each world and character presents a different understanding of Dust.

Every world we see in *His Dark Materials* has its own story of what Dust is and what it means. In Lyra's world, a Muscovite called **Boris Mikhailovitch Rusakov** discovers an unusual elementary particle, one that is hard to detect and that does not interact with other particles in any of the expected ways. The Rusakov particle's most peculiar feature is its attraction to selected people: these particles attach themselves to adults and children whose **dæmons** are fixed, but are less concentrated around pre-pubescent children. News of Boris's discovery reaches the **Magisterium**, who sends an Inspector from the **Consistorial Court of Discipline** to investigate. The Inspector suspects Boris of 'diabolic possession', exorcises his laboratory, and interrogates him under the rules of the Inquisition. Ultimately, however, the Magisterium had to concede that Rusakov is not lying – his particle really does exist.

Having accepted Boris's discovery, the next challenge is how to rationalise it within the Church doctrine. The only way the Church can make sense of his particle is to see it as the physical manifestation of original sin; proof that something physical happens when innocence becomes experience [NL, 5, 21]. Later, his particle becomes known as Dust, after the biblical passage 'for dust thou art, and unto dust shalt thou return' [NL, 21; Genesis 3:19].

For centuries, the Church has preached the wickedness of original sin, that the loss of innocence is a tragic event. But now it has been manifested, can the Church do something practical about it? When **Mrs Coulter** makes the connection between Dust and the fixing of one's dæmons, the consequences are terrifying. Mrs Coulter argues that separating children from their dæmons before the dæmons are fixed might prevent sin from settling. The children would be in a permanent state of innocence. 'Dust is something bad, something wrong, something evil and wicked,' she tells Lyra. 'Grown-ups and their dæmons are infected with Dust so deeply that it's too late for them. They can't be helped ... But a quick operation on children means they're safe from it. Dust just won't stick to them ever again' [NL, 17]. And so the **General Oblation Board** is formed to investigate this hypothesis further [NL, 5, 21].

In **Will**'s world, a parallel line of discovery takes place. The **Dark Matter Research Unit** at **Oxford** is one of several research projects across the world investigating Dark Matter, masses that are hard to detect but must be present in order for gravity to work [SK, 4]. **Dr Mary Malone** and **Dr Oliver Payne** discover strange '**Shadow Particles**' which, like Rusakov particles, do not react in the expected way. Mary and Oliver also spot that anything associated with human workmanship or with conscious human thought is surrounded by these Shadows. Skulls predating the emergence of the human species, approximately 35,000 years ago, were not covered in Dust [SK, 4, 12].

Most amazingly, Mary and Oliver discover that these Shadows respond to human thought and have consciousness themselves. Through **The Cave**, Mary and Oliver are able to 'communicate' with these particles. Learning from Lyra, Mary develops a program to turn images into text and to speak to one another. The results are startling: Mary discovers that her Shadow Particles are the same thing as Lyra's Dust and are also known as angels [SK, 12]. These rebel angels intervene in human evolution for vengeance against the **Authority**, drawing themselves to conscious thought and experience [SK, 12].

On a third world, the land of the **Mulefa**, Mary discovers another understanding of Dust. Here, the Mulefa are able to see Dust, comparing it to the reflection of light off the ripples of water at sunset. Their name for it sounds to Mary like 'sarf' or '*sraf*'. The Mulefa are able to distinguish Mary from the grazers by the *sraf* that surrounds her. Thanks to this ability to see Dust, the Mulefa develop a more profound connection with it than other species in other worlds. The Mulefa believe that Dust is created when they are grown up and comes from the oil but they know that without the trees it would vanish. More alarmingly, they can see that Dust is leaving their world [AS, 17].

The loss of Dust from the Mulefa's world, and indeed all the worlds, began around 300 years previously. The cause was the subtle knife, created by the **Philosophers' Guild** in **Cittàgazze**. With every cut, the knife penetrates 'the emptiness outside'. The fine edge, which Will can feel to close each window, is still big enough to let Dust leak out. In more recent days, however, the outpouring has become catastrophic. First, **Lord Asriel**'s **bridge** rips open a hole between worlds, a vast window. Then the Church's **quantum entanglement bomb** opens a vast **abyss** in the land of the dead [AS, 34, 37]. The Mulefa seek Mary's help in arresting the flow.

Mary is only able to come to a conclusion when she too is able to see Dust through the amber spyglass. She comes to realise a fundamental truth that the Mulefa have understood for generations: that conscious activity – thought, experience and wisdom – were essential for the continued renewal of Dust. Previously, Mary had suspected that, whatever Shadows were, they had something to do with 'the great change in human history symbolised in the story of Adam and Eve' [AS, 17]. Now she knew that without conscious activity, without the **Fall** from innocence and elevation to experience, 'thought, imagination, feeling, would all wither and blow away, leaving nothing but a brutish automatism' [AS, 34]. By not seeing 'wickedness' in Dust, the Mulefa and Mary sought to cherish and preserve it [AS, 17]. By contrast, **Father Luis Gomez**, possessed of the notion of original sin, immediately condemns the Mulefa's use of wheels as 'abominable and Satanic, and contrary to the will of God' [AS, 35].

The second Fall of Man has to take place to ensure humankind can turn once more against innocence and progress to wisdom. Mary likens Will and Lyra's actions to putting a pebble in the right place to change the course of a mighty river [AS, 36]. In gaining experience, they stem the loss of Dust from the worlds. The settling of Dust marks the passing from innocence to experience (*see* **Innocence and experience**).

Perhaps the purest explanation of Dust is given by the angels. **Balthamos** states that 'Dust is only a name for what happens when matter begins to understand itself.' The Authority, the first angel, was created from Dust when matter became conscious of itself [AS, 2]. Later, **Xaphania** reveals that conscious beings make Dust and preserve it by 'thinking and feeling and reflecting, by gaining wisdom and passing it on' [AS, 37]. This is the task to fall on Will and Lyra, to teach people to keep their minds 'open and free and curious'. Only then would there be enough Dust to balance its loss through the window out of the land of the dead [AS, 37]. This is the purpose of the Republic of Heaven.

'What is Dust?' is the question that most regularly possesses the minds of Philip Pullman's readers. Its story is told in so many broken sections and from so many viewpoints that it seems set to puzzle generations of readers.

In *Darkness Visible*, Nicholas Tucker rightly points out the similarities between Dust and pantheism. Pantheism literally means God is all and all is God, that is, that all matter is part of God and vice-versa. Pullman certainly presents Dust as something that connects us all. Furthermore, one of the ideas commonly associated with pantheism is the belief that while individuals have a free will, they are ultimately part of a greater whole of which they may not be aware; they could in fact be responding in a way predetermined by the needs of this greater force. As **Jotham Santelia** tells Lyra, 'the universe is full of *intentions*, you know. Everything happens for a purpose' [NL, 19]. This would seem to corroborate Pullman's views on free will expressed in the books.

However, the pantheistic belief in the existence of a God, no matter how impersonal or non-sentient, is in direct contradiction to Pullman's professed views. The point he seems to be making is that Dust is something that connects all living things without the need for a Godhead – indeed the first Godhead was created from Dust like all others. To strive for the **Republic of Heaven** is to educate people in the virtues of conscious thought – in keeping an open mind, challenging, questioning, and in rejecting doctrines and beliefs that narrow our vision. In simple terms, it is a connection between us all that does not depend on Christian morality.

The ideas for Dust seem to stem from a very literal interpretation of the Bible. Lord Asriel points out to Lyra the origin of the word 'Dust' in God's condemnation of Adam following the Fall: 'for dust thou art, and unto dust shalt thou return' [NL, 21]. The second half of the phrase is the most interesting for this can be read as both a statement of Dust as the building blocks of the universe, and as foreshadowing the release that awaits the ghost in the land of the dead. The first to leave the land of the dead, Roger, is delighted to find himself 'turning into the night, the starlight, the air . . .' [AS, 26]. **Lee Scoresby** too passes through the clouds to the stars 'where the atoms of his beloved dæmon Hester were waiting for him' [AS, 31]. Of course, this idea of a universal connection is not new – Dust is not the only thing that 'surrounds us, penetrates us . . . [and] binds the galaxy together'.

It is probably a mistake to see Dust as any one thing. In the course of the books, Dust is revealed to people in different ways based on their experiences and viewpoints. For the Church, it is original sin. For Lord Asriel, it is the cause of great misery at the hands of the Church (*see* the entry on **Lord Asriel** for more on his complex views on Dust). For Mary, the scientist, it is a fundamental particle. For the innocent Mulefa, it is the source of their conscious lives before which they 'knew nothing' [AS, 17]. The hint that we should perhaps adopt this stance comes in Pullman's recurring use of **negative capability**, the mental state essential for the use of the **alethiometer**, the **subtle knife**, the Cave, the **I-Ching** and for seeing one's dæmon in our world. To be 'capable of being in uncertainties,

189

Mysteries, doubts without any irritable reaching after fact and reason'. To try rationally to understand Dust is unnecessary – it just is.

E

EASTERN ANGLIA – The name given to East Anglia in Lyra's world [NL, 7].

EINARSSON'S BAR – Drinking establishment in **Trollesund** in the yard behind which **Iorek Byrnison** worked as a metalsmith for his keep [NL, 10].

EIRELAND – A country known to the people of **Cittàgazze** [SK, 6].

ENARA, LAKE – A region in the north that is home to **Serafina Pekkala's witch** clan. It is surrounded by forested caves, including the gathering-cave where the council of the witches is held [SK, 2].

ENCYCLOPAEDIA EUROPAICA – A reference work in **Lyra's** world that includes the article 'History of the Magisterium' [Stage play programme].

EXPERIMENTAL STATION – *See* **Bolvangar**.

EXPERIMENTAL THEOLOGY – In **Lyra's** world, a branch of scientific theological enquiry; in our world, fundamental physics. It is said that **Jordan College** has no rival in Europe or **New France** in this field. The principal scholar in this field at Jordan College appears to have been the **Chaplain** whose Chapel was filled with 'philosophical apparatus' [NL, 3; SK, 12]. Scholars in our Europe, for a long time, saw science as a branch of theology, as it was a study of God's creation.

In *His Dark Materials*, experimental theology seems to be concerned primarily with the quest to find the smallest particles of matter. The **Philosophers' Guild** in **Cittàgazze** created the **subtle knife** in order to split the bonds of the atom [SK, 8]. In our world, **Dr Mary Malone's Dark Matter Research Unit** is seeking to understand 'Shadow Particles', subatomic particles like electrons, neutrons and protons that do not interact with the electromagnetic spectrum [SK, 4]. **Intercision**, **Lord Asriel's** **bridge** and **Dr Cooper's** bomb seem to work on similar principles [AS, 24].

F

FAIRBANKS, ALASKA – A location where **Major John Parry** meets up with gold-miner **Jake Petersen** and learns the likely location of the **window** to **Cittàgazze**. It is from here that John sends the letter of Wednesday 19 June 1985 to his wife [SK, 5].

FALKESHALL – The location of pleasure gardens in **Lyra's** London [NL, 3]. Falkeshall is most likely the equivalent of Vauxhall.

FATHER CHRISTMAS – **Lyra** hasn't heard of Father Christmas in the radio version of *The Subtle Knife*, suggesting that the **Magisterium's** version of Christianity must be particularly puritanical and joyless.

FEN-DUTCH – A **gyptian** dialect [NL, 7].

FENS – Region of **Eastern Anglia**, a wilderness of endless marshland stretching for hundreds of square miles, where **John Faa** calls together the **gyptians** for the Roping [NL, 6]. The gyptians have ancient privileges of free movement in and out of the Fens which are to be drained and dyked by Hollanders but it largely remains a network of undrained winding channels and watercourses. The only patch of slightly higher ground in the Fens is the **Byanplats** on which there is an ancient wooden meeting hall, the **Zaal**, where the gyptians met for a Byanroping. **Lyra** was enthralled by tales of Fen-dwellers, the legends of a great ghost dog called **Black Shuck** and 'marsh-fires arising from bubbles of witch-oil' [NL, 7]. In reality, the Fens of East Anglia have largely been drained and are now used for agriculture. Draining began in the seventeenth century but was undertaken intensively from the late eighteenth and early nineteenth century.

FIRE-MINES – *See* **Svalbard.**

FIRE-THROWER – A bombardment weapon that catapults blazing pitch that the **armoured bears** use. **Iofur Raknison's** marble palace at **Svalbard** is defended by fire-throwers and **Iorek Byrnison's** bears use the fire-thrower against the people of **Kholodnoye** who refused to let them moor at their town [AS, 8].

FLOODS OF '53 – **Lord Asriel** fights day and night during these floods, saving the lives of the **gyptians Ruud** and **Nellie Koopman** [NL, 8]. This may be a reference to the floods that hit eastern England in late January 1953 in which over 300 people lost their lives.

FORTRESS – **Lord Asriel's** seat of power in a world where he intends to build a life free from the **Authority**. The fortress is located at the western end of a mountain range, overlooking a great plain in front and a valley behind, and near to a sulphur lake. The battlements are made of single slabs of basalt half a hill high. On the highest rampart is the **Adamant Tower**, Asriel's private chamber where he lives and plans with his **high commanders**. The vast caverns beneath house ordnance factories with blast furnaces, rolling mills, **anbaric** forges and hydraulic presses. An anbaric railway passes through the caverns to munitions stores and to a launch pad for the **intention craft** [SK, 13; AS, 5, 15]. **Ruta Skadi** describes it to her fellow **witches** as 'the greatest castle you can imagine' and believes that Asriel must have the power to control time to have brought it and his forces into existence [SK, 13].

THE A–Z OF *HIS DARK MATERIALS*

G

GABRIEL COLLEGE – A college in **Oxford** adjacent to **Jordan College** that hems in the latter's expansion over the centuries, forcing Jordan to burrow beneath the ground [NL, 3]. The high altar of the Oratory at Gabriel College is home to a holy object called a **Photo-mill** [NL, 9].

GENERAL OBLATION BOARD – *See* **Oblation Board.**

GENEVA – The home of the **Magisterium** and therefore the seat of power of the **Church**. The President of the **Consistorial Court of Discipline** had his base at the **College of Saint Jerome** in Geneva.

Interestingly, in our world Geneva was ruled by the theocracy of **Pope John Calvin**, and is now home to the CERN, the European Organisation for Nuclear Research, and is the world's largest particle physics centre. **Dr Oliver Payne** attends a job interview in Geneva. Geneva is the home to **experimental theology** in **Lyra**'s world and fundamental physics in ours, further mirroring the similarities of the two disciplines.

GERMAN ACADEMY – *See* **Berlin Academy.**

GERMAN OCEAN – In **Lyra**'s world, the tide of the **German Ocean** reaches as far as Teddington on the **River Isis** [NL, 3]. It is presumably the equivalent of our North Sea and English Channel.

GOBBLERS – A nickname given to the agency that abducts children in the weeks preceding **Lord Asriel**'s visit to **Jordan College** [NL, 3]. The name is derived from the initials for the **General Oblation Board** [NL, 5].

GODSTOW – The location of an old nunnery, near **Port Meadow. Lyra** tells the **gyptian** children that a werewolf comes out of the nunnery at full moon [NL, 5]. **Pantalaimon** claims to have seen an old **ghost** in Godstow, although Lyra hasn't

[NL, 9]. In our world the nunnery is a ruin, demolished during the 1540s as part of the dissolution of the monasteries. Of course, in Lyra's world the **Church** would have been more capable of resisting any such action and the dissolution probably did not take place.

GOLDEN COMPASS – *See* **Alethiometer**.

GRAND JUNCTION CANAL – In **Lyra's** world, the equivalent of the Grand Union Canal. **Ma Costa** carried Lyra to the **Fens** for the Roping along this route [NL, 6].

GREAT BETRAYAL – *See* **Lyra**.

GRIMSSDUR – A great whale. The harpoon used to kill Grimssdur was on display in the Library of the **Royal Arctic Institute** [NL, 4].

GROUND-GAS – A naturally occurring gas. **Lee Scoresby** says a good vent of ground-gas fills his balloon in an hour [NL, 13].

GUILD, THE – *See* **Philosophers' Guild**.

GYROPTERS – A flying craft that **Lord Asriel's** forces use. Asriel sends number two squadron in search of **Lyra** when she is kidnapped and held drugged by **Mrs Coulter** in the Himalayan cave [AS, 57].

The name is a hybrid of gyroscope and helicopter. The gyroscope was invented by French physicist Jean Bernard Léon Foucault (1819–68) in 1852 and is often used in vehicles to assist stability. Philip Pullman mentioned that he was a big fan of the *Dan Dare* comic strip as a child – when he was on Earth, Dan was the proud owner of a gyro-car.

H

HANGMAN'S WHARF – A wharf in London where the **Oblation Board** holds children before transporting them to **Bolvangar**. **Mrs Coulter** leads **Tony Makarios** there [NL, 3].

HAZARD – A card game that **Lee Scoresby** and the **gyptians** play [NL, 11]. Hazard is a real card game, much like craps and is played with two dice. The name derives from the Arabic *az-zahr* meaning die.

HEIDELBERG – A place in Germany that **Farder Coram** visits where he sees the books of symbols for interpreting the **alethiometer** in the **Abbey of Saint Johann** [NL, 9, 10].

HIGH BRAZIL – A place in **Lyra's** world. She considers stowing away on the **gyptian** expedition to the Arctic but fears she might find herself on the wrong ship and en route to High Brazil [NL, 9].

HIMALAYAS – A mountain range that is home to **Ama** and the **Pagdzin** *tulku* and the location of the cave where **Mrs Coulter** keeps **Lyra** captive [AS, 2].
   The Himalayan mountain range separates India and northern Pakistan from the Tibetan plateau, now part of China.

HOLDING AREA – The strange shanty town where **Will** and **Lyra** wait until they die so that they can enter the **land of the dead**. It is here that Lyra encounters her **Death** [AS, 19].

HONEY-BREAD – A foodstuff that **Ama** uses to bribe the porter in order to get an audience with the **Pagdzin** *tulku*. [AS, 4].

I

I-CHING – aka the **Book of Changes**. The I-Ching is the oldest of the classic Chinese texts and is traditionally credited to the

Emperor Fu Hsi (c. 2850 BC). It describes the ancient system of cosmology and philosophy at the heart of Chinese cultural beliefs: the ideas of balance through opposites and acceptance of change. The I-Ching is described through 64 abstract line drawings known as hexagrams, which are traditionally represented in a circle arrangement. Followers believe that one can make sense of the world by using the I-Ching for divination. **Dr Mary Malone** uses the book in this way using the yarrow stalks' method of divination. Interestingly, **Lyra** observes that this form of divination requires the same state of being as is required to use the **alethiometer**, the **subtle knife** or **the Cave** [SK, 4; AS, 7].

IMPERIAL GUARD OF MUSCOVY – 'The most ferociously trained and lavishly equipped army in the world'. The Imperial Guard swear to uphold the power of the **Magisterium**. When **Lee Scoresby** collects **John Parry** to take him to another world, he finds that all the buildings in the port at the mouth of the **Yenesei River** are under the control of the Imperial Guard [SK, 10]. The presence of Russian soldiers is perhaps a hint that the Magisterium, as well as dominating Europe, holds sway over nations that are Russian Orthodox in our world.

IMPERIAL MUSCOVITE ACADEMY – An academic institute that has an astronomical observatory on a mountain near **Nova Zembla**. **Stanislaus Grumman** visits the observatory many times. In **Lyra's** world, every philosophical research establishment has to include a representative of the **Magisterium** on its staff to suppress any heretical discoveries. A **Skraeling** is the representative at the observatory; he has a snowy owl **dæmon** who tries to kill **Lee Scoresby** [SK, 6].

IMPERIAL NAVY – Creators of a weapon that fires blended potash and naphtha, which ignites on contact with water. The Imperial Navy developed it for their war against the **Nippon** [SK, 14].

INQUISITION, OFFICE OF – In our world, an office of the Roman Catholic Church that was created to suppress heresy.

Inquisitions were first established in the late twelfth century but had mixed successes. By far the most infamous was the Spanish Inquisition, instituted in the late fifteenth century under the control of the kings of Spain. This Inquisition was founded primarily to force the conversion of Jews and Muslims who had controlled much of southern Spain in the preceding years. Columbus took the Inquisition with him to the New World. In **Lyra**'s world, the rules of the Inquisition are employed to interrogate **Rusakov** for heresy [NL, 21]. **John Faa** hears that the Office of Inquisition is to be revived [NL, 7]. It is **Metatron**'s intention to establish a permanent inquisition across all the worlds.

INSTITUTE OF ARCHAELOGY – *See* **Archaelogy, Institute of.**

INTENTION CRAFT – An agile, well-armed aircraft is created for **Lord Asriel**'s forces in the armoury beneath the **Adamant Tower** [AS, 17]. The intention craft is a mass of pipework, cylinders, pistons, switchgear, coiled cables, valves and gauges that look like 'complex drilling apparatus'. It is mounted on six legs and has the cockpit of a **gyropter**. However, no gyropter controls are truly necessary as the intention craft is directed by the thoughts of its pilot. Human occupants wear helmets while their **dæmons** hold a handle, completing a circuit that allows the 'intentions' of its pilots to guide the craft. It could therefore only be piloted by a human with a visible dæmon. When **Mrs Coulter** first sees it in operation, piloted by Lord Asriel, the craft moves so quickly it appears to vanish. In fact, it springs into the air where it hovers silently before Lord Asriel rapidly despatches a raiding party [AS, 16]. Mrs Coulter steals the intention craft, as Lord Asriel had intended, to make her escape to **Geneva**. She later pilots the craft to the **Clouded Mountain**. Lord Asriel has a later, more advanced model [AS, 16].

INTERCISION – aka **Maystadt Process, the.** The process of separating a person, particularly a child, from their **dæmon**.

This is the focus of the experiments at **Bolvangar** where the **Oblation Board** hope to show that intercision could protect a child from **original sin**. The **Skraelings** have been separating body and **dæmon** by hand for centuries. The main problem for the Oblation Board is the high death rate from shock. The use of anaesthesia and the **Maystadt anbaric scalpel** reduces the death rate to below 5 per cent. The next step forward is **Lord Asriel**'s discovery of an alloy of manganese and titanium that has the property of insulating the body from the dæmon. This gives rise to the creation of the **silver guillotine** apparatus which is used at Bolvangar [NL, 16]. Some adults at Bolvangar volunteer for the process and a whole regiment of warriors are treated in the same way and become as **zombi** [SK, 2]. For the unfortunate children who survive intercision, their lives are filled with a sense of loss for their dæmon as in the case of **Tony Makarios** [NL, 12].

In the books, direct comparison is made between intercision and castration. Lord Asriel says that the Church permits castration because castrati keeps their high treble voice that is 'so useful in Church music' [NL, 21]. Asriel also tells **Ruta Skadi** that the castration of boys and girls is evidence of the wickedness of the Church [SK, 2].

ISIS – In **Lyra**'s world, the river that stretches from Oxfordshire to **Limehouse** [NL, 3]. The River Isis is, in fact, the River Thames, which becomes known as the River Isis within the boundaries of **Oxford**. It would seem that in Lyra's world, the Isis is the name for the whole River Thames.

IZMIR, COLLEGE OF – A college that the Turkish ambassador belongs to in the tall story **Lyra** tells the **gyptian** children at the Roping. Although the story is fiction, the college may, of course, be a real place in Lyra's world [NL, 8].

J

JENNIVER – An alcoholic drink that the **gyptians** favour. Jenniver takes its name from the Dutch for juniper (jenever), the bush that gives the berries that are fermented to make gin [NL, 7].

JERICHO – Part of **Lyra**'s **Oxford** where the **Costa** family regularly moor [NL, 3]. Among its narrow streets, there are small brick-terraced houses and the Oratory of **Saint Barnabas the Chymist** [NL, 3]. **Jericho** is in west Oxford near the canal.

JIMSON-WEED – The basis of an ointment that acts as a kind of insect repellent, which **Lee Scoresby** uses en route to the tribe of the **Yenesei Pakhtar** [SK, 10].

JORDAN COLLEGE – **Lyra**'s home in **Oxford**. Jordan College is the grandest, richest and probably the largest of the colleges in Oxford. It consists of three irregular quadrangles constructed between the early Middles Ages and the mid-eighteenth century [NL, 3]. The College had never been planned as such and grew organically as the needs of the College evolved. As Jordan College jostles for space with Saint Michael's College on one side, **Gabriel College** on the other and the University Library behind, it began to extend underground sometime in the Middle Age. Tunnels, vaults and cellars extend for several hundred yards around the foot-print of the buildings above ground. It is in part of these great vaults that the College's reserves of **Tokay, canary, Burgundy** and **brantwijn** are kept [NL, 3].

The College's riches lay in its vast estates. It was said that one could walk from Oxford to Bristol or to London and never leave Jordan land. This brought in significant rentals from dye-works and brick-kilns, forest and **atomcraft**-works that were built on the College's estates. Every Quarter-Day, the Bursar and his clerks accounted for the value of the College and presented it to the **Concilium**, presumably the College's ruling council. The news was invariably good: swans were usually ordered for a feast, salaries paid, new properties acquired, books purchased and the cellars filled with wine [NL, 3].

Some of the funds raised through rentals was spent on maintenance of the old buildings. Jordan College kept a permanent staff to look after the physical restoration of the College, some part of which was always about to fall down. The **Parslow** family had been retained as stonemasons and scaffolders to the College for five generations. In total, a dozen or so families of craftsmen served the College [NL, 3].

Inside, the College was a maze of rooms and corridors. The grand Hall was the setting for elaborate dinners, laid out with three tables running the length of the room and a high table on a raised dais. The kitchen, where Lyra was observed by **Bernie Johansen** the pastry cook, was adjacent. A door on the dais led to the Retiring Room, the most private part of the College open only to scholars and guests. After a dinner, the scholars traditionally took poppy and wine. Another exit from the Retiring Room led to a busy corridor that linked the Library and the Scholars' Common Room [NL, 1]. The Library filled one edge of the Melrose Quadrangle and burrowed several floors underground [NL, 3]. There was also a Buttery [NL, 3].

From the kitchen, one could walk into a quadrangle between the Chapel and Palmer's Tower and into Yaxley's Quadrangle where the oldest buildings of Jordan College stood [NL, 3]. This included Staircase 12 where Lyra's quarters were located and the Master's Lodging, a grand and slightly gloomy house that opened onto Yaxley Quad and backed onto the Library Garden [NL, 3].

Perhaps the most important building was the stone-pinnacled Chapel which was adjacent to the Library Garden. Jordan College had no rival in Europe or in **New France** as a centre of **experimental theology**. Money from rentals was used to buy the latest philosophical apparatus for the **Chaplain** so as to keep Jordan College ahead of the rest. Nearby was the Oratory, the domain of the Intercessor, **Father Heyst,** whose responsibility it was to lead all College services, conduct prayers and hear confessions. Beneath the Oratory lay the catacombs where Father Heyst once caught Lyra and **Roger** playing [NL, 3, 4].

It was below the Oratory that the **Master of Jordan College** would eventually be laid to rest. The Master was the most senior academic and head of Jordan College. Generations of

Masters were immortalised in portraits in the Hall [NL, 1]. Their bodies were interred in lead-lined coffins in the crypt below the Oratory. Each coffin was adorned with a brass plaque depicting the master's **dæmon**. The former Masters included: **Ignatius Cole**, 1745–48, and his dæmon **Musca**; **Francis Lyall**, 1748–65, and **Zohariel**; **Simon Le Clerc**, 1765–1789, and **Cerebaton** [NL, 3]. The skulls of scholars were also apparently interred there, with small disks of bronze bearing pictures of their dæmon [NL, 3].

The internment of dead scholars demonstrates the strictly hierarchical culture of Jordan College. Within the academic staff there was the Master, senior Scholars, and Under-Scholars. It was also a patriarchy. The Retiring Room itself was never open to women – it was even cleaned by the butler, not the maidservants [NL, 1]. Lyra herself had a 'proper Jordan disdain' for female scholars who 'could never be taken more seriously than animals dressed up and acting a play'. [NL, 4]. **Saint Sophia's**, Oxford's women's college headed by **Dame Hannah Relf**, was even located a distance away, at the northern end of the city [NL, 4].

Jordan College's scholars include the Sub-Rector, Chaplain, Enquirer, **Librarian, Palmerian Professor, Cassington Scholar, Dean** and the **Intercessor**. Staff included the Butler, **Steward**, Chef, Bursar, Clerks and **Mrs Lonsdale** the Housekeeper. Other colleges included Saint Michael's, **Gabriel**, Brasenose, and Saint Sophia's where Lyra studied **alethiometry**.

Jordan College is based on Exeter College in Oxford where Philip Pullman studied.

K

KAMCHATKA – A place which is the focus of attention of the **Tartars** at the time of **Lyra's** visit to the **Witch-Consul** at **Trollesund**. The **alethiometer** informs Lyra that the Tartars are going to pretend to attack it but do not because it is too far away from their position and would stretch them too far. There are gold mines in Kamchatka [NL, 10].

KHOLODNOYE – An isolated village located in central Siberia on the path of a river that flows from northern Tibet to the Arctic Ocean. In the aftermath of the creation of **Lord Asriel's bridge**, the village is affected by floods and earthquakes and the river momentarily flows the opposite way. Father **Semyon Borisovitch**, a local priest encountered by **Will**, believes this to be a sign that the **Apocalypse of Saint John** is coming true [AS, 8].

KINGDOM OF HEAVEN – *See* **Clouded Mountain**.

KING GEORGE'S STEPS – The location of the entrance to a tall warehouse in **Hangman's Wharf** where the **Gobblers** hold children from transport to **Bolvangar** [NL, 3].

L

LACQUER – The **Mulefa** produces a natural lacquer by dissolving the tree sap from the wheel-pod trees in an alcohol made from distilled fruit juice. **Mary Malone** uses repeat coatings of the lacquer to create a hard amber-coloured translucent material that, when polished and oiled, forms the lenses of the **amber spyglass**. The hardened material has the same properties as Iceland Spar, a mineral that splits light rays in two [AS, 17].

LAND OF THE DEAD – In **Lyra**'s world, people believe they will be rewarded for obeying the teachings of the **Authority**. However, on death, every single person is sent to the land of the dead, a prison camp established by the Authority in the early ages. There, the **ghosts** of the dead are sent to be tormented for eternity by the **harpies**. The gate to the land of the dead is on an island that can only be reached by boat. Ghosts are taken to the **boatman** and carried across the stinking water. Unfortunates like **Will**, Lyra and the **Gallivespians**, who arrive in the suburbs of the dead with their **dæmons**, are forced to leave them behind: this is an immutable law, not a rule that can be waived or broken. The land itself is a barren plain where a dim light bathes everything in the same dingy colour. Here, the ghosts of the dead are without substance and only able to whisper. When Lyra sees the land in her dream, she observes ground that has been trampled flat by millions of feet for millennia. 'This is the end of all places and the last of all worlds.' Lyra and Will are able to appease the harpies and gain their help in leaving the land of the dead. Releasing the ghosts is a major blow against the Authority. The land of the dead may be the 'spirit world' referred to by the **Tartars**.

When people cite sources for Philip Pullman's books, they often mention **John Milton**, **William Blake** and **C. S. Lewis**. The land of the dead represents the most striking divergence from the iconography of those earlier writers. All three of them portray Hell – Milton (of course) in *Paradise Lost*, Blake's illustrated Dante's *Divine Comedy* and Lewis in *The Screwtape Letters*. These are lively and vibrant depictions. Philip Pullman's land of the dead goes back to an earlier model, one shared by the Greeks, Mesopotamians and the ancient Hebrews, where the afterlife was seen as a pale shadow of life on Earth. Crucially, both the Greeks and Hebrews felt that all people went to the same afterlife;, there was no reward for the virtuous or punishment for the wicked. Lyra's adventures in the land of the dead are reminiscent of legends of the **Harrowing of Hell**.

LANGLOKUR STREET – The street on the waterfront in **Trollesund** where **Einarsson's Bar**, and **Iorek Byrnison**, can be found [NL, 10].

LAPLAND – Area of the frozen north. The main port of Lapland, and the last large conurbation before the frozen wastes, was **Trollesund**. The **witches** have a consulate there [NL, 10].

LIMEFIELD HOUSE – **Sir Charles Latrom**'s residence in Old Headington, **Oxford** [SK, 7].

LIMEHOUSE – Part of London where **Tony Makarios** lives [NL, 3].

LODESTONE RESONATOR – A **Gallivespian** communication device that **Chevalier Tialys** uses to keep in contact with **Lord Roke** [AS, 5]. The resonator consists of a pencil of grey stone which is 'played' with a tiny bow when sending a message. To receive the reply, a wire is stretched along the length of the pencil and headphones attached. The resonator is in fact one device split in two using the principle of **quantum entanglement**. The device is stored in a wooden box like a violin case that is no longer than a walnut [AS, 13, 14].

LOOKOUT RIDGE – A location in north Alaska, one or two miles north of the **Colville River**, where the '**anomaly**' exists. Eskimos have known of it for centuries. **Major John Parry** finds the 'anomaly' on a spur on the ridge and discovers that it is a **window** to **Cittàgazze** [SK, 5].

M

MAGISTERIUM – *See* **Church, the.**

MAGPIES – The name **Cittàgazze** is Italian for 'city of magpies', because the people there are forced to steal from other cities and worlds as the **Spectres** prevent any form of viable economy.

When asked what his **dæmon** would be, Philip Pullman suggested 'a magpie or a jackdaw, one of those birds that pick up bright shining things' (*Sunday Telegraph*, 27 January 2002), tying in to his comment at the end of *The Amber Spyglass* that 'I have stolen ideas from every book I have ever read'.

MAKE-LIKE – The **Mulefa** word for metaphor. They use the notion of light reflecting off the ripples of water at sunset as a 'make-like' for **Dust** [AS, 17].

MANCHESTER – The **Concilium** of **Jordan College** approves the purchase of an office block in Manchester, paid for from the rents paid to the college for businesses built on college land [NL, 3].

MANDARONE – A wire-strung instrument that serenades lovers, and is played in **Cittàgazze** before the coming of the **Spectres** [SK, 6]. It is probably a kind of mandolin, a musical instrument created in the early eighteenth century and descended from the mandora, a sixteenth-century lute.

MANGANESE AND TITANIUM – An alloy of these two elements is mentioned on numerous occasions, directly and indirectly, in the books. **Lord Asriel** discovers that an alloy of manganese and titanium has the property of insulating the body from the **dæmon**. This leads scientists at **Bolvangar** to create the **silver guillotine** [NL, 16]. Lyra observes that the **window**-cutting blade of the **subtle knife** is made of the same material [SK, 8]. Given the relationship between this alloy and **Dust**, we could guess that the alloy of 'two rare metals', which **Pavel Khunrath** discovers has the mysterious property of pointing to the truth and so used to make the fourth hand of the alethiometer, is the same alloy [Stage play programme]. Equally, an emulsion derived from these metals may be the one used by Lord Asriel in the north that allows him to take **photograms** of Dust [NL, 2].

MARCHPANE – The name for marzipan in **Lyra**'s world [AS, 33]. Marchpane is an archaic world for marzipan derived from the Middle French *marcepain*.

MAYSTADT ANBARIC SCALPEL – A device used in the early attempts by the **Oblation Board** at **intercision** that reduced the death rate from operative shock to below 5 per cent. It was superseded by the **silver guillotine** [NL, 10]. to one of the **ghosts** in the **land of the dead** [AS, 18].

MAYSTADT PROCESS, THE – *See* **Intercision**.

METEORIC IRON – *See* **Sky-metal**.

MINISTRY OF THEOLOGY – A Government department at **White Hall**. **Benjamin de Ruyter** leads his spying party of **gyptians** on an ill-fated break-in at the Ministry. De Ruyter is killed, **Gerard Hook** is captured and **Jacob Huismans** is mortally wounded. **Lord Boreal** is thought to have been a principal member of this department of state [NL, 9].

MUSCOVY – The name for the Soviet Union in **Lyra**'s world [SK, 9].

N

NEGATIVE CAPABILITY – The term for the state of mind required to use **the Cave**, the **alethiometer**, the **subtle knife** and to see the **dæmons** of the people of **Will**'s world. According to **Lyra** it is akin to seeing something from the corner of one's eye [AS, 35].

As **Dr Mary Malone** states, negative capability is a theory put forward by the poet John Keats (1795–1821). In a letter to his brothers George and Thomas Keats dated Sunday, 21 December 1817, Keats wrote: 'I had not a dispute but a disquisition with Dilke, on various subjects; several things dovetailed in my mind, and at once it struck me, what quality went to form a Man of Achievement especially in literature and which Shakespeare possessed so enormously – I mean Negative Capability, that is when man is capable of being in uncertainties, Mysteries, doubts without any irritable reaching after fact and reason.' The last section of this letter is quoted by Mary in *The Subtle Knife* [SK, 4].

Keats was a member of the Romantic movement of the late eighteenth and early nineteenth century. Romanticism was an artistic and intellectual movement that emerged in reaction to the Enlightenment thinkers' belief in the superiority of science and logic. Keats believed that great artists, particularly poets, had the ability to suspend rationality, to accept that some things could not be resolved and thereby to open themselves to experience. In this state – negative capability – one could explore problems rather than seek to resolve them. Keats explored the idea of negative capability in a number of poems including *Ode to a Nightingale* (1819) and his unfinished epic *Hyperion* about the fall of the Titans to the Olympians.

NEW DENMARK – A country in **Lyra**'s world [NL, 5]. **Lee Scoresby** is a New Dane from Texas and we also hear that there is a **New France** that exists outside Europe [NL, 3, 10]. Presumably, the United States of America does not exist but is instead an agglomeration of colonial territories belonging to European powers.

NEW FRANCE – A country in **Lyra**'s world, outside Europe [NL, 3]. *See* **New Denmark**.

NIGHT-GHAST – A nightmare. After changing the coins in the Oratory, **Lyra** has a night-ghast in which three dead scholars, with bloody stumps where their heads should be, stand at her bedside pointing accusingly at her [NL, 3, 9].

NIPPON – The name for Japan in **Lyra**'s world, and the Japanese name for Japan in ours. **Lee Scoresby** believes that the name 'Jopari', given to **Stanislaus Grumman**, might be Nipponese [SK, 6]. The **Imperial Navy** fought a war against the Nippon [SK, 14].

NORHAM GARDENS – A location in **Will**'s **Oxford** [SK, 7].

NORROWAY – A place in the north in **Lyra**'s world, presumably equivalent to our Norway [NL, 10].

NOVA ZEMBLA – A place in the north in **Lyra**'s world where **Stanislaus Grumman** was last heard of alive [SK, 2]. It is also the location of the **Samirsky Hotel**, the occasional host to a number of Arctic drifters including **Sam Cansino** (SK, 6], and the place where **Iorek Byrnison** makes his armour from **sky-metal** after his exile from **Svalbard** [NL, 13].

In our world, the archipelago of Novaya Zemlya is in the Russian part of the Arctic Circle and was the site of atom bomb tests in Soviet times.

NUNIATAK DIG – The name of the fateful expedition, sponsored by the **Institute of Archaelogy**, that hires **John Parry** as a guide. It is during this expedition that John stumbles on the **window** to **Cittàgazze**. Strictly speaking it is a preliminary survey and not a dig [SK, 4].

O

OB – A region near **Nova Zembla**. It is the home of the **Tartars** [SK, 6].

Ob is the name of a major river in western Russia that runs north and west, skirting the western edge of Siberia.

OBLATION BOARD – aka **General Oblation Board, Gobblers, Dusthunters**. An initiative that **Mrs Coulter** establishes and controls. Although sanctioned by the **Consistorial Court of Discipline**, the Oblation Board, like its founder, is not entirely answerable to it [NL, 2]. According to **Professor Docker**, the Oblation Board was established to investigate the reason why **Dust** is attracted to adults and not pre-adolescent children [NL, 5]. The name derives from the mediaeval practice of giving one's children to the Church to become monks or nuns; these children are known as oblates [NL, 5]. The idea was taken up by the Oblation Board who stole children for experimentation. Approximately ten years prior to **Lyra's** adventure, the Oblation Board bought from some **witch** clans the right to establish research stations in witch land. There, under the guise of the Northern Progress Exploration Company, a prospecting organisation supposedly searching for minerals, the Oblation Board began their experiments into

Dust. Early experiments consisted of simply tearing the **dæmon** from the human but this was superseded first by the **Maystadt process** and then the **silver guillotine**. The witches knew the Oblation Board as Dusthunters and regarded **Bolvangar** as a place of hatred and fear [NL, 11]. Children knew them better as Gobblers, a name derived from the initials of the General Oblation Board [NL, 3]. In the aftermath of the second **Fall**, a more liberal faction came to power in the **Magisterium** and the Oblation Board was dissolved [AS, 38].

OPHIUCUS – A constellation across which the **witches** witness a troop of **angels** flying in **Cittàgazze** [SK, 6]. The constellation, more commonly known as Ophiuchus, is also known as the serpent-bearer. Legend has it that Asclepius, the god of medicine and healing, learned the secrets of life and death from serpents. He was killed by Zeus to prevent the human race from becoming immortal. Given the parallels with the story of the **Fall**, and an angry God opposed to the wisdom of the human race, one might presume that Philip Pullman's choice of constellation was significant.

OXFORD – **Lyra**'s home, 'in a universe a lot like ours, but different in many ways'. Lyra's Oxford is a university town, dominated by 21 colleges (there are 39 in our Oxford). **Jordan College**, where Lyra lives, is adjacent to Saint Michael's and **Gabriel**. To the north of the city is **Saint Sophia's** where Lyra studies **alethiometry** under **Dame Hannah Relf**. The other colleges are: Balliol, Broadgates Hall, Cardinal's, Durham, Foxe, Hertford, Magdalen, Merton, Oriel, Queen Philippa's, Saint John's, Saint Edmund Hall, Saint Scholastica's, Brasenose, Somerville, University, Worcester, Wordsworth and Wykeham. Other buildings include Bodley's Library, the Sheldon Theatre, the Ashmolean and University/**Pitt–Rivers Museums**, the Oratory of **Saint Barnabas the Chymist** and the **Botanic Gardens**. Parts of Oxford include **Jericho** and **Port Meadow**. Oxford can be reached by the Rivers Cherwell and **Isis** and was regularly visited by the **gyptians** every year between the spring and autumn fairs. A steam railway service operated between Oxford and London and the **zeppelin** station carried mail to the capital [LO, fold-out map].

Philip Pullman was a student at Exeter College, Oxford, which was the model for Jordan College. He lives in Oxford and has based much of Lyra's world on the Oxford of ours.

OXFORD DIRECTORY – A list of names and addresses in the Oxford area, divided between 'trade' and 'residential' volumes which **Lyra** consults. It is possible that they might also be **telephone** directories, but Lyra doesn't use it for that purpose [LO].

OXPENS, THE – A location near **Lyra**'s **Oxford** where the Royal Mail **zeppelins** set out for London. It is presumably the **aërodock** where **Lord Asriel** lands for his visit to **Jordan College** [NL, 3].

P

PARALLEL WORLDS – The witches of **Lyra**'s world have known about parallel universes for centuries, but the first theologians to prove their existence were excommunicated 50 years before (this is not far from the time when, in our world, Everett put forward his 'many worlds theory' (1956), although the first work on quantum theory, developed by Max Planck, dates from the early 1900s). There are uncountable billions of parallel worlds; far too many for anyone to visit them all. No one thought it was possible to move between worlds until **Lord Asriel** devised a way – again, though some forms of communication between the worlds, such as the **lodestone resonator** exist. The worlds don't match up perfectly – the Arctic of Lyra's world opens onto the Mediterranean (probably Italy) of **Cittàgazze**. A person living in a world other than their own sickens – **Major John Parry** is dying after ten years in Lyra's world.

We see twelve worlds in the course of the trilogy:

1. Lyra's world, where people have **dæmons**.
2. **Will**'s world, 'the universe we know'.
3. The world containing Cittàgazze.
4. The uninhabited world Will sends the **Church**'s bomb to.
5. Asriel's world (where his **fortress** is located).
6. The world of the **land of the dead**.
7. The moonlit world Will travels to in order to rescue Lyra from the Himalayan cave.
8. The world of the **Gallivespians**.
9–11. A world with dunes; one with an industrial landscape and one with strange bison that Will discovers while trying out the **subtle knife** [AS, 2].
12. The world of the **mulefas**.

PEACEABLE OCEAN – The name for the Pacific Ocean in **Lyra**'s world. It is a popular place for 'wave-riders' [AS, 30].

PHILOMEL, SAINT – The order that provides the **Consistorial Court of Discipline** with two stenographers for their enquiry, **Sister Agnes** and **Sister Monica**. Both take a vow of silence [AS, 6].

PHILOSOPHERS' GUILD – Alchemists, philosophers and men of learning, are based in the **Torre degli Angeli** in **Cittàgazze**, who enquire into the 'deepest nature of things'. They become curious about the bonds that hold the smallest particles of matter together [SK, 8]. Three hundred years prior to **Will**'s arrival, they created the **subtle knife** with which they were able to 'undo' these bonds and cut through to other worlds. Aware of the knife's power, but not its own intentions, the philosophers created rules for the **bearer** of the knife: never to open **windows** without closing them after; never to let another use the knife; never to use the knife for a base purpose; and to always keep it secret. The last bearer before Will, **Giacomo Paradisi,** cannot remember if there have been other rules [SK, 8]. Despite these guidelines, previous bearers evidently left windows open – Giacomo confesses to creating and leaving open the window beneath the hornbeam trees in an attempt to lure **Sir Charles Latrom** to his death. Cittàgazze becomes a crossroads between worlds. The philosophers are unaware that with every cut they create a **Spectre** and a means for **Dust** to escape into the **abyss**. In using the knife intensively and carelessly, they unwittingly unleash the Spectres into their own and other worlds, destroying their livelihoods and reducing their city to decay [SK, 9].

PHOTOGRAMS – The equivalent of photographs in **Lyra**'s world. Photograms are usually taken using a silver nitrate emulsion but **Lord Asriel** develops a new emulsion (presumably of titanium and manganese) that allow him to take photograms of the city beyond the **Aurora Borealis** and **Dust** [NL, 2].

PHOTO-MILL – This holy object is kept on the high altar of the Oratory at **Gabriel College** in **Lyra**'s **Oxford**. The device contains a little weathervane with four sails, black on one side and white on the other, which move around when struck by light. The **Intercessor** uses it as an illustration of ignorance fleeing from the light of knowledge [NL, 9]. What Lyra describes here is a Crookes Radiometer, a device created by the Victorian chemist and physicist Sir William Crookes (1832–1919) in the mid-1870s. No one is quite sure how the radiometer works and despite the application of some of the greatest minds to it, including Albert Einstein, the radiometer remains a scientific curiosity. It is believed that photons are not sufficient to move the weathervane, although this is the explanation given to Lyra by the **Librarian** of **Jordan College**.

PILGRIM'S TOWER – Building in **Lyra**'s **Oxford**, adjacent to **Sheldon Building** [NL, 3]. It may be based on Palmer's Tower in Exeter College, Oxford, where Philip Pullman was a student.

PITT–RIVERS MUSEUM – The museum in **Will**'s **Oxford** where **Lyra** finds the trepanned skulls and meets **Sir Charles Latrom** [SK, 12].

The Pitt-Rivers Museum is part of the University of Oxford's Museum of Natural History in Parks Road, Oxford. Permanent displays in the museum are ethnographic and archaeological.

POPPY – Poppy heads are served after feasts at **Jordan College**. The **Master** cooks the poppy heads in butter in a silver chafing dish heated by a spirit lamp. 'Poppy was always served after a Feast: it clarified the mind and stimulated the tongue, and made for rich conversation' [NL, 2].

Chopped opium poppy heads are sometimes used as a narcotic and could explain the effect on the diners.

PORT MEADOW – Part of **Lyra**'s **Oxford**. The Location of a boatyard [NL, 3].

PRE-EMPTIVE ABSOLUTION – Pre-emptive penance and absolution are doctrines researched and developed by the **Consistorial Court of Discipline** but not known to the wider **Church**. The process involves fervent and intense penance, with scourging and flagellation, for a sin not yet committed. Once sufficient penance had been done, the penitent was granted absolution in advance for the sin to be committed. It was developed by the Court to allow assassinations in the name of the Church to be committed in a state of grace. **Father Gomez** had done this penance every day of his adult life and was therefore granted absolution for the murder of **Lyra** [AS, 6].

Pre-emptive absolution is one of those small but immensely clever ideas that are strewn across *His Dark Materials*. The notion provides a rationale for the commitment of sin that is consistent with Church practice yet utterly contrary to the spirit and intention of the scriptures. If ever there was evidence of this Church's corruption it is this.

PROJECTING LANTERN – In **Lyra**'s world, a form of slide projector. The projecting lantern at **Jordan College** runs on oil [NL, 1].

PROPAGANDA – The original Propaganda was a committee set up by the Catholic Church in 1622 to spread (propagate) the faith. So, under the original meaning of the word, Peter Hitchens' assertion that *His Dark Materials* represents 'Anti-Christian propaganda' is a contradiction in terms. The word, though, now has a broader meaning as any work designed to spread a message, usually by telling only one side of the story. *See* atheism.

Q

QUANTUM ENTANGLEMENT BOMB – An immensely powerful explosive that **Dr Cooper** develops for the **Consistorial Court of Discipline** in order to kill **Lyra** and prevent the second **Fall**. Dr Cooper has a device that can direct the bomb towards its target by using the target's genetic code. It is based on the principle of the **Barnard–Stokes** hypothesis. The bomb requires an enormous amount of energy, ultimately provided by the hydro-**anbaric** generating station at **Saint Jean-Les-Eaux** and the severing of **Father MacPhail** from his **dæmon**. The detonation of the bomb in a world adjacent to the land of the dead creates a vast abyss that begins to extract all **Dust** from the worlds [AS, 24, 26].

R

ROLLS-ROYCE – **Sir Charles Latrom**'s large blue car in which he steals the **alethiometer** from **Lyra**. It is driven by **Allan**, Latrom's chauffeur [SK, 7].

ROYAL ARCTIC INSTITUTE – The London-based institution of which **Mrs Coulter** and **Lord Asriel** are both members. Other members include **Colonel Carborn** and **Dr Broken Arrow**. The Institute Library holds an impressive collection of Arctic relics including the harpoon with which **Grimssdur** the whale is killed, a carved stone found in the hands of **Lord Rukh** and a fire-striker used by **Captain Hudson** [NL, 4].

RUSAKOV PARTICLES – *See* **Dust.**

S

SAINT BARNABAS THE CHYMIST, ORATORY OF – An Oratory in **Jericho, Oxford,** with a great square tower [NL, 3]. In our Oxford, the Church of Saint Barnabas is located in Cardigan Street, Jericho, to the west of the city centre. Barnabas was an early experimental theologian who lived in Palmyra in the latter half of the third century. He invented a technique for the purification of fragrant oils and became perfumer-in-chief to Queen Zenobia [LO].

SAINT-JEAN-LES-EAUX – A waterfall plunging between pinnacles of rock at the eastern end of a spur of the Alps. It is the location of a hydro-**anbaric** generating station that the **Church** seeks to use to power **Dr Cooper**'s bomb. The **President** of the **Consistorial Court of Discipline** and **Lord Roke** die here [AS, 24].

SAINT JEROME, COLLEGE OF – An ancient high-towered building in **Geneva,** complete with spire, cloisters and tower, which serves as the chamber of the President of the **Consistorial Court of Discipline. Mrs Coulter** visited the College three times before the events of *The Amber Spyglass*. The College is overlooked by the belfry of the **Chapel of the Holy Penitence** which is located nearby. The guard at the College gatehouse has a pinscher **dæmon** [AS, 6, 24].

SAINT JOHANN, ABBEY OF – An Abbey in **Heidelberg** where **Farder Coram** sees a copy of the book of reading by using **alethiometrists** [NL, 9, 10].

SAINT PHILOMEL, ORDER OF – The order that provides the **Consistorial Court of Discipline** with two stenographers for their enquiry, **Sister Agnes** and **Sister Monica**. Both take a vow of silence [AS, 6]. In our world, there is no Saint Philomel but there is an instructive Greek myth. Philomela was one of two daughters of King Pandion of Athens. Her brother-in-law, Tereus, raped her and had her tongue cut out so that she could not tell her sister what had happened, hence the vow of silence taken by the Order of Saint Philomel. Philomela was turned into a nightingale and today means nightingale in Latin.

SAINT SOPHIA'S – One of the women's colleges at the northern end of **Lyra**'s **Oxford**. Lyra describes it as a 'dingy, brick-built boarding-house of a college' [NL, 4]. The head of Saint Sophia's is **Dame Hannah Relf**, the renowned scholar of the **alethiometer**. On her return to her Oxford, Lyra begins studying the alethiometer at the college [AS, 38]. Lyra uses Saint Sophia's as her home during term time – dinner at seven o'clock is compulsory for all students – but always has her quarters back in Yaxley Quad when she wants them [LO]. Sophia is the gnostic goddess of wisdom and the name means wisdom in Greek. Philip Pullman believes that to strive for wisdom, a state to which we should all aspire, it is necessary for us to lose our state of innocence. The figure of Sophia is crucially important and is discussed further in the entry on the **Fall**.

SAKHALIN – A location where it is claimed that **Stanislaus Grumman** was killed in an avalanche. An Inuit reported the incident to the bartender at the **Samirsky Hotel** [SK, 6]. In fact, Grumman, better known as **Major John Parry**, did not die in this way: he was eventually killed by a **witch**.

SAMIRSKY HOTEL – A hotel at **Nova Zembla**, near the fish-packing station. It is popular with Arctic drifters who stop there to receive news, look for employment or leave messages for each other. **Lee Scoresby** and **Sam Cansino** can both be found at the hotel on occasion. The barman at the hotel is told of **Stanislau Grumman**'s death by an Inuit [SK, 6].

SANT'ELIA – A place in the world of **Cittàgazze** [SK, 3].

SCHOLARS – *See* **Jordan College.**

SEED-PODS – The pods are harvested by the **Mulefa,** and used to produce oil and wheels. **Dust** is collected on the immense trees that are the source of the seed-pods, and the oil they produce is used to create the lenses of the **amber spyglass.**

SEMYONOV RANGE – A mountain range at the foot of which **Lee Scoresby** locates the **Yenesei Pakhtar** tribe of **Tartars** [SK, 6].

SHADOWS – aka **Shadow Particles.** *See* **Dust.**

SHELDON BUILDING – A building in **Lyra's Oxford** with a pearl-green cupola [NL, 4]. The building is Lyra's equivalent of the Sheldonian Theatre, built between 1664 and 1668, and named after Gilbert Sheldon, the Chancellor of Oxford University at the time who funded the construction. The Sheldonian is situated in the grounds of the Bodleian Library, known to Lyra as Bodley's Library.

SIBIRSK – A Regiment of Northern **Tartars** who guard **Bolvangar.** Each soldier has a wolf **dæmon. John Faa** had never met fiercer soldiers [NL, 12].

SILVER GUILLOTINE – *See* **Intercision.**

SISTERS OF OBEDIENCE – An order of nuns based at Watlington. Following **Lord Asriel's** trial for the killing of **Edward Coulter, Lyra** is handed into the custody of the Sisters of Obedience. Asriel, hating all organised religion, rides in one day, takes Lyra and deposits her with the **Master of Jordan College** [NL, 7].

SKY-METAL – aka sky-iron. Metal that falls from the sky, in meteorites according to the **gyptians,** from which the **Svalbard bears** traditionally create their famous armour [NL, 6].

SMOKELEAF – The name for tobacco in **Lyra**'s world [NL, 14]. In **Cittàgazze** it is known as **tabaco** [SK, 6].

SOCIETY OF THE WORK OF THE HOLY SPIRIT – One of the two most active branches of the **Church** in the search for **Lyra**, alongside the **Consistorial Court of Discipline** [AS, 5]. Although once considered impregnable, the **Lady Salmakia** was able to infiltrate the Society and turn on its priests. She convinced the priest's mouse-**dæmon** to perform a forbidden ritual to invoke the presence of Wisdom. At the appropriate point, she appeared before the man and was able to extract information [AS, 5]. The Society had a more skilful **alethiometrist** than **Fra Pavel Rašek** and was therefore more capable of finding Lyra but the **Gallivespians** felt the Society would not act decisively having done so. It was cause for consternation among **Lord Asriel**'s forces when the more determined Consistorial Court came to an agreement with the Society to find and kill Lyra [AS, 9].

SOVIET UNION – aka Union of Soviet Socialist Republics (USSR). Communist state in our world, roughly on the territories of the Imperial Russia, which existed between 1922 and 1991. **Major John Parry** discovers that the Soviets have sent a spy to investigate the **anomaly**. He believes that the spy has been killed by the Eskimo **Matt Kigalik**. The Soviet Union is known as Muscovy in **Lyra**'s world [SK, 5].

SPIRIT WORLD – Eskimo **Matt Kigalik**, believes that the 'anomaly' is a gateway to the spirit world [SK, 5]. **Umaq**, the **Tartar**, who takes **Lee Scoresby** to the **Imperial Muscovite Academy**'s observatory near **Nova Zembla**, claims that **Dr Stanislaus Grumman** might be neither dead nor alive and must therefore be in the spirit world [SK, 6].

SRAF – *See* **Dust**.

STEAM LAUNCH – A vessel in **Lyra**'s world that **Mrs Coulter** uses to transport children who have been abducted by the

Gobblers to the Arctic. It is captained by **Captain Magnusson** [NL, 3].

SUBTLE KNIFE – aka **Æsahættr, teleutaia makhaira**. A mysterious knife created by the **Philosophers' Guild** of the **Torre degli Angeli** in **Cittàgazze**, capable of cutting **windows** between **worlds**. The Guild consists of alchemists, philosophers and men of learning who enquire into the 'deepest nature of things'. They become curious about the bonds that hold the smallest particles of matter together [SK, 8]. Three hundred years prior to **Will**'s journey to Cittàgazze, the philosophers created the subtle knife with which they were able to 'undo' these bonds and cut through to other worlds. Cittàgazze became a cross-road between worlds, as windows were cut and left open. Somehow the Guild's actions brought the **Spectres** upon Cittàgazze and their world fell into decay [SK, 9].

Despite such amazing capabilities, the knife looks nothing special. The cross-piece and the double-edged blade, about eight inches long, appear to be made of a dull metal; the handle is made of common rosewood. On closer inspection, however, one finds that the handle is inlaid with golden wire, moulded into the image of an **angel** with wings folded on one side and an angel with wings upraised on the other. The blade too is not dull but seems to have colours radiating under the surface. 'If there was such a thing as shadow-coloured, it was the blade of the subtle knife' [SK, 8]. The knife is kept in a leather sheath, backed with stiff horn, with buckles that hold the knife in place [SK, 8].

The two edges of the knife are of incomparable sharpness. The steel edge can cut through anything: it slides into the lead roof of the Torre degli Angeli like butter and makes short work of **Iorek Byrnison**'s armour of **sky-metal** [AS, 8]. The 'silvery' edge is just as keen but altogether more subtle. This edge can cut a way out of the world altogether [SK, 8]. **Lyra** believes that the silvery edge is made of the same material as the **silver guillotine** on **Bolvangar**, an alloy of manganese and titanium also used by **Lord Asriel** in taking **photograms** of the city behind the Northern Lights [NL, 2, 16; SK, 8].

Cutting windows between worlds should only be undertaken by the **bearer** of the knife, an individual identified by the loss of his little finger and the finger next to it on his left hand. The knife indicates time to leave one bearer and settle with another by severing the same two fingers on the next bearer, just as Will's fingers were severed [SK, 8]. It is the duty of the bearer's predecessor, in Will's case **Giacomo Paradisi**, to instruct the new bearer in the use of the knife. To create a window, the bearer has to put his mind at the end of the tip and feel for the smallest gap in the world. Giacomo tells Will that he must 'become the tip of the knife' [SK, 8]. Lyra recognises in the instruction the need to find the same state of mind she adopted to read the **alethiometer** and to use **the Cave** – what the poet Keats calls **negative capability**. Once the bearer has found the curious snag, he can make the cut. Over time, Will came to realise that each world had a snag of a different texture: hard and definite; cloudy; slippery; frail and brittle; elastic and resistant. He recognises his own world easier than the rest. Will also discovers that a resonating feeling means that the ground in the other world is on the same level as the one he was in [AS, 2]. He can also only use it when motionless [AS, 9]. The previous bearer was also charged to pass down the rules of the Guild: never open without closing; never let another use the knife; never use it for a base purpose; keep it secret. If there were other rules, Giacomo had long since forgotten them [SK, 8].

Although the philosophers sought to keep it secret, the legend of the subtle knife, or at least its abilities, spread through the worlds. In Cittàgazze, the inhabitants spoke of a mysterious spell that allowed the philosophers to walk through an invisible door into another world. Some believed it was not a spell but a key that could open even when there wasn't a lock [SK, 6]. On Lyra's world, **Major John Parry**'s interest in the Spectres leads him to explore Cittàgazze in his spirit body and to hear more about the knife. As a result, an old hunter in **Tunguska** believes that **Stanislaus Grumman**, John's alter-ego, knows the location of some kind of object that gives protection to whoever holds it [SK, 2]. In creating the spell to heal Will's hand, **Serafina Pekkala** seems to know something of the knife and its origins: 'And when you sliced a single shade / into thirty thousand shadows, / then they knew you were ready / then they called you subtle one' [SK, 13]. The oldest **cliff-ghast** knew the knife as Æsahættr, which **Ruta Skadi** translates as *god-destroyer* [SK, 13]. **Lord Boreal** also knew it by this and another name – *teleutaia makhaira*, 'the last knife of all' [SK, 15].

It is Lord Boreal's desire for the subtle knife, and his theft of the alethiometer, that direct Will and Lyra to get it. Ironically, having the knife enables them to turn the tables on Boreal and to take back the alethiometer. At the same time, John calls **Lee Scoresby** to his tribe of **Tartars** to collect him and take him north to Lord Asriel's world. John, as the shaman of the **Yenesei Pakhtars'** tribe, discovers the importance of the knife and knows that he must find and instruct the bearer in his purpose. John had barely enough time to tell Will to take the knife to Lord Asriel before he was killed by **Juta Kamainen**, a witch he had scorned [SK, 15].

Will's first priority, however, is to rescue Lyra who has been captured by **Mrs Coulter**. With the help of the **angels Balthamos** and **Baruch**, Will finds her in the Himalayan Mountains. En route, he meets Iorek, the newly restored bear king of **Svalbard**, and gains his respect. When they finally find Lyra, Will uses the knife to try to escape but his mind leaves the point. The knife shatters into pieces [AS, 12].

Mending the knife poses moral questions. Iorek certainly has the required skill to repair it but questions the sense in doing so. Iorek sees in the knife the capacity to do unlimited harm; it would be better, he claims, if it had never been made [AS, 14]. He senses that the knife has intentions of its own, intentions that Will cannot know or control. Lyra and Will consult the alethiometer. It indicates that the knife can do both, bad or good, but that this fine balance is in the hands of the bearer. The alethiometer also indicates that the knife will be the death of **Dust** and the only way to keep it alive [AS, 14]. They decide that the knife must be restored. After the repair, the knife looks different: the rosewood handle is charred and scorched; the blade is shorter, with dull silver lines where the pieces have overlapped and sealed together. Will thinks that the knife looks 'wounded' [AS, 15].

Again, Will does not proceed directly to Asriel but instead travels to the **land of the dead**. It is here that the knife fulfils its great destiny in the battle against the **Authority** by cutting a way out of the land of the dead. In so doing, Will puts an end to the Authority's prison camp forever, releasing the **ghosts** of the dead from endless torment and unleashing them against the Spectres [AS, 29]. He is able to use the knife again to cut a window into the world of the **Mulefa** where he and Lyra escape to safety [AS, 31].

It is only later that Will and Lyra come to understand the real nature of the subtle knife and find the truth in Iorek's misgivings. **Xaphania** reveals to their **dæmons** that each window creates a means for Dust to escape into the emptiness outside. Unless closed, Dust will escape forever; previous bearers of the knife had not been diligent. Serafina seems to have a sense of this in her earlier incantation: 'But little knife, what have you done? / Unlocked blood-gates, left them wide!' [SK, 3]. Moreover, with each cut the knife creates a Spectre. It is for this reason that Cittàgazze, the cross-road between worlds, has the most number of Spectres [AS, 37]. In this way, the knife is 'the death of Dust' as the alethiometer indicates but, in releasing the ghosts of the dead and allowing Lyra and Will to escape, it has been its saviour. While Xaphania's angels undertake to close the remaining windows, Asriel's **bridge** and the **abyss**, Will and Lyra return to their own worlds. Back in his own **Oxford,** and thinking of Lyra, Will raises the knife a final time and breaks the blade so it cannot be used again [AS, 38].

SUNDERLAND AVENUE – The street in **Will's Oxford** where the **window** to **Cittàgazze** exists beneath the hornbeam trees. **Giacomo Paradisi** cuts the window to try to lure **Sir Charles Latrom** to his death [SK, 8, 12].

SUNGCHEN – A pass in northern Tibet that links the landing point of the bears to **Lyra's** cave east and south [AS, 9].

SVALBARD – The home of the armoured **bears**, which **Lee Scoresby** describes as 'the bleakest barest most inhospitable godforsaken dead-end of nowhere' [NL, 13]. The area is mountainous, with jumbled peaks and sharp ridges and ravines, carved by slow-moving glaciers and ice-floes. The coast consists of great iron-bound cliffs, thousands of feet tall, and is inhabited by the foul **cliff-ghasts**. The intense cold is broken only by the coal-pits and fire-mines where bearsmiths hammer out sheets of iron for armour [NL, 13]. It was in this inhospitable land that many prisoners – politicians, kings, trouble-makers – had been exiled, among them **Lord Asriel** [NL, 21].

At the edge of the 'interior,' lies the palace of the bear kings which is also referred to as Svalbard. Traditionally, the palace was carved from the ice caves but **Iofur Raknison**, in his bid to become more human, built a marble palace at the location instead. The massive walls of the marble palace were covered with representations of bear victories over the **Skraelings** and the **Tartars**, of prisoners of war working in the fire-mines and zeppelins bringing tribute to Raknison [NL, 19]. To humans, however, the palace was a stinking place, covered in bird droppings and surrounded by a cloying rancid smell [NL, 19]. Inside, the palace had a courtyard, prison and large combat ground where Iofur fought **Iorek Byrnison** and died. Iorek ordered the destruction of the marble palace and a return to the ice caves.

Svalbard is an island that belongs to Norway. The isolated location is surrounded by the Barents Sea to the east, the Greenland Sea to the west and the Arctic Ocean to the north.

SVEDEN – A country in **Lyra**'s world. The **gyptians** have silver cups which come from the mines of Sveden [AS, 38].

SWISS GUARD – Feared infantry troops, loyal to the **Church**. They are white men, armed with cross-bows. Each has a wolf **dæmon** [AS, 9, 13]. The Swiss Guard are probably the blue-uniformed soldiers who battle with **Lee Scoresby** at **Alamo Gulch** [SK, 22].

SYMBOL READER – *See* **Alethiometer**.

T

TABACO – The name for tobacco in **Cittàgazze** [SK, 6].

TELEPHONES – It is stated in the stage play that there are no telephones in **Lyra**'s world, and Lyra doesn't know what a 'phone call' is in the radio version of *The Subtle Knife*. However, the gatehouse of the **College of Saint Jerome** has a telephone and the postern in **Lord Asriel**'s fortress has a telephone-bell in the book of *The Amber Spyglass* [AS, 5, 24].

TELEUTAIA MAKHAIRA – *See* **Subtle knife**.

TOKAY – A 'rich golden wine' in **Lyra**'s world. **Lord Asriel**'s favourite vintage was 1898 which was evidently popular with the **Scholars** at **Jordan College** since they were down to their last three bottles [NL, 1]. It was also popular with **Lord Boreal** [SK, 9] and was drunk at various times by **Mrs Coulter**, **Serafina Pekkala** and **Dr Lanselius**. Tokay is a naturally sweet wine from Hungary.

TORRE DEGLI ANGELI – *See* **Tower of the Angels**.

TOWER OF THE ANGELS – aka Torre degli Angeli. The tower in **Cittàgazze** that is home to the **Philosophers' Guild**. The tower itself is located in a small old square and has a great oak door with worn steps to the entrance. Inside, stone flags and darkened oak steps have been worn smooth by the centuries. At the top there is a glass and wood structure surrounded by sloping lead roofing, which leads to a crenelated parapet. It is here that **Will** and **Lyra** fight **Tullio** to rescue **Giacomo Paradisi**, the **bearer** of the **subtle knife**, who instructs Will in its use [SK, 5].

TROLLESUND – The main port of **Lapland** and the last large conurbation before the frozen wastes. The **Witch-Consulate**, effectively an embassy established by the **witches** in order to maintain contact with the people of the northern lands, is based at **Trollesund** [NL, 10]. It is here that **Lyra** and the **gyptians** first encounter **Iorek Byrnison** whose armour is being held by the local townsmen to keep him in the town and make use of his metalworking skills. **Lee Scoresby** is effectively marooned at Trollesund when the expedition he expects to join runs out of funds before it leaves Amsterdam. Lee is recruited by **John Faa** to help the gyptian raid on **Bolvangar**. Trollesund has also been visited by the witch **Yelena Pazhets** and her **dæmon** at some time [LO].

TRUTH MEASURE – *See* **Alethiometer**.

TUNGUSKA CAMPAIGN – A campaign in which **Lee Scoresby** and **Iorek Byrnison** fight side by side [NL, 11]. During this campaign Scoresby rescues Iorek from the Tartars who surrounded his ice-fort [NL, 13].

TURKESTAN – A country in **Lyra**'s world. The **gyptians** had silken tapestries from Turkestan [AS, 38].

TURKISH AMBASSADOR – **Lyra** tells the **gyptian** children an elaborate story about the Turkish Ambassador being forced to drink his own poison [NL, 8].

U

UMIAT – A town in Alaska where **Major John Parry** wrote a letter to his wife on 22 June 1985 [SK, 5].

UPPSALA – A location where **Farder Coram** sees an **alethiometer** being read by a wise man [NL, 7].

V

VAN TIEREN'S LAND – A region in the north of **Lyra**'s world. **Captain Hudson** famously visited there [NL, 4].

VODKA – The preferred drink of **Father Semyon Borisovitch** who introduces it to **Will** [AS, 8].

VOLGORSK – The home of a few renegade **witches** who help the **Gobblers** even after the nature of the experiments at **Bolvangar** are known [SK, 2].

W

WATLINGTON – The location of the convent of the **Sisters of Obedience** [NL, 7].

WHITE HALL PALACE – A Palace where the King holds his weekly **Council of State** [NL, 3]. In our world, the Palace of Whitehall was the principal residence of the English monarch from 1530 to 1698 when it was largely destroyed by fire. In the seventeenth century it was the largest palace in Europe, bigger even than Versailles, with more than 1500 rooms. Almost all that remains today is the Banqueting House, designed by architect Inigo Jones in 1619 and completed in 1622.

WHITE HAM – A wood to the west of **Lyra's Oxford** [NL, 3].

WINCHESTER – A city in Hampshire where Will and his mother Elaine live [SK, 4].

WINDOWS – The name given by **Will** to those gateways between **worlds** created by the **subtle knife** [SK, 1]. Windows are hard to see and only 'spring into being' when approached from the side [AS, 14]. Only the **angels** are able to find them easily. The majority of windows originated in **Cittàgazze** where the subtle knife had been created by the **Philosophers' Guild** of the **Torre degli Angeli**. The **bearer** of the knife can cut a window using the silver-edged blade and can close it using his fingers. However, unbeknown to the Philosophers, each cut creates a **Spectre** and each window left open allows **Dust** to escape into the **abyss**: the Philosophers' Guild, in using the knife carelessly, brought about their own destruction. **Lord Boreal** knew the location of many windows but these shifted once **Lord Asriel** created his **bridge** [SK, 9]. Indeed, Lord Asriel's bridge and the abyss created by the **Consistorial Court of Discipline**'s bomb are simply larger windows, which have a more dramatic impact on the loss of Dust from the **parallel worlds**. In 2006, *Doctor Who* borrowed heavily the concept that a window between parallel worlds left open could result in the end of the universe. At the conclusion of the 'Doomsday' episode of *Doctor Who*, this rift is closed, leaving the Doctor in our world and his companion, Rose, trapped forever in another – in the same way as will and Lyra are parted.

WITCH-CONSUL – *See* **Dr Martin Lanselius**.

WORLD OF THE DEAD – *See* **Land of the dead**.

WORLDS – *See* **Parallel worlds**.

Y

YARNTON – There is an 'Anbaric Park' on the way to **Yarnton**, near **Lyra's Oxford** [NL, 2].

YARROW STALKS – *See* **I-Ching**.

YENESEI RIVER – A river in the north. After **Lord Asriel** creates the **bridge**, strange atmospheric disturbances change the landscape and the river is unusually free from ice [SK, 6].

   The Yenesei River, also spelled Yenisay or Enisei, is one of the longest rivers in Asia. It runs from south to north across central Siberia. Its name means 'great river'.

YORUBA – A nationality in **Lyra's** world. One of the members of the **Imperial Muscovite Academy**'s observatory at Nova

Zembla was a Yoruba [SK, 6]. In our world, Yoruba is a language used in the region of southwest Nigeria and some parts of Togo and Benin.

Z

ZAAL – The ancient wooden meeting hall on the **Byanplats** in the **fens** of **Eastern Anglia,** where the **gyptians** traditionally held their Ropings. The hall has eight carved wooden chairs reserved for the gyptian leader, **John Faa,** the heads of the six gyptian families and **Farder Coram.** There is also a separate 'parley room' for private discussions [NL, 7].

ZALIF – An individual of the **Mulefa** race. **Dr Mary Malone** notices that the word is pronounced slightly differently depending on the sex of the zalif in question [AS, 10].

ZENOBIA, SS – A cruise-liner, owned by the Imperial Orient Shipping Line, which offers trips to the Orient [LO].

ZEPPELIN – A form of air transport common in **Lyra**'s world. The Royal Mail use zeppelins to transport parcels across England [NL, 3]. **Lord Asriel** travels to **Jordan College** by zeppelin [NL, 1], and in the stage version he scandalises the **scholars** by mooring it to the steeple of the college chapel. Both the **Church** and Asriel's forces use zeppelins in the war with the **Authority.** They are powered by gas engines that give a low incessant drone [NL, 8].

In our world, the zeppelin was created by Count Ferdinand von Zeppelin (1838–1917) in the early twentieth century. They fell out of favour after the Hindenburg Disaster (6 May 1937) when the Zeppelin Hindenburg was destroyed in flame as it attempted to moor in New Jersey. The outbreak of the Second World War soon put an end to the zeppelin as a form of air travel.

3. BEYOND THE BOOKS

Like the windows between Lyra's world and others, Pullman's *His Dark Materials* novels offer curious ways in to grand concepts and the work of other writers. Where possible, we've included these references and notes in the entries in the preceding chapters. In this chapter, we look at some of the big themes that are waiting to be explored.

A

ATHEISM – The definition of an atheist is 'someone who doesn't believe in gods'. *His Dark Materials* has been described as 'atheist', but even a glance at it demonstrates that it's a story set firmly in a universe with God, souls, **angels** and an afterlife. *His Dark Materials* is steeped in religious imagery, and demonstrates familiarity with some of the more obscure parts of the Bible. The books take cues and imagery from, amongst others, the work of **John Milton**, **William Blake** and **C. S. Lewis**. Those three writers were very different people, living at different times and their relationship with their religion was often complicated and individualistic, but all three could fairly be described as committed Christians whose best known works

were an exploration of their faith. Significantly, every character in the *His Dark Materials* trilogy takes the existence of God
for granted – there's not one atheist to be found anywhere in
the books. Using the straightforward definition of the word
'atheist', *His Dark Materials* plainly doesn't qualify as godless,
quite the opposite. As Erica Wagner, literary editor of *The
Times* has said, if you take the religion out of the story, 'it is
hard to see what will be left of the whole'.

'Atheist', though, also has a more narrow definition: 'someone who denies traditional religion'. Often, the rulers of a
society would follow a particular god or gods, and if people
didn't follow the same religion, they would be punished for
challenging the social order. Indeed, in Ancient Rome, there's
evidence that early Christians were called atheists. Nowadays
though, in the West, an atheist would be someone who has come
to reject the Christian God's message or the methods of his
followers. For a long time, there have been two main lines of
attack for this kind of atheist thought. The first concerns God,
who is said to be all-powerful, even though there is a lot of
suffering and injustice in the world. If God exists, He could use
his great power to stop suffering. As he hasn't, we might
conclude He is either rather cruel or doesn't care what happens
to human beings – the exact opposite of what Christianity
teaches. The second criticism is more concerned with worldly
matters: the Church, far from being an organisation that inspires
people, is one that scares them into behaving or facing divine
punishment. The Church takes for itself a lot of wealth and
power – bishops and popes preach to us about how we should
live modest lives, but they themselves live in huge palaces. Both
criticisms lead to the same conclusion: instead of making life
better, God and the Church actually make life worse.

Self-evidently, *His Dark Materials* falls into this latter
category. It's difficult to find any sign that religion is a good or
remotely positive thing in the trilogy – the **Church** will do
anything in its self interest: it systematically and deliberately
abuses children, accumulates wealth and sanctions murder.
Those characters who have thought about theology for themselves, rather than just follow what the Church has told them

to do, have renounced their faith. Those people, from **Lord Asriel** to **Dr Mary Malone,** have been enriched and empowered as a result, gained a new and more truthful sense of purpose. Not only that, *The Amber Spyglass* manages to have its cake and eat it by having **Metatron** fulfil the role of the cruel, anti-human God, and the **Authority** as the feeble, neglectful one. The only possible pro-religion argument is that as modern schools and children's entertainment are almost entirely secular, reading Philip Pullman's books at least exposes young readers to questions of faith and religion.

Chris Weitz, the director of the movie version of *Northern Lights* suggested that the Authority could 'represent any arbitrary establishment that curtails the freedom of the individual, whether it be religious, political, totalitarian, fundamentalist, communist, what have you'. In the original books, this is not true. Whatever else communists did, they didn't rule in Heaven, surrounded by angels or control the afterlife, as the Authority is seen to. Weitz would have had a stronger case if he had talked about the **Magisterium** – but even that is steeped in religion, and closely resembles a Christian organisation – there are references to saints, clerics are referred to as 'brother' and 'father', there are chaplains and there are chapels and Churches.

In 1999, before *The Amber Spyglass* was published, Leonie Caldecott wrote an article for the *Catholic Herald* in which she stated that the first two books left children 'with a serious case of conceptual contamination'. If the piece was an attempt to deny Pullman's argument that the Church is wont to ruthlessly suppress any criticism, then it might have been more effective if she hadn't started by suggesting the books were among those 'worthy of the bonfire'. When the third book appeared the following year, whether by coincidence or not, it contained a scene where Lord Asriel reminds us that the Church has long had an instinct to burn those it disagrees with.

Peter Hitchens described the books in a *Mail on Sunday* article as 'deliberate anti-Christian propaganda', but it's not as straightforward as that. Jesus is only mentioned twice, in Chapter 33 of *The Amber Spyglass*, as Mary Malone (who is from our world) recounts her life story. In **Lyra**'s world, there are no references to even the most everyday Christian images, like the crucifix. The *Harry Potter* books are almost simplistically secular, but the wizards of Hogwarts celebrate Christmas – the holiday is never mentioned in any of the books of the *His Dark Materials* trilogy and in the stage play Lyra does not know who **Father Christmas** is. This almost appears coy in places – while characters can utter a relieved 'Thank God' or talk about a place being 'godforsaken' [NL, 9 and 13 respectively], all the talk of religion confines itself to talking about 'the Authority', rather than 'God'. While there are echoes of some apocryphal Christian stories – like the **Harrowing of Hell**, most of the theology comes from the Old Testament, rather than the New. Despite that, it would be disingenuous to suggest that the novels weren't addressing specific aspects of Christian theology. While the story of Adam and Eve occurs in both Judaism and Islam, neither has the same emphasis on the **Fall**. But it's not just an attack on 'Christianity', let alone one type of Christianity. While the **Magisterium** strongly resembles the Catholic Church at the height of its powers, it explicitly isn't the Catholic Church – we're told early in Northern Lights that the Papacy and the bishops have been abolished. It is not a specific institution being criticised, it is all organised religion. The books are concerned with the fundamentals of all religions, using Christianity as a fertile source of mythical, historical and theological examples of bad practice.

The books dramatise the two strands of atheist criticism. The Authority has chained human imagination and freedom, then grown feeble – God is something that needs to be removed if humanity wishes to progress. Down on Earth, the Church is totalitarian, concerned only with maintaining its grip on power. Many writings separate criticisms of God and the Church, or 'organised religion'. The most vehement opponents of churches' behaviour are often the members of that religion, not outsiders. The history of Christianity is full of critics of the Church leaving to form their own version of the faith, which they feel to be closer to Jesus' teachings. For the first two books, it looks like *His Dark Materials* may be heading this way – at the end of *Northern Lights*, Lord Asriel initially talks only about 'the end of the Church ... the end of the Magisterium', not an end to God. So do the books solely criticise 'organised religion'? A number of critics and reviewers of *The Subtle Knife* wondered if the story was heading towards revealing God to be a benevolent force, after all, one whose message had been twisted and hidden by the Church.

In *The Amber Spyglass*, though, Pullman neatly inverts the received wisdom when we finally meet the Authority. Christians have often stated that the problem is that men have neglected God's teachings. Atheists would counter that God seems to have neglected men – to the point that there's no evidence he even exists, let alone that he is benevolent. In either case, if God exists, there is a disconnection between human beings and God, and the solution would seem to lie in more direct contact between man and God. For the original Authority, such contact with a pair of small children ends in His swift death. From there, though, we move to the nightmare scenario. As the new Authority, Metatron is going to make direct contact between God and man – to 'intervene directly in human life' – but this God is vicious and is going to commit all the atrocities that in previous times were 'left to his priests'. Critics of the Church, in our world, have wondered how a benevolent God could allow the Church to do terrible things in His name. The answer in *The Amber Spyglass*, one with a logical consistency if nothing else, is that the Church may be cruel and terrible, but is merely a pale shadow of the cruelty and terror of God Himself. Metatron, we are told, believes that 'the Churches in every world are corrupt and weak ... they compromise too readily'. The message is clear: mankind is better off without either the Church or God.

B

BLAKE, WILLIAM – An English poet, engraver and visionary, who lived from 1757 to 1827. Blake is a huge influence on *His*

Dark Materials, one of the three sources Philip Pullman acknowledges at the end of *The Amber Spyglass*. Blake had a distinctive style of writing and illustration (the latter can be seen on the cover of this book), and used his work to explore the relationship between God and man. He had a complex set of beliefs that, while definitely Christian, were highly personal and aren't always open to easy interpretation. There are three main areas where Pullman draws on Blake's work.

The first is in the portrayal of the **Authority**. Blake's writings about God were particularly obscure and academics have argued about their exact meaning, but essentially he broke God down into a number of distinct aspects, or Zoas, which he gave his own names to. The Authority seems to be closely based on one of these, Urizen, seen in a number of Blake's works, like *The Four Zoas*, *Milton* and *The Book of Urizen*. He is depicted as a contradiction – an ancient man with a long white beard whose body is somehow both athletic and emaciated. When we finally see the Authority in *The Amber Spyglass*, he is the spitting image of the enfeebled Urizen seen in Blake's engravings. Urizen represents the lawmaking and avenging aspects of God, a builder and driver of a chariot. He planted the Garden of Eden. Some academics have suggested that Urizen represents an aspect of God that falls to become Satan – Blake describes him as 'Creator of men, mistaken demon of Heaven', and portrays him declaring pridefully 'Now I am God from Eternity to Eternity.' Pullman also draws on another aspect of God discussed by Blake, Nobodaddy 'the Father of Jealousy', a being falsely worshipped by many in our world as God and portrayed in *To Nobodaddy*.

Philip Pullman, though, sidelines another two main aspects of God that Blake concerns himself with. It was becoming increasingly fashionable in his time to believe that God created the universe and man, but that He was an impersonal, abstract being who didn't interfere with his Creation. It was not possible to understand God or communicate with Him through prayers or rituals. This belief was known as Deism and was held by – amongst others – many of the founding fathers of the United States of America. It was a 'scientific' explanation of how the world and human beings came to exist in an era with no understanding of evolution or the big bang theory. Blake personally hated this ultra-rational idea of God, demanding a more direct, personal type of religion throughout his work. Pullman draws a distinction between the Authority and the Creator, but essentially dodges the issue. Central to Blake's own concept of God, entirely missing from Pullman's, is the notion that, as Blake put it himself, 'God is Jesus', that the controlling instinct of the divine is love, and that God has a profound and passionate understanding of, and connection with, human life.

Blake was a revolutionary, living through the time of the American and French Revolutions, and fervour for social change infuses his work. When **Lyra** ends the *His Dark Materials* series by calling for the founding of the **Republic of Heaven**, there's more than an echo of Blake's poem *Milton*, (more popularly known as the hymn *Jerusalem*), which declared 'I will not cease from mental fight, / nor shall my sword sleep in my hand, / Till we have built Jerusalem / In England's green and pleasant land'. Blake had republican sympathies, but it's hard to imagine he would have taken those as far as Pullman.

Blake's main influence on Pullman comes from his notions of **innocence and experience**. Blake explored these most thoroughly in two linked collections of poetry, *The Songs of Innocence* and *The Songs of Experience*. Blake never defines his terms, but we can see from the poems that children are born into a state of innocence, characterised as a carefree existence full of play, adventure, sunlight, song, comfort and security. Experience is, by contrast, concerned with duty, commerce, desire, politics and death. It is utterly impossible, by definition, to go back to innocence, once you have knowledge of experience, so children should be protected from the often harsh and exploitative adult world. This is a conventional enough view of childhood, and harks back to Adam and Eve's carefree life in Eden (and their loss of it after the **Fall**). Blake and Pullman agree where others might not, though, that for human beings to grow into adults, they must inevitably abandon the state of innocence. To try to prevent the loss of innocence, or to artificially preserve it or return to it, is restrictive, the sign of a stunted spiritual life, not a healthy one.

While they can be read independently, if you read *The Songs of Innocence and Experience* together, you see that some of the poems gain new meanings. 'The Lamb', in *Innocence*, is almost a nursery rhyme about how God created sweet little lambs – but the same God also made 'The Tyger' of *Experience*, a warlike, almost demonic creature. One of the most obvious links is between the poems 'A Little Girl Lost' and 'A Little Girl Found'. The girl in 'The Little Girl Lost', incidentally, is called Lyca. Pullman uses the same sort of dynamic for the structure of *The Amber Spyglass*. In that novel, stories that aren't always directly connected deal with the same themes and inform each other. For example, while **Dr Mary Malone** and **Lord Asriel** never meet, they both, in their very different ways, rebel against God, study **Dust** and come to conclusions about free will. They both see how important Lyra is, and play central roles in her destiny. Pullman – like Blake – leaves the reader to make the association. None of the characters in the *His Dark Materials* books – not even Will or Lyra – get the same panoramic view of events as the reader, but Pullman doesn't spell out the links, or his own conclusions. Blake and Pullman, it seems obvious to say, both have strong opinions, but this method of storytelling genuinely leaves a great deal of room for their readers' individual interpretations, and maintains a lot of moral ambiguities for the complex issues under discussion.

Finally, Blake was the man who first said **John Milton** 'was of the devil's party without knowing it' when he wrote *Paradise Lost*. Pullman has often mentioned the quote in interviews, saying he himself is knowingly of the devil's party.

F

FALL, THE – The Fall refers to the expulsion of Adam and Eve from the Garden of Eden. In the Bible, (Genesis, Chapters

2 and 3 – quoted by **Lord Asriel,** NL, 21) God tells Adam and Eve that they can eat the fruit of any tree in the garden except that of the tree of knowledge. Satan, disguised as a serpent, tells Eve that she will not die for eating from this tree and adds that 'God doth know that in the day ye eat thereof, then your eyes shall be opened, and ye shall be as gods, knowing good and evil.' Eve is tempted, Adam follows and from then on they know shame. They are expelled from Eden. In the New Testament, Paul explains that, by his actions, Adam had brought sin and death into the world (Romans, 5:12). This led Aurelius Augustine (354–430, better known as Saint Augustine) to develop the doctrine of original sin, the belief that Adam's Fall and its effects were passed on through generations. While original sin was rejected by Judaism, it became the central tenet of Catholic Christianity.

At the core of *His Dark Materials* is a radically different interpretation of the Fall. Philip Pullman argues that the Fall was a necessary and desirable stage in the evolution of humankind. The loss of innocence was necessary for humans to acquire wisdom: 'innocence is not wise, and wisdom cannot be innocent'. The fixing of one's **dæmon** symbolises that moment in life when one passes from a state of innocence – or ignorance as Pullman would say – to a state of experience and knowledge. Pullman therefore fundamentally opposes the notion of original sin, rejecting outright that the Fall was anything other than essential.

Behind this picture of the specifics of the Fall is an alternative creation myth. Pullman states that this is partly based on the gnostic tradition, a term used to describe a number of religious sects that operated in the first century after Christ. According to the gnostics, our world was created by a Demiurge or false God who set himself up as the true authority. The true creator is far off and unknowable. Those of us who are conscious must fight to get out of our cruel and sinful world and reach the true one. Critical in the gnostic tradition is Sophia, the goddess of wisdom, and her role in the Garden of Eden. Sophia sent a message to humankind by way of the serpent and thereby gave them *gnosis*, knowledge. This enraged the Demiurge who cast Adam and Eve out of the Garden. For gnostics, the Fall was not the origin of sin but the enlightenment. The name Sophia, which is Greek for 'wisdom', is derived from the Hebrew *SephanyAh* – or **Xaphania** in *His Dark Materials*.

If one digs further, we can perhaps find more clues in the gnostic tradition to the origins of dæmons. In one gnostic story, Sophia sought knowledge of the true creator and in her longing brought matter and soul into the universe, created from the classical elements (earth, air, fire and water). Ignorant of Sophia, the Demiurge created the physical world and humankind. Only later was Sophia able to breathe knowledge into the world and its people, knowledge that would ultimately enable beings to return to the nothingness from which all things had come. Here we have clear distinction being made between three parts of the human being: matter, soul and knowledge – or body, dæmon and consciousness/ghost. Pullman has said that in his creation myth, Sophia 'comes to human beings at a certain stage in their evolution and helps them to realise who they are'. This is the moment when **Dust** is attracted to human beings and their dæmons fix, a personal Fall that happens to us all.

FREE WILL – Free will is the philosophical doctrine that holds that individuals determine their own actions and that these are not predetermined by some wider purpose or intention. Advocates argue that we must be able to choose our own actions because if we cannot, then whatever we do will make no difference to the grander scheme of things, will not influence our redemption or damnation in religious terms. Ultimately, it is a discussion of moral responsibility. The opposing doctrine is determinism.

In *His Dark Materials*, Philip Pullman explores the notion of free will through **Lyra** and particularly **Will**. The world is a very deterministic place. **Jotham Santelia** tells Lyra that 'the universe is full of *intentions*, you know. Everything happens for a purpose' [NL, 19]. Moreover, **Serafina Pekkala** states that Lyra must fulfil her destiny without knowing, otherwise 'death will sweep through all the worlds' [NL, 18]. Likewise, the **gyptians** and even the **Master of Jordan College** have prophecies about Lyra, while **John Parry** knows Will's destiny as the **bearer**. All would seem argue against free will. And yet Pullman throughout argues forcibly for moral responsibility.

The answer seems to come relatively early in the trilogy. In *Northern Lights*, Serafina tells **Lee Scoresby** that 'we are all subject to the fates. But we must all act as if we are not … or die of despair' [NL, 18]. Will is the one who grasps this notion. When **Xaphania** tells him that he has work to do in his world, he decides not to know. Will decides that knowing his destiny may make him resent his lack of freedom, or make him feel guilty should he not follow his calling. 'Whatever I do, I will choose it, no one else.' Free will is an illusion but a necessary one if there is to be moral responsibility. Xaphania observes that Will has taken the first steps towards wisdom [AS, 37].

H

HARROWING OF HELL – A story from the apocryphal Gospel of Nicodemus. From the time of Adam and Eve to the time of Jesus' birth, all human souls without exception went to Hell, as no one can enter Heaven without knowing Jesus. After the Crucifixion, Jesus enters Hell, binds Satan, frees those who are worthy and leads them to Heaven. The story was very popular in the Middle Ages and is the likely template for **Lyra**'s journey to the **land of the dead**.

I

INNOCENCE AND EXPERIENCE – A central concept in *His Dark Materials* is the distinction between the unselfconscious state of childhood, and the pragmatism of adulthood. This is one of the key areas where Philip Pullman draws on the works of **William Blake**, but he develops his own unique, sophisticated and somewhat problematic system.

Most children's fiction places a great value on childhood and assumes that it is desirable to preserve young people in that state for as long as possible. The most obvious example is Peter Pan, a boy who never grows up, but Peter is actually depicted as more than a little spiteful and selfish, not some ideal of childhood innocence. Better examples, including one that is the particular target of Pullman's ire, can be found in the Narnia books of C. S. Lewis.

Like Blake, Pullman sees the loss of innocence as being a normal, even positive, development for a human being. When **Will** meets **Mrs Coulter**, like many of the other male characters, he feels attracted to her. The reason he gives is very telling – 'she seemed like a more complicated and richer and deeper **Lyra**' [AS, 11]. Mrs Coulter loses her innocence, but gains a great deal in return.

Innocence, for Pullman, certainly doesn't mean perfection. Lyra and Will demonstrate that it is possible to lie, steal, question, take responsibility, disobey authority, plot and kill – indeed, commit deicide – while remaining 'innocent'. Lyra's discussions with her **dæmon Pantalaimon** show that she's fully aware of the consequences of her actions, she's *au fait* with the adult world of politics and debate, and that she has a highly developed sense of right and wrong. Will feels guilty for killing a man.

In *His Dark Materials*, the dæmons are a concrete sign of the loss of innocence: children have ever-changing dæmons, and their transition to adulthood is marked by the point when their dæmons fix into one shape. This is simple and accepted by the people of Lyra's world, but it's a problematic concept for us. Can you really mark, to the second, when you stop being a child and become an adult? We're more used to thinking in terms of adolescence; a gradual and erratic process that's different for everyone. A dæmon becoming fixed is not a substitute or synonym for puberty, as that concept is known to the people of Lyra's world. At the very least, there's a case to be made that Lyra's dæmon becomes fixed when she loses her virginity (*see* **Sex**) . . . but presumably, if that was the same for everyone, then some adults (and at the very least, a large proportion of the celibate clergy) would go to their graves with changing dæmons.

Philip Pullman links the concept of innocence to that of **Dust** – and seems to define it in terms of self-consciousness. In the world of the **Mulefa,** towards the end of *The Amber Spyglass*, Lyra swims naked. She has done so many times before, with other children, but she is aware that had Will been with her, it would now have meant something different. It marks a point when a carefree child becomes awkward and self-aware. Around that time, Lyra loses the ability to read the **alethiometer,** but can learn to use it again with discipline and effort.

K

KLEIST, HEINRICH VON – Along with **William Blake** and **John Milton,** one of the three writers Philip Pullman cites as a major influence on *His Dark Materials* in his afterword to *The Amber Spyglass*. His essay 'On the Marionette Theatre' concerns **innocence and experience,** showing how puppets, those who are unselfconscious, and even a bear, possess a grace and ease that it is impossible to deliberately emulate.

L

LEWIS, C. S. – While not cited by Philip Pullman as an influence at the end of *The Amber Spyglass* (unlike **Milton, Blake** and **Kleist**), reviewers were quick to compare *His Dark Materials* to the Narnia books of C. S. Lewis. When Andrew Marr said that 'Pullman does for atheism what C. S. Lewis did for God' (*Daily Telegraph* 24 January 2002), it was meant approvingly. This wasn't the case when Peter Hitchens de-clared Pullman to be the 'anti-Lewis' and the trilogy an attempt to 'dethrone' him. Hitchens' argument – expounded in similar articles for the *Mail on Sunday* (27 January 2002) and the *Spectator* (18 January 2003) – is that the Narnia stories represented a stubborn survival of Christian values in the teaching of children, and that 'the liberal intelligentsia' have used *His Dark Materials* to push their own 'politically correct' agenda, where the good guys 'are gypsies, an African prince, a homosexual angel and a renegade nun'. It's clear that any analysis of Pullman's trilogy needs to address Lewis.

Clive Staples Lewis was born in 1898, and died the same day as President Kennedy in 1963. He was an academic and critic first and foremost, a professor at **Oxford**, then Cambridge. He wrote a great deal, including science fiction and moral essays. His most famous works, though, are the seven volumes of the Narnia stories, which started with *The Lion, the Witch and the Wardrobe* in 1950, and ended with *The Last Battle* in 1956. Each of the books can be seen as a retelling of a specific Christian story, although this was certainly filtered through Lewis's imagination – in the first book, Aslan's self-sacrifice and resurrection have obvious parallels with the crucifixion and resurrection of Christ, but this jostles with **Father Christmas**, fauns and dryads from Greek myth and monsters from Scandinavian legend.

Beyond the standard features of a lot of children's novels, like talking animals and doorways to other worlds, it's hard to point to that many specific parallels between the Narnia books and *His Dark Materials*. **Mrs Coulter**'s offer of chocolate to **Lyra** might spark memories of the White Witch giving Turkish Delight to Edmund, but it's hardly enough to justify links between the two writers. Pullman has made no bones about his loathing for some of Lewis's moral values, though, and his books seem to be a reaction against them in places. Pullman is right that Lewis's depiction of the Calormen feels racist nowadays, but it's hardly the worst example from a 1950s' children's book. The charges of sexism have even less basis to them – while Lewis starts *The Silver Chair* with a little rant against co-education in schools, there are always as many girls as boys on the adventures, and all the children are equally blessed with the two virtues he seemed to value more than any other: bravery and being sensible.

Pullman is on firmer ground when he talks about specifics. He has mentioned Susan's fate in *The Last Battle* a number of times. Susan was the older of the two girls in *The Lion, the Witch and the Wardrobe*. In the final book, the other three children return to Narnia – as do all the children from all the earlier books – but Susan is 'no longer a friend of Narnia' and is 'interested in nothing nowadays except nylons and lipstick and invitations. She always was a jolly sight too keen on being grown up.' Narnia is destroyed, but not before Aslan has ushered them into an 'inner' Narnia, 'as different as a real thing is from a shadow . . . it's all in **Plato**, all in Plato: bless me'. On the last page, it's revealed that all the children but Susan have died in a railway accident. The ending is meant to be uplifting, 'Chapter One of the Great Story which no one on earth has read', but it's undoubtedly problematic. Pullman finds it repellent that Susan is denied entry into Heaven simply for growing up. It's interesting to note that, according to Lewis's own *Outline of Narnian History so far as it is known*, Susan is 21 years old at this point. *The Amber Spyglass* might be read as a response to *The Last Battle* – in both, there is a final, apocalyptic conflict between good and evil, and there's a sense that the fantasy land is damaged and coming to an end. At the end of *The Amber Spyglass*, though, the conclusions are completely different. The children are the masters of their own destiny, the god-figures are dead, there's a concentration on individual responsibility and building a future, the world has been healed . . . possibly as a direct result of two people who are barely teenagers having **sex**.

There is certainly something in Hitchens' analysis that Pullman is the 'anti-Lewis', although he's operating a double standard when he praises Lewis as 'the most influential Christian in modern British culture' but criticises Philip Pullman for being a 'propagandist'. It's interesting that Lewis's science fiction mixes science, religion and myth – *That Hideous Strength*, for example, has a nasty organisation that brings science and Satanic power together in an attempt to exert control over mankind. These have a similar tone to Philip Pullman's books, and a concern with the **Fall**, although the moral compass is almost exactly reversed. Ultimately, Pullman is firm that his story promotes healthy and useful values for children. The irony is that while Lewis and Pullman come to polar opposite conclusions, they are enjoyed for the same reasons Marr identifies: 'I want my children to read him for a reason that Lewis would have understood – because they will be better people afterwards.' Both Lewis and Pullman are telling very moral stories about children looking for answers to big religious questions.

M

MILTON, JOHN – The poet who wrote *Paradise Lost*, the epic poem that serves as the main source for *His Dark Materials* (indeed Philip Pullman's original idea for the trilogy was as a retelling of Milton's poem). Milton lived from 1608–74, and was a Puritan at the time of the English Civil War and Oliver Cromwell's Commonwealth. Milton survived the fall of Puritanism. He suffered a progressive form of blindness. *Paradise Lost* was published in 1667. In it, Milton concerned himself with 'man's first disobedience', the **Fall**. His retelling of Satan's rebellion against God makes the rebel angel a compelling and rather sympathetic character, leading **William Blake** to remark that Milton 'was of the Devil's party' although he didn't know it.

Pullman's debt to *Paradise Lost* is immense, from the broad sweep of the depiction of the Fall to tiny details like Finland being home to **witches**.

O

ORIGINAL SIN – *See* **Fall**.

P

PARADISE LOST – *See* **John Milton**.

PLATO – Plato was a student of Socrates and the teacher of Aristotle with whom he laid the foundations for Western philosophical thought. The influence of Plato can be seen in three aspects of *His Dark Materials*.

First, and most obviously, Plato is directly referenced in **Dr Mary Malone**'s explanation of the **Cave**. Plato develops the notion of the Cave in his *Socratic Dialogues* to explain ideas of perception and knowledge (see the entry on the Cave for further information).

Second, in *Timaeaus*, Plato explores the idea of the Demiurge; a deity who shapes the material world but is not the Supreme Creator. Plato describes the Demiurge as good although presiding over an imperfect world created from chaotic matter. This false God is picked up in the thinking of the gnostics, who believe the Demiurge to be antagonistic to the will of the Supreme Creator. This is one of the inspirations for the **Authority**.

Third, and also in *Timaeaus*, Plato discusses the idea of **dæmons**. Plato says that there is a world-soul of which all individual souls are a subset. Individual souls have two parts: one physical, as in the human soul, and one with no physical presence. The latter are called dæmons and are thought to carry messages between gods and humans. This notion of dæmons originally came from Socrates, Plato's teacher, who said that he had a personal spirit, or *daimonion*, who warned him of events. It is commonly understood to mean intuition.

This division of what we might term the soul into two parts is interesting given Philip Pullman's statement that both the ghost and the dæmon are part of the soul [Radio 4's *Devout Sceptics*, 9 August 2001]. Following Plato, it could be read that the ghost is the incarnate soul and the dæmon the disincarnate. It could also be argued that the world-soul, which provides a connection between living, thinking beings, is **Dust**.

R

REPUBLIC OF HEAVEN – **Lord Asriel** hopes to build the Republic of Heaven, but what he envisions is unclear. It is certainly a world free from the tyranny of the **Magisterium** and the **Authority**. His central belief is that while there is a God, there is no incentive to build a better present life. At the end of the trilogy, with Asriel swept away as part of the vast changes to the universal order, **Lyra** realises that her duty is to build the Republic of Heaven where she is.

Asriel's position has historical parallels. The Puritan Oliver Cromwell deposed and executed King Charles I. At the time, many believed that Kings were appointed directly by God, but Cromwell felt that the King's form of Protestantism was a perversion of God's message. While he called himself Lord Protector, and trimmed away many of the excesses of courtly life, Cromwell quickly became a king in all but name, retaining virtually all the powers of the monarch. It's also notable that **John Milton** was a Puritan, and wrote *Paradise Lost* in the aftermath of his side's defeat. Over a century later, George Washington also rebelled against a king, King George III of England, and America became a republic. This throwing-off of the past inspired generations of revolutionaries, like **William Blake**. Back in America, there was great anxiety – which Washington shared – that the President shouldn't become a king, but that didn't stop Washington from being addressed as 'Your Highness' and (as he preferred) 'Your Excellency', nor from a great amount of power being concentrated in one person.

Some critics of the trilogy feel that the Republic of Heaven represents a weakness in the series. In *The Twilight of Atheism*, Alister McGrath says 'Pullman has secured closure at the literary level – but is this really where the story can be said to end? In one sense it has only begun'. Brian Alderson's *New York Times* review of the three books pointed out that Philip Pullman's rejection of authority figures might seem hypocritical given his position of 'author', being able to manipulate the characters and worlds of his book with his. But, surely, taken together, that is a point Pullman is trying to make. The establishment of the republic shifts the responsibility from authority figures to individuals, from dogma to free will. Lyra says 'we have to be all those difficult things like cheerful and kind and curious and brave and patient and we've got to study and think, and work hard, all of us, in all our different worlds, and then we'll build ... the Republic of Heaven'. Pullman doesn't dictate in loving detail what the future will be like; instead readers are invited to think about and imagine – indeed build – the Republic of Heaven for themselves. That McGrath can only picture 'a new elite' emerging and 'Stalin's liquidation squads' enforcing the new order perhaps tells us more about McGrath's limits than Pullman's.

S

SEX – Many readers have inferred that **Lyra** and **Will** make love at the end of *The Amber Spyglass*. There's clearly a moral movement that would balk at the idea of children's literature dealing with the topic of sexual relationships at all, but modern children's novels, let alone other art they routinely encounter, like soap operas and pop songs, routinely discuss sex and depict it as a normal part of teenage life. The difference between innocence and experience, children and adults, are major themes of *His Dark Materials*, which is a rites-of-passage story, and it would be odd if sexuality was excluded from that.

At the end of *The Amber Spyglass*, **Dr Mary Malone** 'the tempter', gives Lyra and Will some fruit and sends them off alone into the idyllic forest of the world of the **Mulefa**. They feed each other fruit, kiss and say that they love each other. Then it was 'as if all the world were holding its breath' [AS, 35]. **Father Gomez**, watching them, is convinced they are 'walking into mortal sin'. We don't know what happens next, until the children return (hand-in-hand, like Adam and Eve after the **Fall** in **John Milton's** *Paradise Lost*), when they are 'saturated in love' and **Dust** has settled upon them. Their **dæmons**, when we see them next, have fixed into their adult forms. Something so profound has happened that it affects all the universes.

Philip Pullman was well aware that his books appealed to both adults and children, and it may well be that he deliberately crafted an ending which could be read in two, equally valid, ways. There are two readings of what has happened, which we might divide between **innocence and experience**. The 'innocent' reading is that Lyra has a profound but purely mental or spiritual experience, one where she now sees things so differently that she passes from childhood to adulthood. The 'experienced' reading is that it's a profound physical experience – she loses her virginity. Pullman has talked about 'democratic' readings of books, and perhaps there is no 'right answer' in this case.

The book can sustain either reading, but what happens isn't so much ambiguous as *deniable* – we can state categorically that the books don't depict Lyra and Will having sex, so it is impossible to prove that they do. Might that lack of depiction be evidence? We see Lyra and Will kiss and say they love each other, *then* something else happens. Why are we kept from seeing it? By not showing us, isn't that, itself, good evidence that something explicit happens? There are apparent clues that an informed reader could spot (for example, there's a long tradition that female fortune-tellers lose their magic powers when they lose their virginity – as the tarot reader Solitaire does in the James Bond story *Live and Let Die* – Lyra loses the ability to read the **alethiometer** after going into the woods with Will).

One adaptation of the stories is clear on the subject – the stage play states outright 'two children are making love in an unknown world', and while that phrasing might allow for the older, more innocent meaning of the phrase 'making love', Anna Maxwell Martin who played Lyra was in no doubt when she spoke to *The Independent* (7 December 2003) – 'I think she's about 12 to begin with, but it's important to get to a point where it would be feasible that we would fall in love. And make love, you know?', before going on to joke about 'sex workshops'.

Why, in a book that hasn't been afraid to take on big topics and controversial stands, would Pullman want to be coy about the denouement? A serious issue is that the two characters are extremely young. Lyra is barely thirteen years old at the end of *The Amber Spyglass* and is further described as 'small for her age'; Will is twelve. The cover illustrations of foreign editions show them as children. Or, to put it another way, they're the same age Harry Potter and his schoolmates are in their first term at Hogwarts, two whole years before Ron and Hermione even (briefly) hold hands. We can take it for granted that the movie version of *The Amber Spyglass* is going to steer well away from even the possibility of a sexual relationship.

Perhaps, though, we can turn this debate right around. The novel ends with Lyra and Will on different worlds, unable to see or hear each other. As is the nature of stories, we can't know what happens next, but it's hard to imagine either of them moving on to an ordinary life and other lovers, even if Lyra acknowledges the possibility. Even if they did, Lyra and Will would still maintain a unique relationship. It's not whether they had sex, so much as the *meaning* of the act. There is a special bond between the two of them, one that transcends any physicality.

T

TOLKIEN, J. R. R – Author of *The Hobbit* and *The Lord of the Rings*. Philip Pullman has not been critical as much as dismissive of Tolkien's work, seeing 'nothing of human interest or value' in them. His dissatisfaction seems to be two-fold. First, Pullman has commented on the lack of moral ambiguity in *The Lord of the Rings*. Characters tend to be either wholly good or wholly bad. Moreover, once the main protagonists have made their decision, their quest becomes one of endurance rather than moral doubt. Second, Pullman rejects the notion that characters need faith in order to succeed in their quest. While set in a pre-Christian age, Tolkien felt *The Lord of the Rings* was entirely compatible with his Catholic beliefs.

Part Four

THE HISTORY OF LYRA'S WORLD,
AS FAR AS IT IS KNOWN

It is unlikely that Philip Pullman planned a strict timeline for the events of the novels, but this is an attempt to make sense of them. When he says 'six weeks or so', we take this to mean six weeks; a 'couple of days' is taken to mean two days; and 'a few days' is taken to mean three. In the event of 'time passing', we have made a guess and marked them as such.

THE 'EARLY AGES'

'Aeons ago'   Matter becomes conscious of itself. The first angel, the Authority, is formed from Dust and tells all subsequent angels that he is their creator. One of the later angels, Xaphania, discovers the truth about the Authority and is cast out from the Authority's Kingdom.

33,000 BC   The Fall. The rebel angels intervene in human evolution, seeking vengeance against the Authority.
Consequently, it is around this time that 'Shadow Particles' are first attracted to human beings [SK, 4]. Dr Mary Malone tells Lyra that the human brain becomes the ideal vehicle for amplifying the noise from Shadow Particles around 35,000 years ago [SK, 12].

The Mulefa people come into existence. Before this point they 'knew nothing' [AS, 17]. Presumably it is at this time that the Authority creates the land of the dead, to punish humankind for its disobedience.

31,258 BC   In Will's world, a sorcerer puts holes in his skull to let the gods in. His skull is displayed in the Pitt–Rivers Museum in Will's Oxford [SK, 4].

2000 BC   Around this time, Enoch and his brother Baruch live as men. Enoch casts Baruch out. The Authority takes Enoch into the Kingdom of Heaven to become his regent [AS, 5, 30]. Balthamos prevents Baruch's ghost from entering the land of the dead, transforming him into an angel [AS, 11].

AD 1   Jesus Christ is born. He is a prophet who preaches the will of the rebel angels [Pullman interview, *The South Bank Show*].

THE 'MIDDLE AGE'

c. 1314   Jordan College was founded in the 'early Middle Age' [NL, 3]. Jordan College's real-world counterpart, Exeter College, was founded in 1314.

The Middle   The Church popularises the notion of angels. Mrs
Age   Coulter believes them to be a creation of 'The Middle Age' [AS, 16].

1555   The French Bishop John Calvin becomes Pope and sets about radical reform of the Church. He establishes the Consistorial Court of Discipline. After his death the Papacy is abolished and replaced with a collection of courts, colleges and councils known as the Magisterium [NL, 2; Programme of the stage play].

1612   Pavel Khunrath, a scholar working in Prague, is burnt at the stake for his work on the symbol-reader. A few of his devices and a copy of his book of readings survive and are investigated by later scholars who give the device the name alethiometer [Programme of the stage play].

THE COMING OF SPECTRES

1697   In the world of Cittàgazze, the Philosophers' Guild of the Torre degli Angeli create the subtle knife. With every opening they cut, Dust begins to leak out of the universe into the abyss [AS, 27]. In the world of the Mulefa, the seed-pod trees begin to die [AS, 27].

1745   Ignatius Cole becomes Master of Jordan College [NL, 3].

1748   Francis Lyall succeeds Ignatius Cole as Master of Jordan College [NL, 3].

c. 1750 The final phase of the building of Jordan College is completed in the 'mid-eighteenth century' [NL, 3].

1765   Simon Le Clerc succeeds Francis Lyall as Master of Jordan College [NL, 3].

c. 1776 In Cittàgazze, the knife-bearer of the Philosophers' Guild makes a window through to the world of the Mulefa and carelessly does not close it. Mary and later Father Gomez use this window [AS, 7].

1789   Simon Le Clerc dies [NL, 3].

c. 1796 According to Dr Martin Lanselius, alethiometers were last used seriously around this time [NL, 10]. In fact, the Consistorial Court of Discipline, the Society for the Work of the Holy Spirit and

Lord Asriel each had alethiometrists at the time of Lyra's adventure.
Also 'for centuries' the witches have talked about Lyra [NL, 10].

1800s	For a large part of the nineteenth century, the College of Bishops dominates the Magisterium [NL, 2].
1898	The year of Lord Asriel's favourite Tokay vintage [NL, 1].
1925	According to Arctic legend, a Norwegian ship was first seen drifting unmanned from around this time [SK, 5].
c. 1946	Barnard and Stokes became the first mathematicians to prove the existence of other worlds mathematically. They were excommunicated by the Church [NL, 2, 21].
1953	In the floods of '53, Lord Asriel saves the lives of two young gyptians [NL, 8].
1956	Farder rescues Serafina Pekkala from an assault from a great red bird in the Fens of Eastern Anglia. They fall in love. Serafina has a child by Farder but the boy dies in a great epidemic from the East not long after his birth. Serafina is recalled to her clan to become Clan-Queen on the death of her mother [NL, 10, 18]. Thorold joins the service of Asriel and watches his master nurse a growing sense of rebellion against the Church [SK, 2].
1957	In Will's world, Hugh Everett rationalises his 'many-worlds' hypothesis [SK, 12].
c. 1959	Mary is born (assuming she is 37 – 'in her late thirties') [SK, 4].

1983   Around this time, Asriel and Mrs Coulter meet and fall in love. They begin a clandestine affair. Lyra is born. It is immediately obvious that she is the daughter of Asriel and not Edward Coulter. Mrs Coulter pretends that her daughter has died in childbirth. Lyra is cared for by Ma Costa on Asriel's Oxfordshire estate [NL, 7].

1984   Before 24 June, Will Parry is born [SK, 5].

1985   In Will's world, c. 8 May, the Nuniatak dig sets out for Alaska, led by John Parry. The expedition is sponsored by the Institute of Archaelogy at Oxford University [SK, 4].
During May, Matt Kigalik sees a Russian spy searching for the anomaly near Lookout Ridge for a couple of days. The spy does not return (John Parry suspected that Kigalik killed him) [SK, 5].
c. 19 June. The Nuniatak dig reaches the North American Arctic Survey Station at Noatak, Alaska [SK, 4].
19–24 June. John Parry searches for the anomaly and writes letters to his wife, Elaine [SK, 5]. He vanishes without trace and is presumed dead. In fact, John stumbles upon a window to Cittàgazze. From there he discovers Lyra's world and his own dæmon, Sayan Kötör. In his early explorations he befriends the Yenesei Pakhtars tribe of Tartars [SK, 6].

c. 1986 At some time between 1983 and 1986, Edward Coulter discovers that his wife lied about the death of her daughter in childbirth and confronts Asriel. Asriel kills Edward. This is presumably some time after Lyra's birth as Ma Costa is surprised Lyra cannot remember: 'you ought to, little as you were' [NL, 8]. In the subsequent trial, Asriel is stripped of his lands and fortune. Mrs

Coulter turns her back on Lyra. Ma Costa's appeal for custody is rejected and Lyra is handed to the Sisters of Obedience at Watlington.
Asriel takes Lyra from the Sisters of Obedience at Watlington and deposits her with the Master of Jordan College. For 'ten years or more', Lyra is in the care of the Master [NL, 7].
Mrs Coulter begins her ascent to power through the Church.

1987   John Parry adopts the name Dr Stanislaus Grumman and makes his way to Berlin. He presents a thesis to the Imperial German Academy and gains membership by defending it in debate [SK, 6].

c. 1989   About two years after joining the Berlin Academy, John Parry, now known as Dr Stanilaus Grumman, meets the Director of the Imperial Muscovite Academy's astronomical observatory north of Nova Zembla [SK, 6].

1991   c. June. Will and his mother play a game at the supermarket. During the following months, Will realises that the dangers she sensed were not in the real world but in her head [SK, 1, 5].
Before this time, John Parry is initiated into the skull-cult of the Yenesei Pakhtar tribe of Tartars. He is referred to by the name 'Jopari' [SK, 6, 10].

c. 1993   By this time, Mrs Coulter has reasoned that there was a relationship between Dust and the fixing of one's dæmon. She establishes the General Oblation Board under the auspices of the Consistorial Court of Discipline, with the condition that all experiments take place in a remote location. Bolvangar is created [NL, 21].
Around this time ('2–3 years ago') the Gobblers

start abducting children and taking them north to Bolvangar [NL, 6].

1994   Lee Scoresby meets one of Grumman's team when he flies over the Yenesei River. By this time, Grumman had a hole in his head and was a Tartar by adoption [NL, 13].

1995   c. March. Stanislaus Grumman's expedition to the north vanishes without trace. In one of his last messages to the Berlin Academy, Grumman reports a city beyond the Aurora.
Around this time, the Skraeling wars are raging across Beringland. Some Arctic drifters believe Grumman was shot outright during the wars [SK, 6].
Asriel embarks on a diplomatic mission to the King of Lapland. In fact, he searches for Stanislaus' expedition [NL, 2].
Autumn. In Lyra's world, around the time of the horse fair, Lyra and the Collegers capture the Costa's narrow boat [NL, 3]. Since the gyptians came and went with the spring and autumn fairs, and disappeared after every horse fair, it is presumably autumn [NL, 3].
c. October. Asriel visits Jordan College and shows the scholars photograms of Dust and the city beyond the Aurora. He obtains funding for a second expedition to the north to investigate the matter further [NL, 2].
It is probably around this time that Mrs Coulter spends her three months in the north, supposedly in Greenland making observations of the Aurora [NL, 4]. In fact, she helps Iofur Raknison overthrow Iorek Byrnison in order to gain the former's commitment to capturing and imprisoning Asriel on Svalbard [NL, 19].
Iorek is exiled from Svalbard. He makes new

armour from sky-metal, only to have it stolen
from him by the people of Trollesund.
Winter. In Will's world, Will stops taking piano
lessons from Mrs Cooper [SK, 1].

1996   Dr Polstead becomes one in a long line of Lyra's
unwilling tutors at Jordan College [LO].
c. Spring/Summer. Asriel finishes assembling his
laboratory on Svalbard. He awaits the final thing
he needs to complete his bridge to the stars [NL,
21].
c. 15 September. Two weeks before Roger and
Billy Costa are abducted, two children are taken
from Banbury [NL, 3].
c. 29 September. Jessie Reynolds is taken by the
Gobblers [NL, 3].

LYRA'S ADVENTURE

1996   **c. 30 September 1996 – 5 January 1997.**
(continued) *Northern Lights.*

Day 1   c. 30 September. Billy and Roger are abducted by
the Gobblers. This takes place in 'Autumn' [NL,
5], during the horse fair after which the gyptians
usually leave. The fair is presumably something
akin to the harvest festival, and so one could
guess that it takes place in late September. For the
purposes of this timeline, we assume that the
horse fair takes place on 30 September 1996.
On the same day, Lyra first meets Mrs Coulter.
The Master gives Lyra the alethiometer [NL, 3,
4].

Day 2   c. 1 October. Lyra and Mrs Coulter take a
zeppelin to London [NL, 4].

Day 13   12 Oct 1996. 'Not long before' he finds the
window to Cittàgazze, Will witnesses a solar
eclipse [AS, 18]. The nearest eclipse of the sun
was a partial eclipse that took place on 12

	October 1996 (a total eclipse didn't take place until 11 August 1999).
Day 44	c. 12 November. Autumn has turned to winter. 'Six weeks or so' after Lyra's arrival in London, Lyra and Mrs Coulter plan their cocktail party [NL, 5].
Day 56	c. 26 November. After an undisclosed time (we have assumed two weeks pass), Mrs Coulter holds her cocktail party. Lyra discovers that Mrs Coulter is responsible for the Oblation Board and escapes. She is captured by Turk traders but rescued by the Costas.
Day 57	c. 27 November. Lyra wakes on the Costas boat. Before this time, but after Billy's abduction, the gyptians had captured one of the Gobblers and made him talk [NL, 6].
Day 59	c. 29 November. 'Within a couple of days', Lyra feels at home on the boat.
Day 62	c. 2 December. After 'a few days' the Costas arrive at the Zaal in time for the Byanroping. John Faa tells Lyra about her real parents [NL, 7].
Day 65	c. 5 December. The second Byanroping takes place, three days after the first.
Day 66	c. 6 December. In the early hours after the Roping, Benjamin de Ruyter slips away on his spying mission.
Day 67	c. 7 December. Benjamin and his gyptian spies capture Gobblers at Clerkenwell. They discover connections between the Gobblers and the Ministry of Theology and Lord Boreal.
Day 68	c. 8 December. In the 'few days' after the second Roping, news reaches the gyptians of Benjamin's failed mission [NL, 9].
Day 80	c. 20 December. A group of twelve children are

brought to Trollesund by the Oblation Board [NL, 10].

Day 82   c. 22 December. Two weeks after the news of Benjamin's death, the gyptians arrive at Colby. Late at night, they set out for Trollesund.

Day 83   c. 23 December. On the journey to Trollesund, Farder tells Lyra about witches.

Day 84   c. 24 December. Tony Makarios is severed [NL, 17].

Day 85   c. 25 December. After two days at sea, Lyra decides that the sea is the life for her [NL, 10]. The twelve children at Trollesund set out for Bolvangar [NL, 10].

Day 87   c. 27 December. 'One morning' (not 'next morning'), the gyptians arrive at Trollesund. They have only been at sea 'a few days' [NL, 10]. Lyra visits Dr Lanselius and meets Iorek. John Faa hires Lee. Kaisa talks to Farder.

Day 88   c. 28 December. Lyra tells Iorek the location of his armour (it has had time to rust) [NL, 11]. The gyptian expedition sets out for Bolvangar. En route, Lyra and Iorek split and find Tony.

Day 89   c. 29 December. The gyptians continue on to Bolvangar [NL, 13].

Day 90   c. 30 December. Less than a day from Bolvangar, the gyptians are attacked by Samoyeds. Lyra is taken to Bolvangar and speaks to the children, arriving late in the day [NL, 14].

Day 91   c. 31 December. Mrs Coulter arrives at Bolvangar [NL, 15]. Lyra and Kaisa release the dæmons and raise the fire alarm. Iorek and the witches save the children. Lyra walks the children to the gyptians during the 'deep dark Arctic night'. Lyra, Iorek and Roger travel in Lee's balloon to Svalbard.

1997

Day 92   c. 1 January 1997. With the moon high in the sky, the cliff-ghasts attack Lee's balloon. Lyra falls out and is captured by the bears [NL, 18].

Day 93   c. 2 January. Lyra speaks to Jotham Santelia and tricks Iofur [NL, 19]. Iorek is a day's journey away, carried away there by the balloon after Lyra's crash [NL, 19].

Day 94   c. 3 January. Iorek fights Iofur and is victorious [NL, 20].

Day 95   c. 4 January. Iorek takes Roger and Lyra into the interior of Svalbard to find Asriel.

Day 96   c. 5 January. The next day, Asriel takes Roger and opens the bridge to the stars. Lyra crosses the bridge and finds herself in Cittàgazze.

1997
(continued)   **c. 6–12 January. *The Subtle Knife*.**

Day 97   c. 6 January. Will leaves his mother with Mrs Cooper.

Day 98   c. 7 January. Will's house is burgled in the early hours. He makes his way to Oxford where, just before midnight, he finds the window to Cittàgazze.

Day 99   c. 8 January. In the early hours, he meets Lyra who has been in Cittàgazze for '3 days, maybe 4' (we have assumed three) [SK, 1]. After sleeping, they travel to Will's Oxford. Will investigates his father's disappearance. Lyra encounters Sir Charles Latrom and Mary Malone.
In Lyra's world, Lee searches for Stanislaus.

Day 100   c. 9 January. Charles steals the alethiometer. Will and Lyra retrieve the knife from the Torre degli Angeli and use it to take back the alethiometer. Lee collects Stanilaus from the Yenesei Pakhtar tribe of Tartars.

Day 101   c. 10 January. Will and Lyra are rescued from the
           Belvedere by the witches. Serafina tries to heal
           Will's hand but the spell fails.
           Mary leaves her world and enters that of
           Cittàgazze.

Day 102   c. 11 January. Will and Lyra travel through
           Cittàgazze and exchange their stories.
           In Lyra's world, Lee and Stanilaus are attacked
           by the forces of the Church and barely make it
           through the night.

Day 103   c. 12 January. In Lyra's world, Serafina flies to
           Lee's aid but is too late. Lee is killed.
           That evening, Will meets his father. John Parry is
           killed by Juta Kamainen. Lyra is kidnapped.

1997   **c. 13 January – 8 March. *The Amber Spyglass*.**
(continued)

Day 104   c. 13 January. Will sends Baruch to find Lyra [AS,
           2].

Day 105   c. 14 January. Baruch returns to Will and tells
           him where Lyra is being held [AS, 2]. Baruch
           leaves for Asriel's world.

Day 106   c. 15 January. In the Adamant Tower, Baruch
           dies of his injuries. Asriel despatches his gyropters
           and slow-moving zeppelin to find Lyra.

Day 107   c. 16 January. Will travels to Kholodnoye. A
           week or more has passed since Asriel created the
           bridge to the stars. Will meets Iorek [AS, 7, 8].

Day 110   c. 19 January. A 'few days' later, the bears'
           steamer arrives at its destination. Iorek and Will
           are three days' travel away from Lyra's cave [AS,
           9].

Day 113   c. 22 January. Will meets Ama. At night, they
           rescue Lyra but the knife is broken. Amid the
           battle between the Church and Asriel's forces,
           Lyra and Will escape.

Day 114   c. 23 January. Iorek mends the subtle knife [AS, 15].

Day 115   c. 24 January. Lyra and Will travel to the land of the dead. Lyra meets her death.

Day 116   c. 25 January. At first light, they travel to the river. Lyra leaves Pantailamon behind. They enter the land of the dead 'just a few weeks after Roger had died' [AS, 22]. Lyra convinces the harpies to help her. The Church's bomb is detonated, creating the abyss. Will cuts an exit from the land of the dead [AS, 26].

Day 117   c. 26 January. Lyra and Will find their dæmons and narrowly escape the Spectres at the Battle on the Plain. They enter the world of the Mulefa. Lord Asriel and Mrs Coulter drag Metatron into the abyss [AS, 31].

Day 118   c. 27 January. Lyra and Will are reunited with Mary.

Day 119   c. 28 January. Mary tells Will and Lyra why she left the convent.

Day 120   c. 29 January. The next day, Lyra and Will enter the grove. Balthamos kills Gomez. The second Fall takes place [AS, 35]. That night, Serafina visits Mary, Pantailamon and Kirjava.

Day 121   c. 30 January. Xaphania tells Will and Lyra that all windows must be closed [AS, 37].

Day 122   c. 31 January. The gyptians arrive to take Will and Lyra home.

Day 123   c. 1 February. The gyptians set sail. The voyage to Cittàgazze will take two weeks.

Day 137   c. 15 February. The gyptians land at Cittàgazze. Will and Lyra agree to visit the Botanic Gardens in Oxford every Midsummer's Day. They part.

Day 158   c. 8 March. 'Three weeks later', Lyra has dinner with the Master of Jordan College and Hannah

Relf [AS, 38]. At midnight, she visits the Botanic Gardens.

1999 **Lyra and the birds**
c. 8 March. Two years after Lyra and Will have parted. Yelena Pazhets tries to murder Lyra and frame Sebastian Makepeace [LO].